AN OUTLINE OF CHRISTIAN WORSHIP

AN OUTLINE OF CHRISTIAN WORSHIP

GORDON S. WAKEFIELD

T&T CLARK
EDINBURGH

T&T CLARK LTD
59 GEORGE STREET
EDIBURGH EH2 2LQ
SCOTLAND

First published 1998

ISBN 0 567 08610 0

British Library Cataloguing-in-Publication Data
A catalogue record for this book is available from the British Library

Typeset by Elaine Black, Glasgow
Printed and bound in Great Britain by MPG Books, Bodmin

To the Members of the Joint Liturgical Group of Great Britain, 1966–94

'Friends on earth and friends above'

CONTENTS

PREFACE

In 1936 Oxford University Press published *An Outline of Christian Worship* by the Scottish liturgist, W. D. Maxwell. It went through seven editions until 1963 and was a pioneer in the revival of liturgical studies in the Church of Scotland and the British Free Churches. It inspired the interest in worship which has meant that the liturgical movement has involved Protestants as well as Catholics, so that the mainstream in all denominations would flow in the same liturgical direct-ion and agree on the shape of Christian worship. This is instanced in ecumenical compendia such as Jones, Wainwright and Yarnold, *The Study of Liturgy* (SPCK, 1978) and the SCM *A New Dictionary of Liturgy and Worship* (1989) edited by the late J. G. Davies, and the existence since 1963 of the Joint Liturgical Group of Great Britain, instigated by the then Archbishop of Canterbury, Michael Ramsey.

Maxwell's subtitle says that his book is a study of the 'development and forms' of Christian worship. It is in effect a history from the New Testament onwards, with particular concentration on Reformed rites, which had been neglected and misunderstood. It is confined to Sunday morning worship and the liturgy of Word and Sacrament. Initiation is excluded. I have thought this too important in the discussions of our time and in the Christian life to leave out here. The offices are dealt with very briefly, there is a summary account of the Christian Year and a valuable last section on forms of prayer, amplified with more examples in the author's collected papers as a Senior Army Chaplain, *Concerning Worship* (OUP, 1948).

J. S. Whale pointed out the neglect of hymnody. The book was a trail-blazer and as such invaluable, but the bibliography, though large, is now outdated and inadequate and there has been such immense international liturgical scholarship since that a new book needs to be written offering a more balanced and more comprehensive treatment, and taking account of work constantly going on. In addition to the various Commissions ecumenical and denominational, which are perpetually in business, there are associations such as Societas Liturgica and the Alcuin Club and the aforementioned Joint Liturgical Group in the United Kingdom. There is also need to take account of the revival of 'free' worship, evangelical, charismatic and the characteristic fervour of the Black Churches. At the same time, this book, like Maxwell's, must be written from the standpoint of certain principles and convictions, and therefore offer some personal critique as well as accurate and sensitive description. The purpose of this new book is to offer a beginner's introduction to assist the journey through the thickets and minefields of liturgical history and controversy and to inform understanding of the ever-developing ecumenical situation. It also seeks to be a modest help towards right judgement. There is always a danger of bandwagons rushing excitedly if not to heresy then to a jungle of individual or group predilections and fashions.

This cannot claim to be an original work except in certain of the opinions expressed which themselves are doubtless shared by some others. It is shamelessly dependent on many experts. To name Paul Bradshaw, Edward Yarnold, Kenneth Stevenson, W. Jardine Grisbrooke, the late G. J. Cuming, B. D. Spinks, J. D. C. Fisher, known chiefly through their writings, though with some I may claim personal friendship, is by no means to be exhaustive. I suppose my own period is the Reformation onwards and the modern revisions, but one cannot understand these without the worship of the people of God from the beginnings as far as it can be discovered. Twenty-eight years with the Joint Liturgical Group as well as a share in the *Methodist Service Book* of 1975 and its sequels is also some qualification.

The writing was interrupted for some months by illness. That I have recovered and been able to resume and complete the work is very much due to the loving care of my wife.

GORDON S. WAKEFIELD

CHAPTER 1

THE ORIGINS OF CHRISTIAN WORSHIP

Both biblical and liturgical scholarship are less certain of assured results than they were when historical criticism was taking all before it. In the 1920s a devout liberal Protestant teacher of the New Testament could claim that his generation was in a unique position to understand Jesus because so much was known of the world to which he came, not least its religion. Now there is less confidence, in some ways in direct proportion to the increase of knowledge, which may paradoxically expose ignorance, reveal gaps and try to fill them with speculation which is often the result of the suspicious and sceptical approach of the scholar who seeks not to be unduly influenced by the conditioning of inherited belief. This is true of studies of worship.

One problem with regard to the origins of Christian worship, as Paul Bradshaw has shown, is that because accounts of it derive from later periods, there is little certainty as to what precisely Jewish worship was like at the time of Christ. Were proselytes baptised before 200CE? Was the synagogue service what it became later and was daily attendance the practice of every devout Jew in large towns? Was the Last Supper a Passover meal as the synoptists imply or is the Fourth Gospel right in its chronology? If it were a Passover meal, is this a help in understanding the Christian Eucharist since 'we are far from certain about the precise details of the Passover meal in the first century, and it is probable that it was considerably different from the form it took after the destruction of the Temple' (Bradshaw, 1992, p. 51)? Confessing that there is little about which we can be sure either in Jewish or Christian worship in New Testament times, Bradshaw concludes:

> . . . the New Testament generally cannot provide the firm foundation from which to project later liturgical developments that it has frequently been thought to give. We must therefore remain agnostic about many of the roots of Christian worship practices which we observe clearly for the first time in the following centuries. (Bradshaw, 1992, p. 55)

It is particularly dangerous to turn speculations into certainties in accordance with one's own convictions and prejudices. The Eucharist has assumed the greatest importance in church history. It has survived deep divisions, cruel persecutions and the most bitter controversies, yet has exercised perennial allure and inspired the deepest love. It has been reaffirmed in our own time by Protestants as much as Catholics as the central act of Christian worship. After centuries of most bitter division it could become the Sacrament of Unity. At least convergence is possible, as was shown by the World Council of Churches' 1982 Report, *Baptism, Eucharist and Ministry.* The temptation therefore is to think, as Catholics have always tended to do, that our eucharistic faith and practice go back to the New Testament itself and that we have the mind of the historical Jesus. This should not altogether be ruled out. Christians believe that by meditation on the texts of the Last Supper and the words ascribed to Jesus, in the community of dedicated minds, the Johannine promise will be fulfilled and the Holy Spirit will guide us to the truth. But absolute certainty is not possible. There may indeed be eucharistic truth for us in our churches and our lives, but we may be experiencing a development, beneficial to our time, out of origins half-hidden in the fragmentary records and differing traditions of the New Testament.

There may well have been, as Hans Lietzmann and others have recognised, a 'double strand' in the eucharistic worship of the early Church. There was the fellowship meal as in Acts 2:42, 'They met constantly to hear the apostles teach, and to share the common life, to break bread and to pray'. There is no mention here of the upper room or the Lord's death. The apostles' teaching would presumably include the latter, though, if we follows Acts, this would not be as atoning sacrifice but to enable the preaching of the resurrection and make available the gift of the Spirit. There would be no soteriology or doctrine of the atonement. This is reinforced by Acts 10:40, where Peter talks of Jesus's resurrection appearances being not to all the people but to the predestined witnesses, 'even to us who did eat and drink with him after he rose from the dead'.

The other strand follows Paul in 1 Corinthians 11:23ff., in which the meal is the proclamation of Christ's death, a tradition which the apostle claims goes back to Jesus himself and his actions on his betrayal night as also Mark's Gospel later records. Words peculiar to Paul, though found in the longer text of Luke 22:19, are those of the command 'Do this in memory of me'. Their authenticity has been questioned and there may be some reluctance now to base the celebration of the Eucharist on them as an act of obedience, which, since it is to Christ himself, raises this Sacrament, as the Wesleys in the eighteenth century believed, to the supreme means of grace. Did Jesus himself in the upper room, foresee a liturgical community which would continue and require a regular, disciplined practice? Is it not more likely that the command was read back into the concluding hours of Jesus's ministry by those who, like Paul, were already experiencing the actions over bread and cup, within or outside the fellowship meal, as the way in which they could recall 'the whole Christ', that is, his life on earth and the death which was its consummation and the precondition of his risen and exalted life and victory? Thus they would, in the interpretative language of C. H. Dodd, reconstitute the crisis of their Christian origins. Yet if the Last Supper is a historic event, as we have no reason to doubt, since John describes it too though without the eucharistic words, and if we are able from the records to encounter Jesus as a man of flesh and blood and to enter into his mind at all, is it not possible that in that moment of mingled fellowship and lurking grief, he would ask his disciples by means of a rite to remember him whatever happened? Joachim Jeremias interpreted the command to mean, 'Do this in order that God may remember me and bring in his parousia and his kingdom' (Jeremias, pp. 237–55). This has its difficulties, not least in the Pauline context which is concerned primarily with the past, accomplished event of the Lord's death

(Kilpatrick, p. 13), but it could be in keeping with the eschatological reference of the Supper – 'I will drink no more of the fruit of the vine until I drink it new in the Kingdom of God' (Mark 14:25 and parallels) – 'You show forth the Lord's death until he come' (1 Corinthians 11:26). Jesus was still hoping that the Kingdom might come that very night. If not, and he must go the way of the cross, he would want his disciples to take part in a rite which would preserve his memory before God, and through which the Kingdom would eventually come as they prayed as he had taught them.

What must never be overlooked in considering Paul's account is his emphasis on the awesome solemnity of the rite, which if it is abused will result in most fearful judgement. He is reacting to Corinthian scandals, their eating and drinking to excess and a refusal to share supplies, so that the rich are surfeited and the poor deprived. The death of Jesus has been forgotten in a 'fellowship' meal which has become a travesty. Paul did not envisage the spine-chilling effect of the Eucharist in the teaching of John Chrysostom at the end of the fourth century; but the partaking of bread and cup were not actions of an informal matiness, they were the commemoration of the utter self-giving of the Son of God in anticipation of his coming in his Kingdom.

Even so, there is room for different interpretations of the New Testament evidence for the Eucharist. In our time, there has been a renewed emphasis on the meal, even though, as with a meal in children's games, the food is but token. The worshippers gather in a circle around the table, the minister facing them. No longer is he (though not any more always a male in Anglican and Reformed Churches) afar off at a distant altar, repeating the Lord's words of institution *sotto voce* and turning to the people only to elevate the host, the consecrated bread, the very body of Christ, for their adoration more than their partaking. The unity of the congregation is now all-important, hence the revival of the reconciling 'kiss of peace'. To adopt a distinction of W. H. Vanstone's, 'place' in the community has supplanted 'space' for contemplation of the divine mystery. James Dunn, a leading New Testament scholar, has regretted the disappearance of the meal over the centuries and would wish for its complete restoration, the priesthood of all believers realised in lay celebration and a diversity of form and expression as he believes was the case in the primitive Church. He sums up the New Testament evidence like this:

> The picture then is as clear as it can be. The Lord's Supper as a meal, expressive of the shared participation of the congregation in Christ brought to focus in the sharing of the bread at the beginning and the wine at the end. A meal in which the words of institution would be repeated probably by the host, whether man or woman, or possibly by any other member known for his or her commitment to Christ and service of the community. (Dunn, p. 41)

This has to be taken seriously, though not, in spite of the eminence of its author, as undisputed authority. In the last analysis we are all, as the fashionable 'reader-response' school of criticism insists, bound to interpret the evidence according to all those factors which form our own predilections, provided we do not do violence to the texts, or treat our own beliefs as beyond qualification. Dunn speaks as an elder of the Kirk who has become an English Methodist. I, who have no claim to a like New Testament scholarship, write as an English Methodist in the Wesleyan tradition, brought up on Cranmer but with some reverence for Catholic devotion and psychological propensity for the 'vertical' over the 'horizontal' dimension of worship. Therefore against Dunn, who does not show much interest in the meaning of the words of institution, apart from their all-important significance as inviting disciples to participate in Christ's action, and who does not appear to give particular emphasis to the Lord's death, I would turn to the powerful treatment of eucharistic origins in the late Donald MacKinnon's essay on 'Sacrament and Common Meal' (in Nineham, pp. 201ff.).

MacKinnon, who, admittedly, was a philosophic theologian rather than a New Testament specialist, finds the origins of the Eucharist in the table-fellowship of Jesus with the outcasts of society. Luke subtly changes the Marcan account of this (2:15ff.) into a sign of the Kingdom of God, rather than a ritual meal (Luke 5:29f., 15:1ff.). MacKinnon calls attention to Ernst Lohmeyer's *Kultus und Evangelium* ('Cult and Gospel') which sees the meals with sinners as a fundamental challenge to the Temple and its cult. Lohmeyer would have liked to expel from the Gospel any endorsement of the sacrificial, the cultic or ritual aspects of religion. The way of Jerusalem is judged by the way of Jesus. His ministry is of awe-ful mercy as harlots and prodigals feast and the 'righteous' remain excluded in their complacency.

The Last Supper is the climax of the meals which began with the Lord's eating with the riff-raff. And yet with a difference. The crowds have disappeared. They have been reduced to the twelve in the upper room. Does Mark 14:25, 'Truly I tell you: never again shall I drink of the fruit of the vine until that day when I drink it new in the Kingdom of God' imply that the days of 'the gluttonous man and the wine-bibber' are over?

Jesus has introduced a ritual act pregnant with meaning, waiting to be born. It took place at the time of the Jewish Passover, yet the chronology in relation to that feast is uncertain (and there is no mention of the lamb or the deliverance from Egypt). There is sacrificial language in the statement of the body given and the blood of the convenant. All we can say may be 'simply that by his blessing of the bread and thanksgiving over the cup, Christ throws over the things that are coming upon him an overwhelming, in fact a final, significance. By words at once conveying the burden of a most mighty religious tradition and bright with an awful novelty, he reveals the meaning of his death to his own. More than this, as de la Taille's use of the word *oblatio* (oblation) suggests, he makes himself over to God.' This is his unique sacrifice, interpreted in John 17:19, 'For their sake I consecrate myself.' The disciples are drawn in as the sinners and tax-collectors were not. His intimates alone are present, no prostitutes nor profiteers, nor the hungry five thousand on whom he has compassion. Those meals were gestures of a reconciliation which the act foreshadowed here makes possible. 'At the supper table, he lays his consecrating hand upon the life now drawing to its close, at once bestowing its fulness upon his disciples and setting it upon the altar of his Father's will.' The meals of the ministry were prophetic signs of the Kingdom of God. Then there was feasting, joy and celebration; now the woes are at hand, yet these acts with the faithful, though a bewildered and timorous few, are more intimate and more poignant, heavy with the finalities of redemption. And there is the note of eschatological triumph, even as the Jews in the death trains to Auschwitz sang of the meal when Leviathan would be given them for their feast.

There are many layers of meaning beneath these brief records and a rich biblical typology. In the upper room Jesus looked forward; in the Eucharist the Church looks back, looks back from within its chequered history, in which much of Christ's vision at times has been lost. Yet in the rite of the upper room, it has a sacramental continuity with the life of Christ. In some sense the rite is his biography. Like the disciples at the Last Supper, the Church has still to pass through his death, but the table is alight with the promise of the Kingdom and it is by dying with Christ that Christians live.

That interpretation, which is of a deeper spirituality than much academic theology, is no more definitive than James Dunn's. But it has richness and it relates the Supper and the institution to the ministry of the Son of Man, who 'came eating and drinking', to his concern for sinners and offering of himself to bring them to God and his inauguration of God's rule in all the earth. And from the Gospels themselves, it justifies the central place of the Eucharist in Christian worship.

There was non-eucharistic worship in the early Church, much of it spontaneous. There was singing – psalms from the Jewish Psalter, so germane to the New Testament understanding of Christ, hymns such as are found in the early chapters of Luke's Gospel and possibly in such passages as Philippians 2:5–11 and the worship of heaven in the Revelation of John, 'spiritual songs', composed under momentary inspiration. What were Paul and Silas singing at midnight in the Philippian jail (Acts 16:25)? There was a charismatic, pentecostal movement, which burst through any liturgical forms. It brought the freedom of the Spirit, delivered many from inhibitions and restraints, and made it possible for the humblest believer to express a real though not always intelligible joy in Christ. It had its dangers, sometimes of blasphemy, as Paul found at Corinth, which made some liturgical order necessary. Hence his account of the institution of the Supper and the injunction 'Let everything be done decently and in order' (1 Corinthians 14:40). There is a contrast between the Pentecostalism of Acts with its crowd-infecting enthusiasm and its noise and the Johannine teaching of the Paraclete. He is the friend in need, the counsel for the defence of believers in the trials of the world and the guide into the fullness of truth. He is bestowed not in a rushing wind – though this metaphor is found in John 3:8 to describe the mystery of spiritual rebirth, as the wind blowing where it wills. Nor does the Spirit come in tongues of fire, but by the breath of the risen and glorified Christ as the accompaniment of his peace. We must not think that the early Christians all agreed about worship, which seems, as C. F. D. Moule said, to have been a combination of 'chaotic informality' and great reverence, with some contention between parties more inclined to one than the other.

The New Testament has many references to Christians praying, from the teaching of Jesus himself with his insistence on petition and privacy, and the prayers at the beginning of Paul's letters, which are always of thanksgiving (Greek *eucharisteo*) and glory to God, and which merge into the various introductions often describing his own prayers for the churches to which he is writing, always related to some aspect of the gospel relevant to their situation. These are the writer's personal prayers, though after the pattern of the Hellenistic world and they are not liturgical, but it is not unlikely that prayer in this style was sometimes corporate and that it owed a good deal, as extempore prayer always does, to liturgical forms, which in this case were Jewish or from the Qumran community. The opening salutation of most of Paul's letters may well have prefaced the liturgy: 'Grace to you and peace from God the Father and the Lord Jesus Christ'.

There is much exhortation to persist in prayer (e.g. Colossians 4:2; 1 Thessalonians 5:17). It is prayer which helps to hold the scattered congregations together and to support the apostolic ministry. In the Acts of the Apostles, Christians are frequently at prayer together. They would shape their prayers according to Jewish forms and yet these would not be wholly adequate for Christians, for whom prayer, though offered to God the Creator and Father of Jewish faith, was in the name of Jesus. The Lord's Prayer is an exception. This the disciples are said to have learned from Jesus himself and we may believe that it is an instance of the way he prayed, as in the Garden of Gethsemane, when out of his distress he asked that the Father's will, not his, be done (Mark 14:36 and parallels). Its plural form, however, suggests that it was intended for a group and that even if it were used by an individual in private, it presupposed membership of a community. There is no reference to it elsewhere in the New Testament other than in the Gospels of Matthew and Luke, though there may be an echo in Romans 8:15: 'The Spirit you have received is not a spirit of slavery, leading you back into a life of fear, but a Spirit of adoption, enabling us to cry "Abba! Father"' (cf. Galatians 4:6). The Lord's Prayer is given a more liturgical form in Matthew 6:9ff., and the doxology found in some manuscripts testifies to its use in worship, while it is prominent in the teachings of the early Fathers. Tertullian and Origen in the third century both say that Jesus intended it as an outline of prayer. In this it may have resembled the eighteen benedictions of Jewish worship. By the end of the first century these were prayed three times a day, which is the instruction of the *Didache* (whose date remains a 'riddle' though parts may be as early as 60CE), regarding the Lord's Prayer (see Petuchowski and Brocke, eds, pp. 149ff.). Both forms of the Lord's Prayer in the original are metrical, the Matthean especially being redolent of the psalms, while the petitions are addressed to God, whose nature as Father and King is very much of Jewish spirituality though possibly given particular meaning from what scholars such as T. W. Manson and Joachim Jeremias believed to be the deepest religious insights and most intimate experience of Jesus himself. It is important to observe with James Barr and Geza Vermes and contrary to Jeremias and Oscar Cullmann, and widespread belief found as early as the English Puritans, that 'Abba' is not 'Daddy'. There was prayer to Jesus in the New Testament, from the dying Stephen and from Paul for instance, but this was not liturgical. In the Catholic and

Orthodox liturgical tradition, prayer has always been through Christ to God (see Jungmann, 1965, *passim*).

The disciples went to the Temple to pray, but may have held their own prayers in Solomon's portico. Acts 1:13 says that they assembled in the upper room, and Acts 12:12 that they were gathered in the house of John Mark's mother, praying fervently for Peter's release; and it is probable that their meetings, which would include prayer as well as teaching and the meal (Acts 2:42), usually took place in private houses, separate from the synagogue and the Temple.

Whether Christians kept hours of prayer from the first, or prayed three times a day like devout Jews, is not certain. There are hints in Acts, but there is now a lack of conviction about this book's account of the earliest communities. It may reflect the idealism of the second generation about Christian beginnings and an order which did not exist so early. Christians were feeling their way as they sought to come to terms with 'the new thing' which was the gospel, both in the Jewish and the Gentile worlds.

Paul Bradshaw has said that Christianity and Judaism were not so much parent and child as 'two children of the same family who grew up in increasing estrangement from one another and so exhibit a mixture of similarity and difference in their characters' (*Daily Prayer in the Early Church*, 1981, pp. 29f.). In this book he singles out some distinctive characteristics of Christian prayer, including its being offered through Jesus Christ, or in his name, as already mentioned above. Another is the increasing preference for the form 'We, or I, thank God' as the introduction rather than 'Blessed be God'. Also there was a tendency to begin with remembrance, anamnesis, of God's mighty acts in creation and redemption and to hail his sovereign Lordship and then proceed to petition and intercession. Concluding doxologies were in the Jewish tradition as was the use of the solemn 'Amen' to end prayers. The scope of intercession was wide, to include enemies and persecutors as in the teaching of Jesus and, indeed, all humankind, not least 'kings and those who are in high positions' (1 Timothy 2:1–7).

The same is true of the Apostolic Fathers: 1 Clement 59–61 lists in detail those for whom intercession is made and includes an

> extensive prayer for earthly rulers; Ignatius of Antioch bids his readers to pray unceasingly for the rest of mankind 'for we can always hope that repentance may enable them to find their way to God' (Ephes. 10); and Polycarp makes petition for 'all those under heaven who shall one day come to believe', and instructs: 'pray for all God's people; pray too for our sovereign lords, and for all governors and rulers; for any who ill-use you or dislike you; and for the enemies of the Cross' (Phil. 12). (Bradshaw, 1981 p. 35)

There is an eschatological dimension to prayer, that is, it is offered in expectation of 'the last things', the coming of God's Kingdom. This is the heart of the Lord's Prayer, 'thy kingdom come'. It is inseparable from vigilance, 'watch and pray'. This need for a state of readiness may imply fixed times of corporate prayer, e.g. three times a day as in the *Didache*, possibly symbolised in the Mark/Matthean account of the Lord going three times to arouse his sleeping disciples in Gethsemane, and also an eastward orientation: 'as the lightning comes from the east and shines as far as the west, so will be the coming of the Son of Man' (Matthew 24:27). This may have encouraged night prayer and vigils. There is the reiterated statement that the day of the Lord comes as 'a thief in the night' (Matthew 24:43–4/Luke 12:33–40; 1 Thessalonians 5:2f.; 2 Peter 5:10; Revelation 3:3, 16:13).

It may be that Christians knelt in prayer more than Jews. There is no doubt that they also stood; for instance the injunction to forgive as the accompaniment of prayer is introduced with the words, 'When you stand praying', while Jesus himself stood as he said grace over the loaves at the feeding of the five thousand, or thanked God before the raising of Lazarus, or as he prayed his consecration prayer in John 17. But the writer of Ephesians bows his knee to the Father as he prays for his readers to know all the dimensions of divine love. Peter kneels and prays before he revives Tabitha (Acts 9:40). Paul kneels with the elders of Ephesus as he prays with them in farewell (Acts 20:36), and likewise with the Christians on the beach at Tyre, as he takes ship for Jerusalem. In Luke's account of Gethsemane, Jesus kneels. This may betoken the earnestness of Christian prayer, the pleading before God.

Preaching, proclamation, a telling of the Christian story, often leading to dialogue, is essential to the Christian mission in the New Testament, but was there a liturgical ministry of the Word? The story of Acts 20:7ff. of Paul at Troas, preaching at such length that the young man Eutychus slept and fell out of the window, to be revived by Paul, who then returned and broke bread, has been hailed as an instance of the liturgy of Word and Sacrament. This could be so, though it is wrong to generalise from one instance, when there may have been special circumstances and we have no means of knowing whether it was a regular custom. Similarly it is probably as mistaken as it is attractive to see in the story of the walk to Emmaus a liturgy of Word and Sacrament. Breaking bread is a characteristic action of Jesus, as in the feeding of the five thousand (Luke 9:16). The two disciples, who do not seem to have been of the twelve (certainly Cleopas is not named among them), would not have been present at the Last Supper. And there is no mention of wine, though this may not always have been part of ritual meals. Fish accompanied bread in John 21:9 and there are Jewish Christian documents which describe the celebration of the Eucharist with bread and salt. Acts 1:4 is usually rendered '[the risen Christ] was assembled together' with the Christians, or in their company; a literal translation would be, 'he took salt with them' (Cullmann, p. 16).

There was certainly preaching apart from the mission. Although it is no longer possible to be as dogmatic about the influence of the synagogue as in time past, the synagogue custom of exposition of Scripture, often by a visiting Rabbi, as with Jesus in Luke 4:16ff., could well have been carried over into Christian worship and would come to include those writings, apostolic letters and Gospels, which would go on to become part of the Christian canon. It used to be fashionable to argue that the needs of liturgy accounted for the composition of the Gospels, and this tied in with the belief that an early Christian calendar of observances governed their shape. This led to some ingenious and fascinating hypotheses by scholars such as Philip Carrington, who argued that Mark is arranged according to the Jewish cycle of sabbaths and feasts, and more recently Michael Goulder, who has regarded the Synoptic Gospels as lectionaries. Aileen Guilding saw the Fourth Gospel in terms of the Jewish three-year lectionary and Oscar Cullmann aimed 'to show how the Gospel of John regards it as one of its chief concerns to set forth the connection between the contemporary Christian worship and the historical life of Jesus' (Cullmann, p. 37). None of these attempts has gained scholarly consensus and they have rather passed out of consideration, though Michael Goulder does not give up easily. What is unchallengeable is that the Word was central to early Christian worship. Jesus himself left no writings, but he taught in memorable sayings and word pictures. The Church recalled him verbally and with the use of Scriptures old and new. The connection between Word and Sacrament could go back to the upper room itself where Jesus would teach over supper, and may be instanced in the Farewell Discourses of the Fourth Gospel which presumably took place at table, though after the meal, which is mentioned only in passing and does not include the Eucharist. By the time of Justin Martyr's *First Apology* around 150CE, 'the records of the apostles or writings of the prophets are read [in the assembly] for as long as time allows', expounded with exhortation by the president and followed by prayers and an extempore thanksgiving over bread, wine and water, which are then distributed.

It has been said that if St Paul had heard mention of 'the blessed Sacrament' he would have thought it referred to baptism not the Eucharist. This rite of water, according to the New Testament, is the act of initiation into Christ's religion. It is the sacrament of union with him, incorporation into his body. Jesus himself was baptised at the outset of his ministry under the preaching of John the Baptiser. Not all interpreters would maintain that this is central to our understanding of Christian baptism, even though the ancient Syrian tradition believed that the Christian's baptism was an imitation of it – hence the use of oil as well as water to simulate Jesus's messianic anointing.

Paul sees in the immersion in water a sharing of Christ's burial:

> By that baptism into his death we were buried with him, in order that as Christ was raised from the dead by the glorious power of the Father, so also we might set out on a new life. (Roman 6:4)

This did not have the influence on post-apostolic thought about baptism that might have been expected, certainly not in Syria. The font was regarded not as a grave but as a womb, following the Johannine tradition in which baptism is new birth, regeneration: 'In very truth I tell you, no one can enter the kingdom of God without being born from water and spirit' (John 3:5). A mere rite of water will be an empty sign; spirit alone may lead to an esoteric mysticism which could end in weird and superstitious fancy, even the occult. Yet the Spirit is as living water (John 7:37ff.) and water flows from the pierced side of Christ (John 19:34). The first letter of John says 'In fact there are three witnesses, the Spirit, the water and the blood, and these three are in agreement' (1 John 5:8), which may be a reference to an early custom of entry into the Church following the sequence of unction, baptism, Communion. Other ceremonies soon came to accompany water-baptism. We have noted anointing. There was also the laying-on of hands. Some have believed that from early times the laying-on of hands (apostolic and thereafter episcopal hands) was necessary to convey the Spirit. Instances are found in Acts, most notably 8:14ff., where the Samaritans had been baptised but did not receive the Spirit until Peter and John were sent from Jerusalem to lay on hands. (The canonical interpretation would be that 'hands' is in the plural because Peter and John each laid a hand on the baptised. For an apostle or bishop to lay on two hands would be ordination not initiation.)

Geoffrey Lampe argued that this case of the Samaritans is an exception because of the Samaritans and their delicate relationship to the Jews and that the water is itself 'the seal of the Spirit'. In the early Church no other rite was necessary (Lampe, *passim*). There is also doubt as to whether bishops were the successors of the apostles, who were evangelists, and recipients of resurrection appearances rather than the overseers of the Church. In Jerusalem, James the Lord's brother, the episcopal prototype, has a different office from Peter the apostle.

There remains the inveterate question as to whether infant baptism has New Testament precedent or justification. Theology dominates here rather than hard evidence. Hans Urs von Balthasar is emphatic that:

> . . . to say that entrance into God's Kingdom occurs unconsciously – that is, in such a way that the subject involved neither perceives nor understands Christ's gesture – is a fact so alien to Scripture . . . that it must without question be regarded as an exception . . . infant baptism obscures the normal image of the personal encounter with Christ and the decision for Christ that takes place in every Sacrament (thus making of it *merely* an *opus operatum*) [an objective work or ritual act valid irrespective of the response or faith of the participants]. And also because all Christian existence is therefore grounded upon a *fact* which is quasi-natural because it is not initially ratified by the subject.

On the other hand, he does recognise the powerful and moving argument from prevenient grace – 'while we were yet sinners Christ died for us' (Romans 8:5) – without our prior consent. Although he does not refer to it precisely, he seems to be questioning F. D. Maurice's belief that Calvary was the world's baptism. Has the Church then a cosmic responsibility towards all humankind (Balthaser, pp. 579f.)?

On the New Testament evidence it has been argued that baptism of families included babies (Acts 16:25) and even that baptism for the dead allowed the legitimacy of vicarious faith on behalf of those who could not take a conscious decision (1 Corinthians 15:29). And Polycarp's testimony before his martyrdom (*c.* 159CE), 'eighty and six years have I served him and he has done me no wrong' could imply that he was baptised as a baby.

CHAPTER 2

THE DEVELOPMENT OF CHURCH ORDER

In *The Search for the Origins of Christian Worship* Paul Bradshaw gives an invaluable account of the discovery in the nineteenth century of ancient church orders, rule books and constitutions on organisation, ethics and liturgy, which purported to be of apostolic origin. They were in fact claiming apostolic authority for disciplines which may have been more what their compilers wanted to be the rule in local churches than evidence of any uniform practice in the first days of the faith. We cannot be certain that these give an exact account of the practice of the churches from which they came. We like to imagine that if we use or adapt them we are worshipping in the same way as our distant forbears near to the events they celebrated, but this may not be so.

There are problems of translation. Some of the orders have not come down to us in their original languages. The so-called *Apostolic Tradition* of Hippolytus, so influential in modern eucharistic revisions, was presumably written in Greek, the liturgical language of the second-century Roman Church from which it is believed to have emanated. The original has to be reconstructed from translations into Latin, Arabic, Ethiopic, Sahidic and Bohairic, the oldest of which, the Latin, was probably not made until the fourth century. Even more, there is a feeling among modern scholars that this and other surviving documents may be products of 'armchair liturgists dreaming up what the perfect liturgy might be like if only they had the freedom to put into practice what their idiosyncratic tastes and personal convictions longed for' (Bradshaw, 1992, p. 72; cf. Stevenson, ed., p. 136). At the same time these documents must represent a tradition not very far removed from the apostolic age. They did not simply descend from heaven by way of devout imagination.

The *Didache* is a problem not only as regards dating, on which there has been a wide divergence of opinion (Joan Hazelden Walker thinks it even older than Mark's Gospel), but also provenance. Does it come from Egypt, Palestine or Syria, a mainstream community or a backwater? It is undoubtedly a composite document and parts may be primitive and parts much later. As to its place of origin, while it was obviously known in Egypt where versions and fragments of the text were found, the reference to the piece of bread 'scattered upon the hills' can hardly be to the flat lands of the Nile Delta, and the provision for an alternative to living water would hardly be necessary in the Nile valley. The possibility of a Syrian origin is reinforced by the invocatory formula, 'in the name of the Father, Son and Holy Spirit', which scholarly opinion believes was peculiar to Syrian Christianity until fairly late.

Content is also a puzzle. Does it describe a Eucharist or an *agapē* (lovefeast)? There are Jewish models, but the order creation-redemption is reversed. The cup precedes the bread and is the symbol of Christ the vine of David (Psalm 80:8,9). The broken bread prompts thanksgiving for the knowledge of God in Christ and prayer for the unity of the Church, that it may be made one even as the corn scattered on the mountains is made one in the loaf, broken that it may be distributed to the faithful. Only the baptised may eat and drink.

Are there teachings from St Matthew and phrases from St John? What is clear is that the *Didache* is not Pauline. There is no specific reference to the death of Jesus, though he is the revelation of the Father. The model prayer thanks God for himself, his holy name, 'for the knowledge and faith and immortality made known to us through your child Jesus', and for creation. The prayers for the Church and its unity have been much used since the document was rediscovered in 1873. They have become part of the treasury of the Churches in ecumenical times.

In Chapter 14, which may be later than what precedes, there seems evidence that the common meal was becoming a

Sunday Eucharist, 'on the Lord's day of the Lord'. There is assembly, breaking of bread, thanksgiving after confession. Are we to infer that these were also after the fraction and partaking? It is almost certain that the items are not in order. The confession is 'that your sacrifice may be pure', a spiritual sacrifice undoubtedly. For this purpose reconciliation with fellow Christians is a *sine qua non*.

The whole is summed up in the words of Malachi 1:11, much quoted in later writers, 'For this is that which is spoken by the Lord. "In every place and at every time, offer me a pure sacrifice; for I am a great king says the Lord, and my name is wonderful among the nations"'. The Old Testament injunctions still apply, but republished in Christ, in whom they are fulfilled. Kenneth Stevenson notes that 'the reference to incense in the passage is not included' although it is among subsequent authors (Stevenson, ed., p. 15).

It is easy to see how sacrifice in this metaphorical sense could evolve into the belief that the only perfectly pure sacrifice is that of Christ himself; there are the roots here of the later Latin Mass and the underlying belief that our sacrifice is only fitting if we enter into Christ's sacrifice and prayer. Stevenson points out that

> Although no reference (or allusion) is made to the heavenly offering of Christ, the 'pure offering' could refer to the joining of praise with the angels in heaven, which is part of late Jewish spirituality and is also to be found in the Book of Revelation (Rev 4:1ff.). Moreover, in apocalyptic, the only altar in the heavenly sanctuary is the incense altar, where no animal offerings are made, but only offerings that are *logikos* (reasonable), again in the Platonic sense of 'rational' as 'spiritual'. This term becomes important later on both in the East and the West, as a crucial definition of the eucharist as the Christian sacrifice, since it describes in vivid terms the way in which the eucharist joins in the heavenly ministry of Christ, as interceding (eternally) thereby bestowing the benefits of his saving work to his people (in history). (Stevenson, ed., p. 16)

The account of baptism in the *Didache* is brief. There is instruction, probably through the reading and possible exposition of the document of the 'Two Ways', one of life and one of death, which precedes. This does not necessarily presume a lengthy preparation, though the emphasis is on ethics rather than theology. Christianity is primarily a way of life. Nothing is said as to who baptises. Water, preferably running or living water, is the only element. There is no mention of oil or laying-on of hands. Immersion is not explicitly stated. There is nothing about the symbolic significance of water, as in Romans 6:3ff., where baptism re-enacts Christ's death and resurrection, or John 3:3ff., where baptism by water and the Spirit is rebirth. The baptism is by the trinitarian formula and is preceded by a fast for one or two days in which any others may join.

Liturgy is taking shape with Justin Martyr, writing at Rome (c. 150CE). In his account of Christian worship in his first *Apology* there are rites of baptism and Eucharist, the latter, as we have seen, describing a ministry of Word and Sacrament. The theology is of the Logos or Word incarnate, as in the Fourth Gospel, but one notices a concentration on the elements, which are not common bread or common drink but given either 'by the prayer of the Word who is from him', or 'by a word of prayer that is from him [God]', or 'by a prayer of the word that is from him'. Some might read out of this the adumbrations of the belief that the Eucharist is an 'extension of the incarnation'.

In the *Dialogue with Trypho,* the Jew, the Jewish offering of flour is presented as a type of the eucharistic bread. The Old Testament sacrifices are types of the Christian sacrifices, handed down by Christ in remembrance of his suffering. Malachi is quoted, with the reference to incense, as prophecy of the things that, on 'Jesus the Christ's' institution, are to be done and 'are done in every place of the world by Christians'.

A difficulty with the *Apology* is that Justin is explaining Christian worship to the Emperor Antoninus Pius to defend it against charges of occult and sinister practices, and he gives only such details as are necessary for his purpose in terms intelligible to an outsider. He does not enter deeply into matters for Christian instruction, such as whether 'President' is the usual term for the chief minister, or the extent of the scriptural readings, or how they were chosen, or what baptism involved in preparation or whether there were ceremonies other than dipping in water. E. C. Ratcliff made much of this, as did Gregory Dix. He believed that the *Dialogue* supplements the *Apology* with regard to both Eucharist and baptism; the former, as we have seen, fills out the sacrificial interpretation, the latter advances the theory that there is incipient confirmation in the implicit assertion to the Jew that what makes a person a Christian is the gift of the Spirit of God as promised to the Christ in Isaiah 11. Justin does not think is necessary to describe to Trypho how the Spirit is given to the new Christian. Ratcliff, on the analogy of Christ's own baptism and the following gift of the Spirit, and various hints in Justin, is convinced that he did not think water-baptism the whole of Christian initiation (Ratcliff, pp. 110ff.).

This is highly speculative on the part of Ratcliff and others, who were anxious to establish that almost from the beginnings of Christianity confirmation was the essential completion of baptism because through it the Holy Spirit was given by the laying-on of episcopal, that is apostolic, hands. Ratcliff was convinced that both Roman and Byzantine Fathers would have accorded confirmation the greater dignity for this reason (Ratcliff, p. 133). But this leads on to matters which had better be postponed for a slightly later discussion.

The Apostolic Tradition of Hippolytus, who died a martyr in the Sardinian mines, is a tract written during a quarrel by a man who could be venomous, to assert its author's views as to what liturgy should be. Emanating from Rome its theology as well as its liturgical shape is that of Justin Martyr. The most interesting feature and the most influential in our time is the Eucharistic Prayer following the ordination of a bishop. Since at this time the prayer was extempore, this is not an invariable form, authorised and with place in a liturgical book to be used on every occasion. It has a brevity, a lucid terseness, devoid of grandiloquence, characteristic of the West as against Eastern Christianity, which is far richer and with more words. It has certain constituents which become universal: the opening dialogue, 'The Lord be with you', the *Sursum Corda*, 'Lift up you hearts' and the response, the Preface, rehearsing belief about Christ, his relation to God and to creation, his incarnation through the Virgin, and work of redemption. The absence of any direct thanksgiving for creation contrasts with the Jewish meal blessing on which it may otherwise be modelled, but as in much Christian liturgy, it is the difference not the similarities with Jewish worship, as far as it is known, which are important. There follow the words of institution, the anamnesis, the offering of bread and cup. Then there is an epiclesis, an invocation of the Holy Spirit, upon offering and people. This may mark a transition to the prayer, dating at least from the fourth century, that the Spirit should enter the oblation and effect a change in the bread and wine as well as the people. The Spirit is invoked to gather the communicants into one and that they may partake of the Spirit as they partake of 'the holy gifts'. There is a final doxology. There is no *Sanctus*, 'Holy, holy, holy'. E. C. Ratcliff thought that the *Sanctus* was the original conclusion, so anxious was he to insist that authentic anaphoras ended in the adoration of heaven. His argument is powerful but flawed, if only because there is no evidence that the *Sanctus* formed part of Roman liturgy at that stage (Ratcliff, pp. 18ff.; and see *Journal of Ecclesiastical History* I (1) (1950) pp. 29–36).

Some of the phrases have spoken to modern hearts. 'He stretched out his hands when he should suffer' has found echo in the second Eucharistic Prayer of the new Roman missal and the third of the Anglican *Alternative Service Book*. There is a following paragraph which concludes the Preface and introduces the institution:

> And when he was betrayed to voluntary suffering that he might destroy death, and break the bonds of the devil, and tread down hell, and shine upon the righteous, and fix the limit, and manifest the resurrection, he took bread . . .

It is interesting to try and decide how many of these declarations would be acceptable to modern theology. Evil is personalised. There is assertion that the death of Christ has fixed its limit. Henceforth it can go thus far but no farther, something hard to believe in our terrible times. There is the harrowing of hell. Some of the images belong to the language of Christian belief still, though there are those who would argue that liturgical revision has not paid sufficient attention to symbols that come from an outdated cosmology.

Some have thought that the narrative and the anamnesis are later insertions, though Justin had sought warrant for them by quoting Matthew 26:26, implying that the institution narrative and the Eucharistic Prayer went together. If so, they are demanded by logic. As Jungmann pointed out:

> Thanksgiving and remembering are very closely connected. If we look at the content of thanksgiving it is seen to be nothing else but 'thinking of' . . . The meaning of the thanksgiving prayer is essentially this: in prayer before God we call to mind what we have received, and what the basis of our hope is: the great outlines of the work of redemption and the history of redemption, climaxing in the death and resurrection of Christ. (Jungmann, 1978, pp. 6f.)

Jungmann, giving the lectures originally in 1952–3, assumes the integrity of Hippolytus's original Eucharistic Prayer. Scholarship has advanced beyond his magisterial works, but even his slighter, more popular contributions still strike to the theological heart of the matters with which he deals.

As to initiation, *The Apostolic Tradition*, so much more detailed than the *Didache* or Justin, gives instructions on the examination of new Christians, their marital and social status. Regularity in marriage is essential. Heathen masters shall be required to give references and must be pleased. The demon-possessed shall not be allowed to hear the word until they are pure.

Certain crafts and professions are forbidden: brothel-keepers, actors, even teachers, presumably because they had to teach pagan myths, though they may have permission if otherwise they would be unemployed. But charioteers, gladiators and those who go to the games are to be rejected. Sculptors or painters must not make idols. Pagan priests and keepers of idols must abandon their professions. A soldier must not kill, nor take the oath which accorded the emperor divine honours. A magistrate, for similar reasons, cannot be baptised, nor must a catechumen cherish military ambitions. Prostitutes are profligates and eunuchs are out and all types of magicians, astrologers, necromancers and those who cut fringes or tassels on clothing which were believed to be protection against evil spirits.

Hippolytus undoubtedly belonged to the Christian rigorists and some of his instructions seem a long way from the one who received sinners and ate with them. Christ's compassion is somehow missing from these rules. Callistus was a slave who, after bitter punishments for some financial misjudgements on behalf of Christians, was denounced as a Christian. He acknowledged this and confessed his faith, and was sentenced to the Sardinian mines. He was released on the intercession of a Christian concubine of the Emperor Commodus, recovered his shattered health, became papal archdeacon and eventually Pope, an office for which Hippolytus had hoped. This made him Callistus's bitter enemy. He opposed his doctrines and his policies. Callistus's 'Decree on Penance', a few years later than *The Apostolic Tradition,* allowed for those who had fallen into sins of the flesh after baptism to be restored after due penance and absolution. This clemency infuriated Hippolytus as it did his contemporary Tertullian, though it has been the dominating factor in the casuistry of the Church ever since. Hippolytus therefore must not be regarded as other than the representative of one view of the rules of admission to the Church and its membership. (Dix, 1968, pp. xiii ff.).

The catechumenate is to last for three years, though conduct is more important than length of time. Ethics is more prominent in the period of preparation than theology, behaviour more than intellectual understanding. When instruction is finished, the catechumens are to 'pray by themselves, separated from the faithful'. The sexes are segregated throughout. The catechumens are not yet ready for the communal intercession, any more than for the Eucharist. Nor is their kiss holy for the Peace. Yet if a catechumens is arrested and possibly killed before receiving baptism, his sins are forgiven. He has received the baptism of blood.

The examination of those to be baptised is concerned with good lives and with works of care and mercy not faith. 'Religious experience', the story of conversion, does not enter into the matter. The gospel is heard only when the sponsors have testified to the catechumens' practical Christianity.

The catechumens are set apart and the process of exorcism through daily laying-on of hands begins. 'And when the day of their baptism approaches, the bishop shall exorcise each one of them, in order that he may know whether he is pure.' 'Possession' by the Alien, or Evil Spirit, is assumed to be the case with all. The Thursday before the Sunday of baptism is the day of ablutions. Menstruation means postponement for a woman. Friday is a fast day, Saturday the day of prayer, kneeling, while the bishop lays on hands and exorcises them again, after which he breathes on the candidates' faces, signs their foreheads, ears and noses and raises them to their feet.

The whole of Saturday night is spent in vigil, with readings and instruction. The candidates bring with them their eucharistic offerings but nothing more.

At cockcrow, prayer is made over the water, which must either flow in the font or be poured over it, 'living water', though in urgent necessity any water will do. The candidates take off their clothes. The 'little ones', children, who may not have reached the age of speech and whose parents therefore speak for them, are baptised first. The men follow and then the women, their hair loosened and all jewellery removed.

Two oils are prepared by episcopal thanksgiving, one the oil of thanksgiving, the other of exorcism, which is itself exorcised. A priest is flanked by two deacons bearing the oils. There is renunciation of Satan, personally addressed, and then the anointing with the oil of exorcism and the words, 'Let every evil spirit depart far from you'. The candidates are then handed over naked to the bishop or to the baptising priest. A deacon descends with the candidate into the water and there is a threefold baptism, each time in response to an affirmation of faith, in 'one God the Father almighty', in 'Christ Jesus, the Son of God' the events of whose life from birth to parousia are rehearsed, and in 'the holy Spirit and the holy Church and the resurrection of the flesh'. Ascending from the water, the candidate is then anointed by a presbyter (priest) with the oil of thanksgiving. Wiped and clothed, he, or she, enters the church where the bishop lays on hands, and prays that thus with their sins remitted, 'though the laver of regeneration of the holy Spirit', they may have grace to serve God according to his will. There is one more anointing with the oil of thanksgiving, this time of the head. The forehead is signed, a kiss given and there is the greeting 'The Lord be with you' with the response 'And with your spirit'. Then and only then the candidates may join with all the people in the prayers of the faithful. 'And when they have prayed they shall give the kiss of peace.'

The Apostolic Tradition is now regarded as the source of all the other church orders. The *Canons* of Hippolytus derive from *The Apostolic Tradition* and probably date from between 336 and 340. They deal with the same issues at a later date. There are still prohibited occupations for Christians, very much the same as before. The threefold orders of ministry, bishops, priests and deacons are clear. There is to be a certain magnificence about their dress at the altar to distinguish them from the people. The readers too must be ceremonially clothed. The altar is to be treated with reverence and the sanctuary veiled from the worshippers; if an insect or foreign body falls into the cup through carelessness an evil spirit may have power over it. Women and men are to be segregated and the kiss of peace is not to be exchanged with a member of the opposite sex.

The Eucharistic Prayer of the *Tradition* is left out, as well as prayers over the oil, cheese and olives. Paul Bradshaw who has produced the only English edition of the *Canons*, presumes that this is because 'they did not correspond sufficiently with those in use in CH's own tradition for them to be acceptable' (Bradshaw, 1987, p. 13).

The final canon is not found in the *Tradition*. It concerns the paschal celebration on the eve of Eastern. No one is to sleep until morning and the worshippers are to be bathed, purified and 'illuminated', in expectation of the coming of him who has made the whole creation free. There is much condemnation of those who have been baptised and have received communion, declared themselves Christians and then returned to the ways of the world. The true Christian should seek to resemble Christ. There is a whole catalogue of vices to be avoided and virtues to be practised. There is to be generosity, mercy and no contempt for slaves, on the part of masters, but no dealings with the 'Gentiles' nor mixing with them, sentiments taken over from Judaism, though 'Gentiles' must now refer to pagans and adherents of false faiths and worldly values. It is not racist. Celibacy and total avoidance of women are *de rigueur* for those who would be as the angels. Such a Christian, who apparently is of the male sex only, must live humbly, in voluntary poverty, supporting himself by the work of his own hands, done, it would seem, without tools or mechanical aids. He must give to the poor and to the Christian community from what he earns in this way. He is to pray and fast much and be willing to bear suffering. 'Let him carry his cross and follow the Saviour and be ready to die at any moment for the sake of Christ in faith.'

Gluttony, pride and love of gold are the temptations, similar to those of Christ in the wilderness, most to be resisted by those who would be perfect. Pride is the sin of sins, love the supreme virtue, the foot-washing the model. Matthew 25:31ff. carries the promise of great reward, for Christ is served in these afflicted 'little brothers', presumably Christians in distress.

What is imperative is that ethics and liturgy should be inseparable.

The longest of the church orders is the *Constitutions of the Holy Apostles according to Clement,* known for short as the *Apostolic Constitutions,* and dated about 375CE. It includes almost the whole of the *Didache* and the third-century *Didascalia,* the latter of Syrian origin. It is a huge compendium, almost certainly compiled in Antioch. What follows is taken largely from W. Jardine Grisbrooke's edition and introduction (1990).

The nature of its theology is problematic, which is understandable given the ferment of fourth-century Antioch. It has been charged with Arianism, though this may be due to the fact that it is conservative and lives in the theological milieu of second-century Origen, some of whose archaic terms were being interpreted by heretics in support of their own doctrines. The christology is unclear, but the doctrine of the Holy Spirit seems to rank it among created beings, which is incompatible with the declarations of the Council of Constantinople in 381.

There are interesting accounts of the arrangements of the church building on the model of a ship. The deacons are the mariners, the 'brethren' passengers. The building is oblong, like a boat – the presupposition is, of course, that it is rowed. It is turned towards the east and the celebrants and congregation face east during the Eucharist. There is no evidence of the westward position in Syria, much less of worship in the round. The ambo or lectern and the bishop's throne are in the centre, the presbyters' seats on either side of the latter, the deacons standing. The sanctuary is screened, to heighten the sense of heavenly awe. It is all rather different from the house churches of earlier days.

> As everywhere in the early church standing is taken for granted as the posture for prayer; in VII, 45, 1, the newly-baptised Christian is told to pray the Lord's Prayer standing, because 'of necessity he who is risen (with Christ) ought to stand up and pray because he that is raised stands upright'. Kneeling is prescribed for certain prayers (cf. VIII, 10, 2, p. 27) while at times the whole congregation or a particular group within it is required to bow or to prostrate. (Grisbrooke, 1990, p. 14)

The congregation is seated for the readings apart from the Gospel, but they may have sat on the floor. There is no indication that seats are provided. The laying-on of hands is clearly of importance in various contexts. The sign of the cross is mentioned but once, though it would surely be made more often. The priests washed their hands ceremonially before the Eucharistic Prayer, a practice found in the Jewish Passover, though Kilpatrick does not regard this as mutual influence. It goes back to first-century practice (Kilpatrick, p. 40). There is distinctive dress for the clergy and the bishop is to put on his 'shining garment' before the Eucharistic Prayer. Women must cover their heads. Two of the deacons on each side of the altar, 'each hold a fan of thin membranes, or of the feathers of a peacock, or of fine cloth, and let them silently drive away the flying insects that they may not come near the cups' (VIII, II, 12. 1, Grisbrooke, 1990, p. 31).

The liturgy is, one may think, inordinately long in the Syrian and Eastern style, not the Latin, which is more terse and more tight. Grisbrooke sets out the order in detailed outline. The surviving service follows the ordination of a bishop.

There is no entrance rite. It begins with the Liturgy of the Word. The number of lessons is uncertain. Were there three or as many as twelve? If the former, the provision would be as in modern revisions – Old Testament, 'Epistle', Gospel. Grisbrooke thinks there may have been four – Law, Prophets, Epistle, Gospel – a pattern which still survives in some Eastern rites. The new bishop then greets the people in the words of 'the Grace' and preaches a sermon.

There follows a whole series of dismissals by the deacon. There are five categories. First those who are 'hearers' only and unbelievers. Then the catechumens, after a litany and a trinitarian prayer by the bishop asking for their renewal and union with the Church to share in its mysteries. To the biddings all the people are to respond 'Lord have mercy', and especially the children to whose prayers was ascribed a particular power. Next those possessed by evil spirits with a prayer for exorcism which is largely an eloquent invocation of the Christ who cast out devils, a piling up of scriptural ascriptions. Then the 'illuminands' are dismissed, catechumens in the last stages of preparation for what Justin Martyr called the 'enlightenment' of baptism, and, finally, penitents, those who have transgressed against the law of Christ and the Church but who, after a period deprived of the sacraments and the full fellowship of the Church, are to be restored. They pray prostrate.

Those who remain, the faithful who would have left only on pain of excommunication, join in the common prayers of the Church. These consist of a lengthy litany of twenty-one petitions, the basis of what is the intercession in the liturgy of St John Chrysostom to this day. They ask for peace in the world and the Church, pray for the parish, which probably means diocese, for 'every episcopate under heaven', and every order of ministry, for those who bring forth the fruit of good works and make offerings, for the 'newly enlightened', for the sick, for travellers, exiles, prisoners, the oppressed, for enemies and persecutors, for those outside the Church, the unconverted, for the children, for one another and for every Christian soul. This is followed by a prayer by the bishop, largely for the people's perfection and sanctification in the truth.

There is next the kiss of peace, men greeting men and women women. The children stand near the 'bema', a raised platform in the centre of the church which contains the lectern, the bishop's throne and the seats for the presbyters. This is in order that they may see the action, but also that they may be in sight of a deacon so that they do not misbehave. Similarly a deacon is to watch over the men and women so that they do not disturb the proceedings, or whisper, or sleep. The men's and women's doors, separate, must remain shut. No one is to enter or leave during the anaphora. Solemn warnings precede the Offertory.

This begins with the greeting and the 'Lift up your hearts'. There follows praise to God and thanksgiving for creation, which tells the whole story to include the celestial as well as the terrestrial, angels as well as human beings, every element, all creatures and plants, the seasons, the weather and man as a citizen of the world and its adornment, given dominion over 'the fish of the sea and the birds of the air', an immortal soul and a mortal body, with reason and moral judgement, five senses 'and the ability to move from place to place'. Then there is thanksgiving for salvation history – the whole story of Israel from the disobedience of Adam to the miraculous entry into the promised land under Joshua.

The congregation joins in the *Sanctus* with the heavenly host whose incessant song this is (cf. Isaiah 6:11–13). These latter are named in all their numerous degrees, ten thousand times ten thousand and thousands of thousands. They are not simply comprehended in the brevity of 'angels and archangels and all the company of heaven'.

The prayer then continues with thanksgiving for the new covenant in Christ who, eternal Son of God, did not abandon lost mankind throughout previous history but then became incarnate with the Father's consent, 'to become man who was the creator of man; to become subject to the laws who was the lawgiver; to become a sacrifice who was the high priest; to become a sheep who was the shepherd'. The story of Jesus, the appeaser of God and reconciler of God and humanity is told, his virgin birth and full humanity, his revelation of God in preaching and teaching and mighty works, his betrayal, arrest, trials, sufferings, death and his rising again and his being taken up, after forty days, to the right hand of God.

The institution narrative follows. Nearly all such have differences from those of the New Testament, possibly due to their extemporisation in early days. This depends to some extent on 1 Corinthians 11:23ff., but there are many elaborations:

> For in the night in which he was betrayed, he took bread in his holy and undefiled hands and looking up to you, his God and Father, he broke [it], and gave [it] to his disciples, saying: This is the mystery of the New Covenant, take of it, [and] eat, this is my body [which is] broken for many, for the remission of sins. In the same way also [he took] the cup, mixing it of wine and water, and sanctifying [it] he gave it to them, saying: Drink of it, all [of you];

> this is my blood [which is] shed [or poured out] for many for the remission of sins; do this for my memorial. For as often as you eat this bread and drink this cup, you proclaim my death until I come.

The anamnesis includes the whole work of God in Christ from the Passion to the final coming and judgement and the offering of 'this bread and this cup', controversial words in the Church of England revisions of our time. A sacrifice is being offered in the oblation of the elements and those who make it are ministering as priests, or, literally, following Grisbrooke, 'priestizing'.

The epiclesis asks that the offering be accepted and the Holy Spirit sent down upon it 'that he may make this bread the body of your Christ and this cup the blood of your Christ'. The root meaning of the Greek translated 'make' is 'to show' or 'manifest'. In this context it undoubtedly has overtones of 'transform'. The consequence of the descent of the Spirit is that the partakers themselves are filled with the Holy Spirit and their own spirituality is made secure in their becoming worthy of Christ and obtaining eternal life. The Holy Spirit is said to be 'the witness of the sufferings of the Lord Jesus'. This is echoed in one of Charles Wesley's *Hymns on the Lord's Supper* in which the Spirit is invoked, 'Come thou witness of his dying'. Grisbrooke points out that there is possibly a different interpretation of this phrase and that it is the sacrifice and not the Holy Spirit which is the witness. He agrees that this is not likely (Grisbrooke, pp. 38f.).

There are then further intercessions. Modern Western revisers would regard these as redundant, an unnecessary repetition. The prayers of the faithful in response to the Ministry of the Word would be enough. Whatever may be the historical explanation of their entry into the anaphora, the theological rationale is that intercessions would be most truly effective if they were made as close to the most awesome acts of the service as possible, in the presence of the consecrated species. Alexander Schmemann, giving a modern justification, has said that it is as Christians are about to partake of the heavenly feast that they must remember the world and human needs (Schmemann, 1966, p. 53). The anaphora concludes with a doxology and the 'amen' which Jerome said should be like a thunderclap. There follows one more litany reinforcing the intercessions, which ends with a commendation, what Grisbrooke calls a 'prayer of humble access', said standing. It asks that, sanctified and 'cleansed from all filthiness of flesh and of spirit', we may be worthy partakers of the good gifts set before [us].

The invitation includes texts that have become familiar throughout the Churches: 'The holy gifts of God for the holy people of God'; 'One is holy, one is Lord, Jesus Christ to the glory of God the Father'. There is a *Gloria in Excelsis,* the angels' song at Bethlehem with the Palm Sunday 'Hosannas'.

The communicants partake in hierarchical order: the bishop first, then the presbyters, deacons, subdeacons, readers, singers and ascetics; then the women deacons, the virgins, the widows; the children and after them all the people approach, with reverence and godly fear. The bishop gives the oblation; the deacon the cup. The recipient says 'amen' to both. Psalm 34 is read during communion – the psalm which has the words 'O taste and see that the Lord is good . . .'.

There is a final, quite lengthy, thanksgiving by the bishop, a prayer over the people and a dismissal by the deacon. The 'blessed bread' which has been offered by the people but found surplus to requirements and not consecrated, is distributed as it still is in Eastern rites, but, here, to the ministers in hierarchical order, the bishop getting four parts, the presbyters three, the deacons two, the rest. i.e. subdeacons, readers, singers, deaconesses, one.

I have dealt with this liturgy at length because it illustrates the Eastern development. It has the rudiments of the Orthodox liturgies used to this day.

There is much else in the *Apostolic Constitutions.* The liturgical year is described, beginning in what is April to us. The great feast of the Nativity is celebrated on the twenty-fifth of the ninth month (December), the Epiphany on the sixth of the tenth month (January). This is the feast of the manifestation of Christ's divinity. The coming of the wise men is celebrated at Christmas. There is a fast in Lent and Holy Week, probably for nine weeks, though it may have lasted only from Monday to Friday each week, Saturdays and Sundays being days of no fasting. Was Holy Week included in Lent? It is all rather complex. There must be no confusion with the Jewish Passover at Easter. The Christian Passover will be kept at the vernal equinox and the resurrection will always be celebrated on a Sunday. The Sunday following, after eight days, is to be observed with great honour because of the convincing of Thomas. The Ascension is to be celebrated on the Thursday, forty days after Easter and on the fiftieth day is the great feast of Pentecost. These will be days of rejoicing. There must be no mourning; but there will be a fast the week after the week of Pentecost and thereafter fasts on Wednesdays and Fridays except at festivals.

As in the *Didache,* the Lord's Prayer is to be said three times a day. There are to be prayers 'in the morning, at the third hour, at the ninth, in the evening and at cockcrow'. The third, sixth and ninth hours represent times in the Lord's crucifixion. There were to be morning and evening services in church, possibly coinciding with the above hours. The *Gloria in Excelsis* is sung in the morning – two different texts are given – and there is an evening hymn of praise, ending with the *Nunc Dimittis.* Psalms and litanies are prescribed. There should be no prayers with catechumens, heretics or those who are having sexual relations with slaves.

There are three baptismal rites due to the state of transition of initiation practices in fourth-century Syria. A post-baptismal anointing is introduced and the pre-baptismal anointing hitherto required, which in our terms meant that confirmation preceded baptism, is somewhat downgraded. Although it is in this liturgy that there is found the sentence so cherished by some recent scholars, 'But if there be neither oil nor chrism, the water is sufficient', Grisbrooke points out that 'there is the implication that the other actions are required (i.e. the anointing and the sealing), even if they can only be performed with water' (Grisbrooke, p. 62). The reference seems to imply that baptism of the dying is in mind. Some element other than water was generally thought necessary, possibly because of the model of the baptism of Jesus and the descent of the Spirit upon him.

The first anointing is preceded by a renunciation of the devil and all his works, an 'adhesion' to Christ and a profession of faith, virtually the Nicene Creed. The summarised prayer for the blessing of the oil reflects the changes. This anointing is now primarily for the remission of sins and preparation for baptism, but the oil is sanctified that the 'grace of the Spirit' may be imparted to it. The water is blessed with a preface of adoration for the incarnation and God's rescue of mankind from the Fall and then the actual prayer of blessing with echoes of Romans 6:3ff. There is no mention of Christ descending into the waters of Jordan. This blessing which gives spiritual power to the water, so that it is no longer in its natural state as in Jewish baptisms, is essential to the validity of the sacrament. Baptism is in the threefold name, presuming three immersions, and then the post-baptismal anointing with the scented chrism, representing 'the sweet odour' of Christ which makes Christian lives fragrant, since they have died and risen with Christ.

Finally the newly-baptised stands upright as risen with Christ and prays towards the east on the example of 2 Chronicles 5:13. First there is the Lord's Prayer, now permitted, and then the petition for 'a body undefiled, a pure heart, a watchful mind, a knowledge without error and the presence of your Holy Spirit that I may be founded in the truth and have full assurance of the same, through your Christ, through whom glory be to you in the Holy Spirit for ever.'

Many other eucharistic liturgies and expositions have come down to us from the first five centuries. These may be classified according to their places of origin.

Egypt

The so-called *Sacramentary of Sarapion*, in spite of being judged by some scholars to be Arian and heretical and as late as 456CE, could well be the compilation of Sarapion, Bishop of Thmuis in the Nile Delta (340–60), friend of Athanasius. The intercessions come after the sermon, though the preface to the anaphora prays for the worshipping congregation and the commemoration of the departed is within the anaphora. Sacrificial language is used regarding the bread and the cup:

> Full is heaven, full also is earth of your excellent glory, Lord of the powers. Fill also this sacrifice with your power and your

> partaking, for to you have we offered this living sacrifice, this bloodless offering.

The term 'bloodless offering' or 'unbloody sacrifice' has a long history. It is found in the second-century *Testament of Levi*. It is not confined to the Eucharist. It both describes the perfect worship of heaven and contrasts Christian worship with pagan holocausts. It is closely connected with the 'living sacrifice' of Romans 12:1, the offering of ourselves. It is Eastern and in contrast to the theology of the West which was, later, so concentrated on the 'bleeding sacrifice' of Calvary. It is also found in the anaphoras of Chrysostom, James and Mark (K. W. Stevenson in G. Austin, ed., pp. 103–30). The bread is 'the likeness of the holy body'; the cup 'the likeness of the blood'; the action makes 'the likeness of the death'. The words imply similitude rather than what would in the philosophic categories of the medieval West be change of substance, but there could be a hint that the liturgy re-enacts Calvary.

This is a sacrament of reconciliation. The institution is lengthy for there is commentary on the words, including the passage from the *Didache*, slightly amplified:

> And as this bread was scattered over the mountains, and was gathered together and become one, so gather your holy Church, out of every nation and every country and every city and village and house, and make one living Catholic Church.

As we have already noted, it may be thought incongruous in the Nile Delta to pray about bread 'scattered over the mountains'.

The *Liturgy of St Mark*, the liturgy of the patriarchate of Alexandria, had reached the shape in which we know it, though with fewer words, by the time of the Council of Chalcedon in 451. The discovery of papyri and various fragments in the twentieth century would date parts of it two hundred years earlier. There are distinctive features before the anaphora, though these vary in various manuscripts. After preliminaries such as prayer over the incense and prayers for the emperor and the patriarch, the Ministry of the Word is succeeded by intercessions. These, again, are not invariable in different versions. They are followed by the 'Three Prayers' for peace, the patriarch and the congregations, a distinctive feature of Egyptian rites. Some of these intercessions are found expanded in the anaphora where they have an unusual position in the Preface, which offers 'this reasonable and bloodless service'. They are lengthy and comprehensive. The last, which consists of short petitions derived from the first letter of Clement of Rome, is said with all standing, presumably even the weak and infirm, and is followed by the deacon's summons to turn to the east and an adoration, which has reference to the heavenly hosts, leading to the *Sanctus*. This, from Isaiah 6, had its liturgical origin in the synagogue. In spite of E. C. Ratcliff's contention that it may well have been found in the second century and 'that the spiritual locus of ancient Christian worship . . . is not the church-building on earth but the sanctuary of heaven' (Ratcliff, p. 33) most scholars believe that it was not among the earliest elements of the anaphora, but was included in the East around 300CE and in Rome one hundred and fifty years later. There is an epiclesis which, usually, introduces, rather than follows, the institution: 'fill, O God, this sacrifice also with a blessing from you through the descent of your [all-] holy spirit' (G. J. Cuming, 1990, *passim*).

The anaphora of St Basil of Caesaria may represent the use of Cappadocia in the first half of the fourth century, having been brought to Egypt by the Cappadocian Father, St Basil, around 357CE. He may have amplified it into the *Liturgy of St Basil* which is still in use in the Orthodox Church, though only on ten days in the year. It is extant in two Coptic versions and one Greek form.

In this anaphora, the Preface addresses God as 'I AM' and celebrates creation, visible and invisible, before the *Sanctus*. Afterwards there is the story of the Fall and the salvation wrought by the incarnate Christ, who gave himself over to death, descended into hell, rose again and ascended into heaven where he awaits the day of his appointment to judge the world. The institution follows 1 Corinthians 11:23, but includes the mixed chalice. The anamnesis is of the whole work of Christ in his sufferings, triumph and 'glorious and fearful coming again', but not in creation. The epiclesis asks that 'your holy Spirit may come upon us and upon these gifts that are set before you and may sanctify them and make them holy of holies'. The intercessions, succinct and without elabration, and the commemoration of the saints and the departed follow. This anaphora, used in Egypt, resembles those of Antioch.

Syria

The Christianity of East Syria with its centres at Edessa and Nisibis retained the influence of Judaism and resisted attempts to bring it within the Hellenistic orbit. It was in conflict with the Byzantine developments, not least in christology, and after the Council of Ephesus in 431, it drifted into the doctrines of Nestorius to be condemned, somewhat unfairly one may think, as heresy. Nestorius insisted that there were two distinct persons in Christ, human and divine, but laid stress on his humanity, against the orthodox tendency, and in spite of the Chalcedonian definition, to think of Jesus more as God than as man.

The *Liturgy of Addai and Mari* is so named after the traditional founder of the Church of Edessa who was said to be one of the seventy, or seventy-two, disciples sent out by Jesus in Luke 10:1. Is he the Thaddeus of Mark 3:18 or in some manuscripts of Matthew 10:3? More probably, he is to be identified with a shadowy figure of the second century. Mari was a disciple of his.

The anaphora is to be said privately by the priest apart from the *Sanctus* and 'amen'. Part is addressed to the Father and part to the Son. But the great puzzle is the absence of an institution narrative. Scholars have made erudite and ingenious attempts at reconstruction. There is no consensus and it is important to remember that early anaphoras were fluid, being extempore compositions of the presiding minister or bishop, though like all such they would have common and repetitive elements. The absence of the institution may chiefly be a problem to those who believe that it is these words which effect consecration. E. C. Ratcliff thought that the rite was a transition from the *agapē* (lovefeast) to the later Mass, *eucharistia* (thanksgiving), rather than *anaphora* (offering). But the argument that it was too awesome to be publicised, put forward by those who believe that an original institution narrative, possibly addressed to the Son, dropped out due both to being recited from memory and to the discipline of secrecy, is intriguing (cf. Spinks, 1993, *passim*).

Theodore of Mopsuestia (*c.* 350–428), mentor of Nestorius, was the great liturgical theologian of the East Syrian Church. And he is especially important in his doctrine of the eucharistic offering. The rites both of baptism and the Eucharist have become awe-inspiring, almost spine-chilling, different both from the Last Supper and the worship of the early house churches. The Christian thanksgiving should be equal to the praises of the seraphim (Spinks, 1993, p. 78).

> What we perform in the liturgy is a kind of sacrifice. *The duty of the High Priest of the New Covenant* (i.e. Christ, whose part the bishop enacts) *is to offer the sacrifice which revealed the nature of the New Covenant*. It is clearly a sacrifice, though it is not something that is new or accomplished by the efforts of the bishop; it is a recalling of this true offering. (Yarnold, p. 209, emphasis in the original; cf. p. 201)

The bishop represents Christ, the High Priest, the deacons the angels, the invisible powers whose liturgy goes on in heaven. Vestments 'give them a more impressive appearance than they possess on their own account'. Stoles were originally sweat rags, cloths carried to wipe perspiration from the face. They were elongated and were wrapped round the neck like a student's scarf. A great many liturgical customs and appurtenances, utilitarian in origin, have become sacralised and given meaning symbolic of spiritual and evangelical realities. The stole, now no longer draped round the neck like a scarf but worn on the shoulder as a servant might, is yet a sign of freedom in Christ. If the bishop represents Christ sacrificing himself, the deacons are as the 'invisible ministering powers' who bring the symbols of Christ's sacrifice to 'the awesome altar'. They are like the angel in Gethsemane (according to Luke) who strengthened Jesus. The liturgy is a solemn if shadowy image of what took place in the historic Passion. This anticipates medieval spirituality in both West and East which saw in the actions of the Mass a correspondence with what happened to Christ. 'By means of the signs we must see Christ now being led away to his passion and again later when he is stretched out on the altar to be immolated for us.' The Offertory is the symbol of Christ proceeding along the dolorous way to his Passion and lying dead upon the altar. The angels do not as in Henry Hart Milman's Palm Sunday hymn, with its echoes of Eastern liturgy, 'look down with sad and wondering eyes /To see the approaching sacrifice'. They are like the spectators at the games shouting Jesus on to the glory, which after pains, short in comparison to their benefits for all believers, will be his (cf. Yarnold, pp. 214ff.).

The bread placed on the altar completes the representation of the Passion. It is as though Christ has already undergone suffering and death and the altar is his tomb. Some of the deacons spread cloths on it as a winding-sheet for him, while, as in funerals of the great of the earth, others fan the air above the body to prevent insects or bird-droppings settling on it. (Fans were essential in the climate of Syria.)

This takes place in silence simulating that of the followers of Jesus in recollection and fear after he had died. The angels too wait, but in glorious expectation of his rising from the dead, which they announce to the women who come to honour the body.

The Offertory recalls Christ's death, but this itself proclaims the resurrection. The prayer of the bishop over the offerings gives thanks for salvation and the Sacrament and for his own ministry and asks for the grace of the Holy Spirit that he may be worthy to celebrate the mysteries which are beyond him as a natural man. The prayer ends with the response of affirmation, 'amen'. There is then the Peace. Paul always puts 'Grace before it, since it is only by God's grace, not our own efforts, that we receive it'. The response to the bishop's 'Peace be with you' is with the phrase 'And with your spirit'. Theodore maintains that 'spirit' here refers not to the bishop's inner self, but to his grace of ordination. The response really is a wish that God's peace may dwell in the whole heart and life of the one about to perform this awesome duty, that his conscience may be clear, that he may be free from all evil, worldly anxieties and from undue tension as he fulfils this ministry. The kiss of peace is exchanged as an expression of unity and mutual charity and reconciliation as in Matthew 5:22–4.

The bishop and all priests present wash their hands as a sign of the cleansing of their hearts. The diptychs are read, the names of the living and the believing dead, for we learn from this the effects of the incarnation, the universal scope of what God has done in Jesus Christ, which benefits all, the living as they contemplate their future hopes and the dead who sleep, 'waiting in the hope for which Christ accepted the death we commemorate in this sacrament'.

The deacon now summons the people: 'Turn your eyes to the offering' for the real offering is not the bread and wine offered to symbolise Christ's death, but the prayer about to begin in which these elements become Christ's body and blood. The bishop blesses the people with the apostolic benediction, 'so rich in meaning and so solemn in character'. Theodore relates it to John 3:16, 'God so loved the world that he gave his only-begotten Son that whosoever believeth in him should not perish but have everlasting life.' The *Sursum Corda,* the summons which fixes minds and turns hearts to heaven, is soon followed by the *Sanctus,* though some words of the Preface may have dropped out. The thrice-repeated 'holy' proclaims the doctrine of the Trinity, recently formulated, but revealed in advance to Isaiah from whose vision in the Temple the seraphic hymn comes. Just as Isaiah when he heard these words fell on his face and uttered lamentation for himself and all his race, so all are to stand in fear and trembling, eyes cast down. In the Sacrament at this moment Christ rises from the dead and pours out his grace, which can happen only by the action of the Holy Spirit so that there is an immediate epiclesis. Theodore maintains that 'our Lord's body was clearly revealed as immortal when it had received the Spirit and his anointing'. So by the invocation of the Spirit the bread and wine, anointed by grace, become the body and blood of Christ, free of corruption and change like his body after the resurrection. There is then an epiclesis over the people that they may not partake to their judgement and ill, as Paul warns in 1 Corinthians 11:29. The Spirit overcomes divisions, quarrels, arguments, envy and jealousy. There is further prayer for the living and departed. The bishop takes the bread and breaks it, looking up to heaven. The bread is dropped into the chalice piece by piece. The words of institution are quoted in Theodore's exposition and presumably repeated in the rite, though this is assumed rather than specifically stated. Fr Yarnold points out that Theodore may be too subtle. The bread is broken for distribution; also it may be mixed with the wine as representing the whole Christ. For this reason, the bishop traces the sign of the cross over the blood with the bread and over the bread with the blood. The third reason is that Christ may be 'shared out' as he was to small groups of disciples in his resurrection appearances. This may seem a strange interpretation, yet it is redolent of the way in which the risen Christ appeared to his various followers, who were able, albeit briefly, to enjoy 'sublime communion' with him and anticipate the delights of the resurrection life in the world to come. Theodore nowhere says that the broken bread represents Christ's broken body, as some Fathers do, presumably following the manuscripts which read 'broken for you' in 1 Corinthians 11:24, which version in fact he quotes in describing the institution. He thinks of the breaking of the bread especially in terms of the resurrection, as at the end of the walk to Emmaus (cf. Luke 24:35). There is a Christian sensuality about Theodore's exposition. In receiving one little mouthful we receive Christ whole, just as the woman with the issue of blood received all of Christ by touching the hem of his garment, or a kiss on the mouth is intended to embrace the whole body (Yarnold, p. 235).

The Eucharistic Prayer concludes with prayer for those who have donated the bread and wine and asks that the sacrifice may be approved of God and that the grace of the Holy Spirit may come upon the world. The sacrament is 'holy things for holy people'. Only the baptised may receive it. The response to the invitation is 'One holy Father, one holy Son, one Holy Spirit', followed by the *Gloria Patri*. Our holiness comes from the one holy God and to acknowledge this prompts our praise.

Communion so unites us with Christ that we become his body. The bishop receives communion first because he needs to communicate just as much as anyone else. There is equality here not precedence. The communicants come by the mercy of God which alone makes them worthy and with all the fervour of those who are Christ's own, fed, as by a natural mother with her own body. Yet joyful as we are, we approach with eyes cast down and both hands extended, the right stretched out to receive the offering, the left underneath to support it. As he gives communion the bishop says, 'The body of Christ' and the communicant in fear and love replies 'amen'. And so with the chalice. There is much guidance as to receiving. The bread should be placed on the eyes, kissed and addressed in prayer as to Christ with confession and adoration. Then the bread is swallowed and personal thanksgiving offered. We should not abstain from communion in knowledge of our sinfulness. Communion will strengthen us and if we live careful and disciplined lives, eager for the good, our faults will be undeliberate and not harm us. Like the live coal the seraph placed on Isaiah's lips after the *Sanctus,* which had made him cry out in realisation of his sinful nature, the mysteries will cleanse us and cancel our debts and abolish our sins as fire consumes thorns. The bishop is as the tongs by which the coals were taken from the altar and brought to the prophet's lips, the intermediary. The grace of ordination makes him as such. It is interesting that in later Orthodox liturgy, the Theotokos, Mary, the Virgin, the God-bearer, is seen as the tongs of Isaiah 6.

There are rules for admission to communion. A serious sin demands abstinence from the Sacrament, the counsel of a priest and penance before restoration, but there is no suggestion of total rigorism, or that repentance is not possible after post-baptismal sin (Yarnold, pp. 243–50). For Theodore the two sacraments of baptism and Eucharist are closely connected. Baptism is birth in anticipation of the birth of the resurrection, or rather it is the seed of new life to be brought to birth; the Eucharist is the food which we receive as growing children, suitable for our life in this world. It is symbolic of our being fed with the grace of the Holy Spirit.

In baptism the devil is renounced, the candidate standing barefoot on sackcloth, outer garments removed, hands stretched out in an attitude of prayer. The renunciation is followed by a covenant with Christ, solemn vows made kneeling; and the first anointing by the bishop wearing 'a delicate, shining linen vestment', to inspire both fear and love. This anointing – like everything else, in the name of the Trinity – is the seal to mark the candidate out forever as the sheep of Christ. It is like branding or the tattoo on a soldier's hand to mark his identity and whom he serves. The seal is on the forehead. The candidate's sponsor stands behind, spreads a linen stole over the candidate's head and raises him to his feet.

There is then a complete stripping and a total anointing before the candidate goes down into the blessed water. There is a triple immersion guided by the bishop's hand, once for every person of the Trinity. The bishop does not say 'I baptise you', but 'N [naming the candidate] is baptised', for no man, only divine grace, can convey the gift of second birth. When the candidate emerges from the water a dazzling white garment is put on and there is a further seal on the forehead in the triune name. Baptism is once for all. It cannot be repeated.

Theodore, whose christology was later condemned as Nestorian, was right in his belief that baptism does not unite us with the divine life of Christ, but gives us a share in his human life and resurrection from the dead. Our baptism is the baptism Christ himself received in his humanity. The declaration at the Jordan that he is the Father's 'beloved son' refers to our adoption in him. Christ was baptised in the name of the whole Trinity, as the descent of the dove, the form of the Holy Spirit, shows.

There does seem to be something like confirmation in Theodore, though not after an interval, in that, as with Jesus at Jordan, the Holy Spirit is given after baptism by a further anointing. This is unlike most Syrian liturgies where the Spirit is conferred in the course of the ceremony. There was, of course, no oil at the Lord's baptism, but the descent of the Holy Spirit as a dove and the declaration of his divine sonship. And G. W. H. Lampe argued that the word 'anoint' in Theodore may be metaphorical (Lampe, 1967, p. 202 n.4). This is unlikely and we have to assume with Fr Yarnold that there was a sealing with oil after baptism as the text implies and that this represents an evolution from rites near contemporary (Yarnold, pp. 165–200).

Jerusalem

Cyril (*c.* 313–86) had a chequered career as Bishop of Jerusalem from 350, being banished several times, but he was in a liturgically strategic position after Constantine had in effect made Christianity the religion of the empire both in West and East. There followed the Arian controversy, which rumbled on and affected Cyril, but after centuries in the shadows of dispersion, poverty and paganism, Jerusalem gradually assumed the prominence one might, from a study of at least Lukan Scripture, have expected. The holy places were opened up, through the particular interest of Constantine and his mother, Helena, which may have been tinged with paganism as well as a Caesaro-papalism, which replaced the Gospels' 'vision of humility' (Yarnold, p. 66; MacKinnon, 1986, p. 105 and in many other places in his writings). They became centres of pilgrimage, notably by Egeria in 381 (Wilkinson, 1971), though datings differ. She gives an account of Holy Week in Jerusalem, a historical commemoration based on the days recorded in the Gospels, not unitive on the Saturday night–Sunday morning as in the earlier Church. Cyril's catechetical lectures seem to have been given about 348, possibly when he was still a presbyter. He was able, as he stood by Golgotha and in the chapel which contained the Holy Sepulchre, to illustrate the Christian's following of Christ by pointing to the actual sites of the Passion and resurrection.

The consequences of all this was that 'the holy city set the liturgical fashion in many distant places in Christendom and the Christian Year came into being'. In at least three matters, all attested by Egeria, Jerusalem practice influenced the Roman rite *viz.* (1) the Feast of the Presentation of Christ in the Temple; (2) the Palm Sunday procession; (3) the Adoration of the Cross on Good Friday (Cross, pp. xix f.).

As with Theodore, Cyril's lectures were given to neophytes *after* they had been baptised. They had the experience first and then were instructed in its meaning, a good method of teaching.

Baptism begins with renunciation of the devil and the candidates face West, the abode of darkness. The 'pomp' of Satan includes 'the mad world of the stage, horse racing, hunting and all such futility', as well as food offered to idols.

There is then a turning from West to East to make the affirmation of trinitarian faith after which the candidates move from the forecourt to the baptistery. The reading is Romans 6:3–14, the emphasis is on dying and rising with Christ rather than on new birth. There is a complete stripping, symbolic of putting off the old nature, and an anointing from head to toe with exorcised oil prior to the descent into the water. The neophyte is led by hand to the pool even as Christ was borne from the cross to the sepulchre, for baptism is death which is simultaneously new birth. Our imitation of Christ is symbolic – we are not literally crucified with Christ – but the salvation is a reality and the sign has the power of making present Christ's sufferings and death for us, just as the eucharistic bread and wine consecrated by the Holy Spirit make present his body and blood.

The chrism, anointing after baptism, makes the neophytes Christs, not simply his possession – there is no apostrophe – but also the anointed of the Lord. The chrism is not mere ointment; through the Holy Spirit it is God's grace, the oil of gladness. The anointing is on the forehead, which Cyril seems to regard as in effect the face, on the ear, the nostrils, since Christians must be as a fragrance in the Church, and on the chest as a putting on of the breastplate of righteousness. The anointing is anticipated in the Old Testament in the cases of Aaron and Solomon, but these are mere figures, whereas the anointing of Christians is a reality. As is said in 1 John 2:27, it abides.

The eucharistic teaching emphasises the indisputable change in the bread and wine according to the Lord's own words, 'This is my body', 'This is my blood'. There are again Old Testament types of this, especially in Psalm 23. The Eucharist should be received spiritually as in a white garment, the garment of salvation and the robe of gladness (Isaiah 61:10).

The rite demands the lavabo and the kiss of peace. The dialogue, begun with the *Sursum Corda,* is awesome for it means that we lay aside the cares of this life and all worldly thoughts. The Preface begins with thanksgiving for all creation, the whole of what we call the universe, whether endowed with reason or not, whether seen or unseen and calls in the hosts of heaven to 'magnify the Lord with me'. This is both a riposte to those who say that Christianity has ignored the natural order and a rebuke to those rites which have inadequately made the whole creation a part of celebration. It culminates in the *Sanctus*.

The epiclesis is next, to effect the change of the offerings into the body and blood of Christ. There is a general intercession in which 'we all make entreaty and offer this sacrifice for all who need help'. The commemoration of the dead asks the departed saints to pray for us and also prays on their behalf. It will help them even if they are sinners, just as a king may relax the punishment of those for whom some gift has been offered him. 'We believe that these souls will obtain the greatest help if we make our prayers for them while the holy and most awesome sacrifice is being offered.' The Eucharist is a sacrifice, not only of our praises and ourselves. 'We offer Christ.' And so we appease the merciful God.

The Lord's Prayer follows, which Cyril, like other Fathers, expounds. Communion must be received as in Theodore later. No crumb of the consecrated bread must be dropped, for this would be like losing a part of our own body and we would also receive less of Christ.

What is clear in Cyril is, first, that there is a real change in the eucharistic species and they must be treated with the utmost reverence, for they are Christ and bring all the powers of his life and Passion to the recipient. Second, that we offer the bread and wine as a bloodless sacrifice, but thereby we offer the slain Christ as a propitiatory sacrifice, though its very existence proves the divine mercy. And, thirdly, there is a philosophy of types and antitypes. 'Type' is from the Greek for 'stamp' or 'die'; 'antitype' is the impression it makes. Some Fathers thought the former the symbol, the latter the reality. For Cyril both are distinct from the grace they signify.

Cyril seems to be more rigorous than Theodore. It would seem that all sin debars from communion (Yarnold, pp. 67–97).

There is in all these rites an increase in reverence and solemnity before what has become the awesome mystery both of baptism and the Eucharist. There is also the inference that adult baptism was the norm. Some indeed postponed baptism till the time of death because post-baptismal sin was regarded so seriously in some parts of the Church, though the dying would not have been able to receive the catechetical teaching. Many could be baptised only as adults because they came from pagan homes. As we have seen, Hippolytus assumes the baptism of young children.

CHAPTER 3

DIVISION BETWEEN EAST AND WEST

The East

What in the West are known as the Middle Ages saw in both East and West a unification of liturgical forms and practices.

The Byzantine liturgy became the norm in both the Greek and Slavonic Churches. This includes three rites. The *Liturgy of St James the Brother of the Lord* is used only on his feast day and not universally, though its use has increased in recent years. It derives from Jerusalem, hence its ascription, though it belongs to the fourth rather than the first century. The Offertory is especially awesome, sung in modern Western churches as the hymn 'Let all mortal flesh keep silence and with fear and trembling stand'; the significance of the Offertory in the Byzantine rites will occupy us later. St James has a very long anaphora concluding with immense intercessions and commemorations of the departed. The *Liturgy of St Basil the Great* is used on the eves of Christmas and Epiphany, on the feast of St Basil (January 1st), on the Sundays in Lent except Palm Sunday, and on the Thursday and Saturday of Holy Week. The anaphora seems certainly to be the work of St Basil, a considerable enlargement of an older form.

The liturgy in regular use is that of St John Chrysostom, though it did not bear his name until three hundred years after his death. Yet it may be the liturgy used at Antioch during his episcopate (379–98) and the language of his sermons bears some resemblance to it.

The development of the church interior and furnishings are essentials of these rites. In the period before Constantine, the building in which Christians gathered for worship had no special significance. It was utilitarian. The Church and the believer were living temples, as Paul says, and the building was subordinate, for according to Stephen's speech in Acts 7, 'the Most High does not dwell in temples made with hands'. There is an echo of this in Chrysostom himself. In his treatise *On the Cross and the Robber,* he says: 'But when Christ came. . . He purified the whole earth and made every place suitable for prayer. If you wish to know how the whole earth finally became a temple . . .' But there developed a new piety which Chrysostom is trying to restrain. It is Dionysius, or Denis, the Areopagite who defines the church as a sacred building, separated from the profane. And this together with the veneration of holy places – Jerusalem was the object of no special veneration before Constantine – caused a fundamental change in Christian spirituality. It was due in part to the Church's victory over paganism and the need for the gaps it left in popular culture to be filled. The ceremonial of the imperial court influenced Christian worship because it was religious in character and also seemed to have divine approval by the conversion of Constantine. Other facts were the change from the eschatological to the historical, less expectation of the end and a greater interest in history, not least in the events of the gospel, and the affirmation of the orthodox faith hammered out in the fourth-century controversies (cf. Schmemann, 1975, pp. 86–101).

The building became the focus of worship and everything within it had a sacred meaning. Altar rails were to become a screen, the iconastasis, separating the worshippers in the nave, on earth, from the altar which is, symbolically, in heaven and from which the divine voice speaks and the mysteries are celebrated as in the eternal order. The screen is covered with icons which are devotional pictures, not realistic portraits, which convey the heavenly transformation of those they represent and in some ways constitute an antechamber of heaven. All this seems to date from no earlier than the late fourteenth century in Russia; and in the Armenian and Coptic Churches there is no iconastasis, though a curtain may be drawn across the sanctuary at certain points in the liturgy.

The iconastasis has gates or 'holy doors', north, central and south, from which the ministers emerge to read the gospel or give communion, even as God in Christ came down from heaven in the incarnation. The theological foundation of the Orthodox liturgy is the origin and end of the historic events of the gospel in the eternal kingdom. All is seen in the Latin phrase '*sub specie aeternitatis*', in relation to eternity.

The liturgy has become more elaborate over the centuries; primitive simplicity has been overlaid by detail due to the increasing association of ideas. There is now a rite of preparation, the prothesis, not earlier than 1600 in its final form. It now consists of two principal parts, the preparation of the ministers and the preparation of the gifts. The former has three parts. The first takes place outside the sanctuary gates and includes a plea for mercy to the Trinity and to the Theotokos, Mary the Godbearer, the veneration of the icons of Christ, the Mother of God and John the Baptist on the screen, the hymn of the saint in whose name the church is dedicated, a prayer for strength to offer 'the bloodless sacrifice' and a request for the people's forgiveness. The second part is a service of vesting which relates each priestly garment to a relevant text, mostly from the Old Testament and not to the items of Christ's Passion as in the medieval West; and, third, there is the washing of hands to Psalm 26:6–8. These second and third acts may take place in a vestry, if there is one, to the south of the sanctuary.

The preparation of the gifts is done in a vestry to the north of the sanctuary, which has the name of the whole of this introductory rite, the prothesis. The priest takes the eucharistic loaf in his right hand and a lance in his left and cuts from the loaf a square which will correspond to what in Western rites is called 'the host'. In the Orthodox liturgy it is known as 'the Lamb' and as he cuts it, the priest recites texts from Isaiah 53, John 1:29 and the piercing in John 19. The preparation of the chalice consists of blessing water and wine and pouring them in. This is followed by the cutting of various particles from the remainder of the loaf when the Lamb has been removed to represent the Virgin, the archangels, the saints of the past, and the living and departed associated with the worshipping congregation. The pieces are placed beside the Lamb on the paten. The whole is then censed together with the congregation, and the vessels are veiled.

The first part of the liturgy proper, the liturgy of the catechumens, when those who are being prepared for baptism are present, begins with 'the great petition for peace'. This and petitions which follow constitute the congregation as a community. The prayers end with the familiar petition which found its way into Cranmer's litany and thence into the 1662 offices, though they derived from a 1528 Latin translation which misreads the Greek. The prayer in the liturgy reads:

> Thou who hast given us grace to engage in common prayer and hast promised that when two or three are gathered together in thy name thou wilt grant their requests; fulfil now the petitions of thy servants as may be most expedient for them, granting us knowledge of thy truth while on earth and life everlasting in the world to come.

There is great emphasis on both the ineffability of God and his love for humankind, on the holiness and beauty of the house of worship, and on our prayers being offered in union with the Theotokos, who is not seen as our intercessor but as the chief of saints and our supreme partner in prayer.

The 'little entrance' follows, a procession with lighted candles and the elevated Gospel book. The Reformed liturgist, Willy Rordorf, likes this because 'it recalls for each believer the fact that the book of the gospels, no less truly than the eucharistic species, symbolizes the incarnate presence of the Lord, who was dead and is alive' (*Studia Liturgica* Vol. 26, 1996, No. 1, p. 43). There follows a reading from the New Testament and from the Gospels, interspersed with hymns and prayers. The sermon should follow the Gospel but is often deferred until just before communion in the Greek usage, or until the end of the service in the Russian. Instead, there are prayers of intercession comprising three litanies – for the living, the departed and the catechumens. The catechumens are then dismissed. The relevant prayers are always used in the Russian Church even when there are no catechumens; in the Greek Church the litanies and the dismissal are commonly omitted. The liturgy of the faithful then proceeds.

This consists of preparatory prayers for purity said secretly by the priest as the eiliton, or corporal, on which the holy vessels will be placed, is unfolded. Then comes the 'Great Entrance' or Offertory:

> The process by which a once so totally insignificant act as the transfer of gifts evolved into a high-point of the Byzantine Liturgy is the stuff from which the history of human culture is woven. (Taft, p. 3)

It may have replaced the simple approach to the altar by which, in the primitive Church, the faithful brought the gifts for the Eucharist. The Hymn to the Cherubim, with interruptions, covers the whole act. During the first part, the priest prays in acknowledgement that none is worthy to enter that service which 'is great and awesome even to the heavenly powers'. It is the incarnate High Priest who has entrusted these mysteries to mortals and the priest prays for the cleansing of his conscience and his acceptance as worthy to offer the gifts. 'For thou art he who offers and he who is offered, he who receives and he who is received and distributed.'

The details of the procession are too elaborate and too variable to warrant description here. Robert Taft quotes a nineteenth-century account by the Russian author, N. V. Gogol. It is a procession to Christ's grave. The angelical host looks down in wonder at the Lord of all, 'in the humble guise of the Lamb lying on the paten'. The procession pauses before the Royal Gates 'to remember before the Lord all Christian men, beginning with those whose obligations are the heaviest, upon the fulfilment of which depends the welfare of all and the very salvation of their souls'. The choir concludes the cherubic hymn with a thrice-repeated 'alleluia' and the procession makes its way through the Royal Gates. After deacon and priest have greeted one another, the priest lays the chalice and the bread representing the Body of Christ 'on the altar as in a grave'. The Royal Gates are then closed, like the doors of a tomb, though not for the liturgy of a bishop or archpriest with pontifical privileges and not in Easter week (Taft, pp. 4–10).

There follows the 'litany of the holy gifts', a prayer of offering, and the kiss of peace, though this is not passed through the congregation. It may be shared among the concelebrating priests. This position differs from that in the West where it immediately precedes communion after the Eucharistic Prayer. Pope Innocent I justified this not only in terms of Matthew 5:23, which might support its connection with the Offertory, but as marking the people's assent to what was done in the mysteries and setting their seal upon it. The deacon announces 'The doors, the doors, in wisdom let us attend', an archaism going back to the time when the liturgy was kept from the world, only the faithful being permitted to share it, for safety's sake as well as to confine it to the truly committed. The Nicene-Constantinopolitan Creed is then said or sung in the first person singular.

Robert Taft stresses the aesthetic impact of 'this stately hieratic ceremonial', which cannot be communicated in words and must be seen. He quotes an ancient Russian chronicle which claims that this was a primary factor in the conversion of Russia. There was no attractiveness nor glory in Bulgarian or German religion, but a patriarchal liturgy in Sancta Sophia left Russian emissaries speechless. They did not know whether they were in heaven or on earth. 'We only know that God dwells there among men, and . . . we cannot forget that beauty' (Taft, pp. 10–11 n.15).

All is now ready for the anaphora. The apostolic benediction of 2 Corinthians 13:14 introduces the *Sursum Corda*. Here the liturgy is better understood by reading than by participation, for the greater part is said secretly by the celebrant and covered by congregational or choral responses.

The Preface piles up epithets to adore the ineffable majesty of the triune God who has made us and raised us up after our fall and will accept this liturgy from us, though adored by the myriads of heaven in the triumphal hymn of the *Sanctus*.

The praise of God's glory seen in the giving of his Son (John 3:16) – very brief compared to that of St Basil, which gives thanks for the whole history of creation and redemption – leads to the words of institution and the anamnesis. 'We offer to thee thine own from thine own, in all and for all.' Then comes the epiclesis or invocation of the Holy Spirit, whose descent effects the change in the elements, making the bread Christ's body and the wine his blood. The change makes possible for those who partake 'sobriety of soul, remission of sins, communion with the Holy Spirit and the fulness of the Kingdom of heaven' and gives access to God, 'not for judgement, nor for condemnation'. In Justin, the Alexandrian Platonists and, later, Athanasius, the consecration is due to the descent of the Logos. It would seem that the Church was not able to concentrate upon the theology and work of the Holy Spirit until the christological controversies had been resolved in the fourth century. Thereafter there is the teaching about the Spirit of the Cappadocian Fathers and the earliest reference to an epiclesis is in Peter of Alexandria, the successor of Athanasius, who refers to 'the holy altar where we invoke the descent of the Holy Spirit'.

'This reasonable worship' (Romans 12:1) is offered for the faithful departed of all offices, and especially for the Theotokos, 'more honourable than the cherubim and beyond compare more glorious than the seraphim'. This is followed by the diptychs, a term derived from the hinged board on the wings of which were written the names of persons, living and departed, for whom prayers were requested at the Eucharist. When the board had long disappeared, the custom prevailed of naming those for whom intercessions were desired and in as close proximity to the sacred mystery as possible. The Lord's Prayer is preceded by a litany for the acceptance of the gifts upon the heavenly altar and for our own worthiness to receive the mysteries. It concludes with the doxology found in some manuscripts of Matthew 6:13, though not those from which the Latin Vulgate, the Bible of the West, was translated. To say the Lord's Prayer is to be ready for communion, though the prayer made its way gradually into the liturgy from the fourth century. Communion is first received by the priests. The Lamb is broken into four parts and arranged on the paten in the form of a cross. The breaking was originally for distribution, but now it has become a sign of the broken body of Christ on the cross, which, nevertheless, is 'broken but not divided, is ever eaten but never consumed'. The Lamb and the particles are then transferred into the chalice and taken outside the screen to be distributed to the faithful. There are concluding prayers and the blessings. Prayers are said as the priest consumes what is left of the elements and the *Nunc Dimittis* is said as he disrobes.

Initiation

The Byzantine rite has become universal in Orthodoxy. It dates from 790 and is derived from the Syrian liturgical tradition. It is similar to that which Chrysostom describes and parts are almost certainly written by him.

It assumes Easter as the baptismal season as Tertullian had done in the third century, though Pentecost is also appropriate and Christmas and Epiphany are suitable too; but at all times, even today, the celebration is referred to as 'Pascha – a Three Day Feast'. The French Oratorian, Louis Bouyer, has said that 'all Christian worship is a continuous celebration of Easter' (Bouyer, p. i) and this is above all true of its initial rites.

The start of the service is supposedly on Good Friday with the renunciation of the devil. This happens as the catechumens, disrobed and barefooted, turn to the West. When they have repeated the formula after the archbishop, or presiding minister, they are asked three times if they have renounced Satan and after the threefold affirmative answer, they are told to blow upon him. Then, turning to the East they three times declare their adherence to Christ. They are then exhorted in terms of a business contract they have made and told 'Make no mistake about the capital upon which interest will be required of you.' A terrible and irrevocable judgement awaits those who are unmerciful and abusive, despisers of the wicked, thieves, slanderers, gossips. They must be forever vigilant if they are to be received into the Kingdom prepared for the blessed. After this they are told to raise their hands and they join in brief intercessions, before the archbishop signs the people. The catechumens resume their clothes, the archbishop enters the sanctuary to pray for those 'who are preparing for the holy enlightening' (Justin Martyr's term for baptism), while the deacon offers a public prayer for them and the priest lays on hands. He offers peace to all and concludes with a prayer for light for all and for their being united 'to thy holy catholic Church'.

The baptism itself is envisaged as taking place on the evening of Holy Saturday. There is a prayer for the sanctification of the waters, that they may be blessed as Jordan, cleansed by the Trinity to the drowning of the enemy, that all who draw and partake of them may be cleansed and, baptised, may appear as the lights of heaven. The priest prays silently that, in spite of his sins, he may not be a castaway, but have the power from on high to be given 'strength to administer this great and heavenly mystery'. He prays for those to be reborn through his 'piteous' ministry that they may be planted in the Church to advance in reverence and glorify the holy, triune name. There is then the great thanksgiving of baptism, rehearsing God's power in creation and his awesome and ineffable majesty, God beyond bounds who yet came to earth and took the form of a servant to save us. The work of Christ is not mentioned after Jordan, as though it was all proleptic (anticipatory) there. So there is a long blessing of the water that it may be the means of refashioning those who enter it for baptism so that 'being planted together in the likeness of the death' of Christ they may share also in his resurrection. There is then the blessing of the oil and the making of three crosses with it in the water, after which the priest sings 'alleluia' three times with the congregation. The catechumens are then anointed by the priest upon the forehead and breast and back and by the deacon on the whole body. The baptism follows not by the priest saying 'I baptise you', but 'Such a one is baptised'. There is another prayer said silently by the priest praying for the gift of the Holy Spirit upon the baptised, while the deacon recites a prayer aloud. After this the priest anoints those who have been baptised, making the sign of the cross on the forehead, eyes, nostrils, mouth and both ears, saying 'The seal of the gift of the Spirit'. The divine liturgy then begins.

There is no need for any rite corresponding to the Western confirmation. It is all there: baptism, burial and resurrection with Christ, new life and the gift of the Spirit. It is an adult rite, which for centuries has been administered chiefly to infants, who could not undergo the long preparation which the catechumenate envisaged. The renunciations and declarations of adherence are made on their behalf. The Byzantine liturgy has a rite for the naming of a child on the eighth day after birth. The child is named which gives identity as a person and affirms uniqueness. The eighth day is the day beyond time, the day of the Kingdom of God. It was the day when Jesus Christ was brought into the Temple and given the name foretold by the angel. The name of the child is given in the Holy Name of Jesus. The infants would be made catechumens with three exorcisms although this presupposed adulthood and a period of disciplined preparation.

The West

As Byzantium came to be dominant in Eastern liturgy, so did Rome in the West, though until the eighth century what have been called the 'Gallican' liturgies had a wide provenance. These had Spanish (or Mozarabic, a name which arose through the Moorish occupation since it was used by Christians who lived under it), Milanese, Celtic and, geographically, Gallican forms.

The style of these rites is verbose and lacks the tightness and economy of Roman liturgy. They include three lessons – Old Testament, Epistle and Gospel – and place the kiss of peace before the Eucharistic Prayer, which is a set of variables placed around the *Sanctus* and the institution narrative. The former is introduced by a florid preface, while the latter, said secretly, has an elaborated account of Christ's actions. There is often no anamnesis and no epiclesis. The Mozarabic liturgy survived longer than the other Gallican types, in fact until the eleventh and twelfth centuries. Like the other Gallican liturgies it bears marks of the struggle against Arianism, asserting the consubstantiality of the persons of the Godhead rather than the mediatorship of Christ, and addressing prayers indifferently to the Father and the Son. Sometimes a prayer begins by addressing the Father, continues to the Son and ends with the glorification of the Trinity.

The name Jesus is preceded by the title 'Lord', found often in the writings of Ambrose of Milan, whose *De Sacramentis*, 'Concerning the Sacraments', presupposes a rite different from the Roman and yet with some affinities in, for example, its sacrificial doctrine and its reference to the pre-Mosaic sacrifices of Abel, Abraham and Melchizedek, which are not those of the ritual law abrogated by Christ. It is from Ambrose that we have the suggestion that the term *'missa'* or 'Mass' was beginning to be used of the whole service and not simply of the dismissals, as in *missa catechumenorum* and *missa fidelium*. It did not, however, become the general Western term before the sixth century. Not only did the words of institution have a place in the liturgy Ambrose knew, but he regards them, as will be the Western belief, as effecting the consecration of the Sacrament (Srawley, pp. 153f, 156). These are not the words of the priest, or those prescribed for him, but the words of Christ: 'So then the word of Christ consecrates the sacrament.'

From the writings of Ambrose we detect the emergence of a central consecration prayer of the Eucharist, which unlike earlier custom, as for instance in Justin Martyr, now attained a fixed form and is known as the Canon, from the Greek word for 'rule' or 'measuring rod'. This is generally considered to be the part of the prayer following the *Sanctus*, although Jasper and Cuming include the whole Eucharistic Prayer from the greeting and *Sursum Corda* to the final doxology.

Jungmann thinks that the Gallic liturgies deteriorated into a 'misty formlessness' (Jungmann, 1976, p. 66). It was Charlemagne (c. 742–814) who imposed the Roman liturgy in his territory to bring good order. He was advised by an Englishman, Alcuin (d. 804). It is to him that we owe the Collect for Trinity Sunday and the Collect for Purity. He presupposes a daily Eucharist, which was not the Eastern custom, although Father John of Kronstadt urged this in nineteenth-century Orthodoxy. Alcuin devised votive masses, or masses for special occasions, for instance in honour of the Trinity, the Holy Cross, Mary, and one most interestingly treated in an essay by Ruth A. Meyers, 'of Wisdom', in which Wisdom, feminine in Scripture as in *hagia sophia* or *sancta sophia*, 'is both Word and Spirit, an agent of creation, revelation and salvation' (Dudley, ed., pp. 39ff.). Alcuin wrote a commentary on Hebrews in which he emphasised that Christ is not sacrificed anew in our offering, which is 'in order to make remembrance of his death'. But he believed that the sacrifice of the cross becomes truly present in our offering.

From Alcuin onwards, the Mass became more clerically dominated. The priest offers the prayers rather than the whole congregation. Latin was no longer understood by most people, which made the service even more a clerical monopoly.

Much was said inaudibly and secret prayers were added. Unleavened bread came to be used and there was a general heightening of reverence before the mystery which priestly monopoly and a dead language served to increase.

The Roman Mass as it emerged between the fourth and eighth centuries begins with Psalm 43, in which the celebrant prays for the light and truth of God to bring him to the holy hill and goes with joy to God's altar. Then there is confession and absolution, an introit psalm, the *Kyries* (prayers for mercy retaining Greek, the original liturgical language of Rome), the *Gloria in Excelsis,* transferred from an office of the Eastern Church and the collect of the day. Collects are a classic Western form of prayer, with certain parallels in the East, which serve the purpose both of constituting the Christian assembly for worship and gathering up the themes of previous devotions. They are properly constructed under strict rules and syllabic rhythms. Normally, they consist of five parts: invocation, relative clause, petition, statement of purpose and conclusion of doxology. Examples have been seen in 1 Maccabees 4:30–3 and 2 Maccabees 1:23–4, although these do not have the verbal economy and succinctness of the Western forms, which breathe the very spirit of Latin; a further example is in Acts 1:24–5, the prayer before lots were cast for Judas's replacement. Cranmer, as we shall see, was the English master of collects, though the revisers of 1661 showed a delicacy of touch which perfect some. Percy Dearmer argued that a collect must have 'colour, rhythm, finality, a certain conciseness as well as vigour of thought; but it must be a unified petition, or it becomes something else than a collect. We might indeed say that it must be one complete sentence, an epigram softened by feeling; it must be compact, expressing one thought, and enriching that thought so delicately that a word misplaced may destroy its whole beauty' (Dearmer, pp. 149f., see Maxwell 1936, pp. 176–9). The Roman Collect for Palm Sunday, literally translated, is a good example of the collect form, although it was much improved in its English versions of 1549 and 1661:

> O almighty and eternal God, who wouldst have our Saviour become man and suffer on a cross to give mankind an example of humility; mercifully grant that we may improve by the example of his patience, and partake of his resurrection. Through Jesus Christ our Lord.

There is no Old Testament lesson but an Epistle, followed by a gradual psalm or sequence and the Gospel, which a sermon should follow, though this tended to be confined to special and episcopal days as the Middle Ages proceeded. The Nicene Creed follows.

The Offertory is first the presentation of the unblemished offering by the unworthy and sinful priest. It is offered 'for all who stand around, and for all faithful Christians alive and dead; that it may avail for my salvation and theirs to eternal life'. The mixed chalice represents the divinity and humanity of Christ. The cup is offered that, rather strangely, it may ascend 'in the sight of your divine majesty for our salvation and that of the whole world, in a sweet-smelling savour'.

Finally there is the offering of 'our humble spirits and contrite hearts', the blessing of the incense, the plea for the intercession of Mary and John the Baptist, Peter and Paul and all saints and the answered request of the priest for the prayers of the people that 'my sacrifice and yours' may be acceptable to God.

The Thanksgiving or Consecratory Prayer probably changed from a more orderly original form through numerous insertions from the fourth century onwards. Some have argued that the *Sanctus* was one of these as also in the East. E. C. Ratcliff believed that a brief preface was originally followed straightaway by the prayer asking God to accept the thank offering which is thought by majority opinion to begin the Canon. Ratcliff thought that the prayer 'conducted the worshippers in the spirit of thanksgiving, by means of the sacrificial symbols of the passion, into the courts of heaven, where they joined with the martyrs and the

Seraphim in the adoration of the Lord of Sabaoth'. Hence the *Sanctus* may have concluded the prayer (Ratcliff, p. 104).

The Canon is now a muddle, not least through the interpolation of two lists of saints. These may have been recited aloud by the deacon as the priest was saying the Canon silently, a practice which may have begun as early as the sixth century, though this is not certain. The first list consists of twenty-five names, probably originating with local saints honoured at Rome to whom Mary and the apostles were added as their cultus increased. Local martyrs were commemorated before the apostles and the cult of Mary was not taken over by Rome from the East until the seventh century. Nor was there a Latin equivalent of the title Theotokos.

The second list may be an enlargement (with further names, mostly of martyrs, many of them women) of a petition which immediately followed the request that the sacramental gifts, the consecrated species, 'be borne by the hands of your angel to your altar on high'. This brings the Canon into the courts of heaven and the adoration of the heavenly host, but it is brought down to earth again by the acknowledgement that we are sinners and cannot be admitted to the fellowship of the saints apart from the bounteous forgiveness of God through Christ. The angel whose hands bear the gifts is Christ himself from the septuagint title in Isaiah 9:6 and, also, Justin's first *Apology* and the Eucharistic Prayer of the *Apostolic Tradition*. There is also a reference to Revelation 8:3: 'And another angel came and stood at the altar with a golden censer; and he was given much incense to mingle with the prayers of all the saints upon the golden altar before the throne.' This is an ancient notion in the West. In the East it came later since the Apocalypse was not there accepted as Scripture so early.

The heart of the Canon is the institution narrative with its consecratory words. Hardly any such narrative in a Eucharistic Prayer quotes one of the New Testament accounts exactly and without some embellishment. This narrative adds adjectives to Scripture: he 'took bread in his holy and blessed hands'; he 'lifted up his hands to heaven, to you his almighty God'; 'taking this glorious cup in his holy and reverend hands'. But it does, infers Ratcliff after a long and thorough examination, belong 'to a liturgical tradition for which the careful preservation of the scriptural form and character of the narrative was held to be vital'. He says, a little later:

> For the function of the Narrative in the Canon is not merely to revive the memory of a significant historic event, or to provide a rationale for the celebration of the Eucharist as the Greek Narratives do; its function is rather to make the significant historic event continuously present and operative. By means of the Narrative, therefore, the Church's *actio* in the Eucharist is identified with and becomes the *actio* of Christ at the Institution.

The narrative is a dramatic recital, enhanced by the taking of bread and cup into the priest's hands in the sight of the people (Ratcliff, pp. 61f.).

Where the narrative fails and deserts Scripture is in the absence of an eschatological note. There is no mention of 1 Corinthians 11:26, 'For as often as you eat this bread and drink this cup, you proclaim the Lord's death until he come.'

As the Middle Ages went on, the Mass became more elaborate and removed from the people, who became increasingly spectators of a distant mystery performed by clergy at a high altar separated from the nave by a screen on which was a rood. The screen was not as impenetrable as the Eastern iconastasis and the altar could often be seen through it quite clearly, while in screens which cut off the sanctuary more obviously, there would be squint holes. In some churches in Lent a huge veil was suspended within the sanctuary to within a foot or so of the ground, making it impossible for the laity to see anything; but this was a symbol to heighten the value of what was temporarily concealed.

In our modern jargon, the worship was 'vertical', not 'horizontal', though this led to intense devotion on the part of the few, for whom it became the supreme act of contemplation. By the end of the Middle Ages, pews were installed to aid the quietness and privacy of those for whom the Mass was the background to acts of devotion, although this was encouraged for all that they might say the rosary or use many of the prayers provided as the action at the altar was going on. From 1200, it became customary to elevate the host after consecration and this became the most awesome moment of the Mass, calling to genuflection the people in the nave of the church, who otherwise may have been discussing business or other affairs, though this was deplored. The liturgy of priest and people 'converged only at the climactic moment when earth and heaven met in the fragile disc of bread he held above his head, and everyone found some heightened words to greet and petition the sacramental Christ for salvation, health and blessing' (Duffy, p. 118). Some would leave after that and hurry to the next church where they might catch that numinous moment. On the other hand, in large churches Masses might be said simultaneously at the many altars, with the elevation staggered, which offered several opportunities for the blessed sight. Communion of the people was infrequent and generally only at Easter.

Eamon Duffy (pp. 92f.) has challenged the charge of individualism which is levelled against the medieval Mass. The Sunday Mass might be distant and essentially a spectacle, but weekly masses at side altars allowed the people to come closer. And 'the unitive and co-operative dimension of the Blessed Sacrament is in fact repeatedly insisted on in late medieval sources'. The guilds made the Mass a corporate celebration with processions and plays. 'The sense that the Host was the source simultaneously of individual and of corporate renewal and unity is perfectly caught in the striking prayer regularly printed in early sixteenth-century primers for use before communion', in which the 'saving victim' is greeted and the final request is for incorporation into Christ's body, the Church.

Eamon Duffy has brilliantly presented medieval religion in *The Stripping of the Altars* and delivered it from some of the grosser misunderstandings of Protestant prejudice. Yet there is enough in his account to warn of dangers. Looking to the host as the climax of the Mass meant that those who disbelieved might be afflicted with blindness, while there are several gruesome stories of doubters being shown the host dripping with blood. There was also the danger of appurtences stealing prominence and the obscuring of what was scriptural and essential. This is notable at Candlemas. In the Gospel story of the presentation of Christ in the Temple, candles are not mentioned, though old

Simeon does speak of 'a light to lighten the Gentiles'. By the later Middle Ages candles had taken over the feast, to the consternation of some clerics. The blessed wax could put the devil to flight. 'The people took blessed candles away from the ceremony, to be lit during thunderstorms, or in times of sickness, or to be placed in the hands of the dying.' Such sacramentals could be diverted to nefarious ends: 'witches were known to drop wax from the holy candle into the foot prints of those they hated, causing their feet to rot off' (Duffy, pp. 102f., 15f.).

There was also the danger that the Mass might be seen as a repetition of Calvary and of the sacrifice which Scriptures says was done once for all. Each detail symbolised some event of the Passion, which the Mass books provided for the laity encouraged their readers to observe, until there would come a time when the priest would be thought to preside at the sacrificial death of Jesus. Unlike what we have noted as the Orthodox symbolism, the priestly vestments recalled the garments of Christ's Passion – the maniple the rope by which he was led from Pilate to Herod and back, the chasuble the purple robe in which he was mocked.

Sometimes there is a wider reference; the gifts of the Magi are remembered at the offertory, while the departure of the priest after Mass is likened to Moses leading the children of Israel through the Red Sea. But the Passion dominated the Mass.

Blessings might be inserted before the doxology of the Canon: of the chrism on Maundy Thursday and water, milk and honey at Pentecost, a custom going back to the *Apostolic Tradition* of Hippolytus. The Lord's Prayer succeeds the Canon, without the doxology, but with an 'embolism' that is an expansion of the final clause 'Deliver us from evil'. The host is broken into three parts as the embolism concludes and the Peace is given as the priest makes three crosses within the chalice with the third part of the host. The *Agnus Dei* is said privately by the priest, deacon and subdeacon and the third part of the host is put down into the chalice, the mingling of Christ's body and blood in the whole of redemption. The Peace is then passed through the choir (who had become from earlier times intermediaries between the people and the priests), beginning with the eldest, and communion prayers follow. After the communion and post-communion and dismissal, it became customary to read the first fourteen verses of the Prologue to St John's Gospel. Sometimes extra Gospels would be inserted immediately before St John, to meet the wishes of the laity who had paid for a particular Mass.

In the later Middle Ages there was an unofficial vernacular insertion in the Mass known as 'prone', a response to pastoral need. This consisted of a sermon, possibly some instruction in the Lord's Prayer and the Decalogue, and 'the bidding of the bedes', that is 'the praying of the prayers'. These last were quite lengthy intercessions. From the seventh century this element had largely disappeared from the Mass.

There were different usages of the one Roman rite in medieval England, but by the sixteenth century only three remained, those of Sarum, York and Hereford. Of these Sarum was dominant in England and indeed in Scotland and Ireland. Its ceremonial was elaborate, the movements of the richly vested priests virtually an art form. It was the Sarum liturgy which the English Reformers had in front of them both to reject and, in parts, retain. When its limitations and, some would think misdirections, are recognised, it must not be forgotten that seventy-five per cent of the population attended Mass every day.

> In the Mass the redemption of the world, wrought on Good Friday once and for all, was renewed and made fruitful for all who believed. Christ himself, immolated on the altar of the cross, became present on the altar of the parish church, body, soul, and divinity, and his blood flowed once again, to nourish and renew Church and world. As kneeling congregations raised their eyes to see the Host held high above the priest's head at the sacring, they were transported to Calvary itself, and gathered not only into the passion and resurrection of Christ, but into the full sweep of salvation history as a whole. (Duffy, p. 91)

And although the Reformation sought radically to remedy what were believed to be its errors and superstitions, it did not change that solemn and mighty memorial of Christ, which has never lost its power to draw his people to himself.

Initiation

Infant baptism demanded a shorter rite than one extended, in theory at any rate, over the three days of Easter, while Easter saw fewer baptisms as time went on, since parents did not wish to wait possibly for many months for their children to be baptised. It was thought dangerous to delay and risk them dying unbaptised and thus denied entrance to heaven.

The Sarum rite of baptism, which was the one used most widely in the high Middle Ages, is the fundamental Roman rite but baptism, like all liturgy, has attracted accretions: oil as well as water from early on; salt, 'a saving sacrament to drive away the enemy', originally given periodically with bread in Lent during the catechumenate, was retained in the Roman rite of infant baptism until 1969. There was also the 'effeta', from *ephthatha,* 'be opened' in Mark 7:34, when Jesus put his fingers into the deaf man's ears and spat and touched his tongue to cure the impediment in his speech. The story of the Lord blessing the children in St Matthew's Gospel is inserted between the exorcisms and the effeta. This derived from Gallican rites in the preparation before Easter when children were brought to church for exorcism and unction and the laying-on of hands. Its place in the Sarum liturgy marks the beginning of its long association with infant baptism and its citation as justification for the practice, which reaches a climax in Philip Doddridge's eighteenth-century hymn 'See Israel's gentle Shepherd stand', sung for many decades in Free Church baptisms. There is the signing of the cross on the infant's right hand, which is found in the Stowe Missal. At the end of the preparation, the candidate's name is asked and by it he or she is bidden: 'Enter into the temple of God that thou mayest have eternal life and live for ever and ever, Amen', implying that the whole of the preceding section is to take place at the church door.

Those to be baptised, though infants, are first made catechumens. Males are set on the priest's right hand, females on his left. There are many signings with the cross throughout. After preliminary prayers, from the Gelasian Sacramentary, for the effects of baptism, with a mention of the entry of the baptised into the new covenant, there is then the exorcism of salt and its placing in the mouth, with the words 'N receive the salt of wisdom for a propitiation of God unto eternal life'. After a prayer that those, male and female, who have tasted the first morsel of salt may hunger only until filled with heavenly food, there are different exorcisms for males and females. These do not differ much and nothing in them relates to differences of gender. The Lord's Prayer, the Hail Mary and the Apostles' Creed are to be said by godfathers and godmothers 'and all that stand around'. This first part of the service ends with the signing of the cross on the right hand and the entry into the church.

The blessing of the font is the next section. The water is frequently to be renewed lest it grow stale, though never in deference to a person of distinction. This would not always be necessary and sometimes this part of the service would be left out and the priest would proceed straight to the baptism. The water in the font must be distinguished from holy water and not either by accident or design sprinkled on the people, for they must not be rebaptised. This could happen carelessly, at the asperges, the sprinkling of holy water after unction, or at the consecration of a church building, or, as happens in our time, at the renewal of baptismal vows. This is prefaced by a litany which is introduced by an exhortation in the vernacular to the godparents, a later interpolation. The godparents are to charge the parents with the child's protection to the age of seven years when he or she having learned the Our Father, Hail Mary, and I Believe, must be brought to the bishop for Confirmation.

The litany was presumably sung in procession to the font. It is an invocation of saints from Mary and the archangels to John the Baptist and the unnamed patriarchs and prophets. The apostles and evangelists follow, name by name, and a whole list of martyrs and saints, male and female, few of whom would be known to the worshippers.

The actual blessing opens with a prayer from the Gelasian Sacramentary, followed by the *Sursum Corda* and a long thanksgiving corresponding to the Eucharistic Prayer, which celebrates water from first creation to the flood, which was a type of washing of regeneration, so that 'by the mystery of one and the same element there might be both an end of vices and a beginning of virtues'. There is an epiclesis over the water as the priest divides it with his right hand in the form of a cross. He exorcises it and blesses it (recalling many scriptural references from the separation of the sea from the dry land and the four rivers flowing out of paradise, to the miracle of Cana, Christ's walking on the water and his baptism by John) with the great commission of Matthew 28:20. He breathes upon the water three times in the sign of a cross, drops wax from a candle into it and divides it with the candle, both in the form of a cross. This is accompanied by the prayer that the water may have power to regenerate, to blot out the stains of sins, restore the divine image and be cleansed from the filth of age. The candle is lifted from the water and the prayer ends with a petition for rebirth through the Sacrament and a doxology. This part of the rite may be used to bless the water when there are no baptisms. It will then be veiled and kept until there are. Before baptism oil is poured into the water with a billio, a small metal rod, or more likely a spoon, kept for the purpose. Chrism, the mixture of olive oil and perfume, usually balsam, consecrated by the bishop on Maundy Thursday, is also poured in similarly.

The baptism itself requires the renunciation of the devil, accompanied by unction applied to the breast and shoulders of the infant, and the declaration of faith made by the godparents on behalf of the child. After the baptism, which is a triple dipping, the child is anointed with chrism, clad in a white robe, the property of the church, and given a candle, the latter practice being first attested in the eleventh century.

Confirmation was understood to mean the completion of baptism. It was a giving of the Holy Spirit in his sevenfold gifts of Isaiah 11, to sanctify the whole life which had been born again by the power of the Spirit in baptism. It was reserved for the bishop, who might not be at hand at the time of baptism, and so an interval was required, which came to be thought of as an opportunity for an infant to grow in understanding and be able to recite the basic texts – Our Father, Hail Mary and I Believe. It was hoped that Confirmation would not be postponed beyond the age of seven. The service consists of a prayer for the sevenfold gifts of the Holy Spirit and the bishop making the sign of the cross on the forehead of the child with his thumb dipped in chrism and saying 'I confirm thee with the chrism of salvation in the name of the Father and of the Son and of the Holy Ghost.' There is a final prayer for the 'humble family' of the confirmed that they may be a temple of God's glory indwelt by the Holy Spirit, and blessings.

CHAPTER 4

THE REFORMED RITES

There was something of a revival of Reformation studies in the middle decades of the twentieth century. The great Protestant theologian Karl Barth was dominant and the ecumenical movement demanded a rediscovery of confessional sources; and there was the attempt to show 'the Catholicity of Protestantism', indeed that the word 'Protestant' was not the antithesis of 'Catholic' as had long been assumed, but to its upholders meant very much the same thing, the affirmation of authentic Christianity. Catholics regarded Protestant theologians no longer as total heretics, but sought to understand their teaching and recognise the validity of some of it, while the Second Vatican Council, in Protestant eyes, represented a reformation and opened the doors to a rapprochement with Protestantism.

In liturgical studies there was a recovery of confessional sources, which had often been neglected under pressure of controversy, and an attempt to show that Protestant worship was not mere libertarianism coupled with hostility to Rome, but was based on ordered principles. The Church of Scotland *Book of Common Order* of 1940 sought to return to the classical foundations of Presbyterian worship and to reaffirm the doctrinal basis of the Church of Scotland as stated in the First Article of her Constitution: 'The Church of Scotland is part of the Holy Catholic or Universal Church.' In 1948, four Congregationalists, John Huxtable, John Marsh, Romilly Micklem and James Todd, published *A Book of Public Worship*. It rested on two premises: one, that although Congregationalists 'rejected the imposition by the State of a uniform liturgy', they 'accepted the constraint of the Gospel to a common liturgical structure'; and, two, that 'Congregationalist worship is to be understood in terms of Holy Communion', this in contrast to the then predominance in the Church of England of mattins and evensong. The book owed much to W. D. Maxwell's *Outline of Christian Worship.* Its sources include the sixteenth-century Prayer Book from Middleburg in Holland, which was accepted by some Congregationalist exiles and had influence on English worship, and Richard Baxter's *Reformed Liturgy* of 1661. Prior to this was the Mansfield College, Oxford, symposium edited by Nathaniel Micklem in 1936, *Christian Worship.*

Meanwhile Methodists were rediscovering the Wesley hymns and their Catholicity, in some cases close affinities with Western medieval spirituality such as devotion to the five wounds of Jesus, while the Free Churches generally, through such historians as Bernard Manning and Erik Routley, were emphasising the importance of hymns in liturgy, not simply as relief for the congregation, or to cover other liturgical actions such as processionals, but as vital elements in the whole movement of worship, adoration, penitence, praise, the application of Scripture, the proclamation of the Gospel, and offering. The Church of England celebrated the *Book of Common Prayer,* of which some Anglo-Catholics sought to recover the pre-Reformation vestiges and there was a rehabilitation of Cranmer and his achievement by Charles Smyth, E. C. Ratcliff, Norman Sykes, and the Methodist Gordon Rupp. The Methodist 1936 rite of Holy Communion was that of the 1662 Prayer Book with some slight revisions by that compulsive editor John Wesley, and this was much prized by some.

Recently Protestant enthusiasm has waned. Able Roman Catholic historians such as J. J. Scarisbrick and Eamon Duffy have revised the more favourable estimates. It is not difficult to see the Reformation as a movement as much political as religious, violently iconoclastic, persecutory, robbing the common people of devotions which were dear to them and sustained their lives in a harsh world, and as bitterly divided within itself, between radicals and the more conservative and not least in liturgy and the understanding of Christ's presence in the Sacrament.

Yet the Reformation was a religious revival and the

doctrine which united its protagonists was that the sole determinant of salvation is God's grace. The whole Catholic system seemed like an attempt to haul oneself up to heaven by one's own bootlaces, with the danger for most of falling into Purgatory which in G. G. Coulton's phrase was 'old hell writ small'. Whatever St Paul meant by justification by faith (and E. P. Sanders, for instance, has revised the Lutheran view of this), for Luther and the Reformers it meant that the moment the sinner turned in penitence and trust to God, he or she was treated as though already righteous; through this psychological deliverance he or she was able to grow in grace and although still a sinner was, if chosen by God, given the strength to persevere. Liturgy had to proclaim this, to be an offer of forgiveness and a visible sharing in all that God in Christ had done. It must be in a language 'understanded of the people', not mumbled in an unintelligible tongue but for the most part spoken loud and clear and always with communion of the people in both kinds. It must be a union of Word and Sacrament, the hearing and exposition of Scripture, the breaking of the Word, together with obedience to the institution of Christ, through which he was made present to his people. But here was the rub. Was he present to all, or only to those who had faith? And was he corporally present in the bread and wine, or were they tokens of a spiritual presence?

The hatred of the Mass astonishes those of us who see its power as well as its limitations and dangers. Martin Luther felt that the Mass encapsulated all that was wrong with the Roman system. The Offertory and the Canon reeked of oblation, of our offering of Christ not his of himself. To surround the institution of Christ with these idolatrous superstitions was like placing the ark of the Lord in the temple of Dagon. But Luther believed that we enter into the sacrifice of Christ as we offer ourselves.

In his *Formulae Missa* of 1523, all that remained of the Canon was the *Sursum Corda,* the institution narrative, which contained the words of consecration, the *Sanctus* and the *Benedictus*. He was uncertain about the mixed chalice, though inclined to think that pure wine 'symbolized beautifully the purity of the Gospel'. He retained the elevation, both of bread and cup, because he did not want to bewilder or hurt those who were used to it. The service was enriched, and the people given increased part, by congregational hymns. At first he thought there should be a daily celebration throughout Christendom. By 1523 he had decided that it should be the Sunday service, unless there were those who wished for more frequent communion.

He was slow in producing the German Mass of 1526. When he did so it was set to music and ready for use; but others had anticipated him as we shall see. In Luther's Mass, there was a liturgy of the Word, with Epistle, Gospel (followed by the Apostles' Creed during which the elements were prepared) and sermon. The liturgy of the Sacrament began with a paraphrase of the Lord's Prayer, without an embolism. Luther reduced the Canon simply to the words of institution. But he kept elevation because it typifies the spiritual elevation of Christ in Word and Sacrament. Hymns were sung at appropriate places throughout and the services concluded with the Aaronic blessing, which Luther thought was used by Jesus as he blessed his disciples in parting from them at the ascension. Luther took literally the words of Jesus, 'This *is* my body', as in his argument with Zwingli, though there is no verb in the original. He believed that through the words of consecration, the body and blood of Christ were joined to the elements.

Zwingli meanwhile, at Zurich, replaced the Canon completely by four prayers, the last of which concludes with the institution narrative to which is added, as consequence, the invitation 'Come unto me all you who labour and are heavy laden and I will give you rest.' The first ends with the Lord's Prayer. There is a completely orthodox affirmation of God's offering of his Son for our redemption and of the reconciling effects of Christ's death. He thus offers himself to be 'the food of our souls under the forms of bread and wine'. Faith in the atonement is a *sine qua non* but Zwingli takes his stand on the Johannine words that the flesh profits nothing but the Spirit gives life.

Zwingli was dubious about the word 'sacrament' because it was not used by Christ, it is an unhappy translation of 'mystery' in, for instance, Ephesians 5:32, and it is not likely to be understood by Germans. But he was impressed by its original meaning as 'a pledge which litigants deposited at some altar and the winner got back his pledge or money'. It was also an oath and came to mean the oath by which soldiers were bound to obey their general. So he declared 'a sacrament is nothing else than an initiatory ceremony or a pledging. For just as those who were about to enter upon litigation deposited a certain amount of money, which could not be taken away except by the winner, so those who are initiated by sacraments bind and pledge themselves and, as it were, seal a contract not to draw back.' But he had a profound suspicion of outward things, fostered by his Augustinian neo-Platonism and the medieval attachment to the material and holy rites and objects which could be bought for money. He attacked those who 'attribute to symbols what belongs only to the divine power and the Holy Spirit working immediately in our souls'. Judas received the Sacrament but it did not save him. Only the Spirit brings us to penitence and faith.

Yet he did not abolish the sacraments. They were instituted by Christ, testify to an actual historical event, are as a ring which Christ gives as a token of his love and to cause him to be remembered as if he were present and eating with his people. Interestingly, Zwingli finds virtue in the fact that sacraments make use of the senses. The elements speak and suggest to the senses what the Word and Spirit do to the mind. But it is faith alone which gives the sacraments efficacy. And fundamental are the sovereignty of God and the freedom of the Spirit (Stephens, 1984, 1985).

The Zwinglian rite is bare, lacking the numinous, with no heavenly dimension, nor sense of the communion of saints. There is no consecration, no intercessions. No longer is Communion the Sunday service. It is confined to four times a year. And communion is to be received sitting, a practice which originated with Zwingli. One of the differences between Reformed rites is that some reduce the Sacrament to a minimal simplicity with no reverential aids and others, unable to shake off the tradition of the Mass, retain the sense of awe and mystery.

At Strasbourg, Diebold Schwarz celebrated the first German Mass in 1524, two years before Luther. It is an almost literal translation of the Latin Mass. Most of the ceremonial was kept and a doctrine of the real presence in the elements was implied. But all suggestions of the Roman doctrine of sacrifice were removed, invocations of the Virgin and the saints were omitted, and the whole was said in an audible voice. Martin Bucer (1491–1551) had been a Dominican friar, who grew weary of Aquinas and Scholasticism through reading Erasmus and then became enraptured with Luther and his preaching of God's love for sinners, the undesirables, not for those who are attractive to him as with human love. 'The love of the Cross, born of the Cross is this: it transfers itself not where it finds some good to be enjoyed but where it may confer some good to a sinner or to an unfortunate' (Hall, pp. 129f.). Bucer became one of the first Reformers to marry, with papal dispensation, but was excommunicated for this by the Archbishop of Speier and had to leave Wissenburg where he had been, briefly, a parish priest. He sought refuge in Strasbourg in 1523, where his father had citizen's rights, and became the leading churchman there. The dominant theme of his preaching was that 'the whole law is fulfilled in loving thy neighbour as thyself'. He was no doctrinaire theologian, which may account for the prolixity and obscurity of his style, which he himself admitted. He was an eirenical theologian, involved in the colloquies between Catholics and Protestants from 1539 to 1541. On the Eucharist he sought to reconcile Lutherans and Zwinglians. Luther, indignant at his search for compromise, called him a 'Klappermaul' ('chatterbox'). He corresponded with Cranmer for many years until in 1549 he was told to leave Strasbourg owing to a conservative reaction, not un-connected with the fortunes of Charles V after his victory at Muhlberg in 1547. Bucer came to England where he was made Regius Professor of Divinity at Cambridge and had increasing influence on Cranmer's liturgical views, though they differed on certain points.

Only the faithful receive Christ in the Eucharist: 'But by means of the holy meal, he who fitly partakes is drawn up by faith to heaven and receives his own Christ, as celestial food, by which he may have more fully his own citizenship of heaven' (MacCulloch, pp. 381f.). Bucer had no truck with the view that by the consecration of the Eucharist, Christ was drawn down to earth. The movement was the other way on. He would have been appalled at the notion that the Sacrament was 'an extension of the Incarnation'. On the other hand, Bucer condemned the Reformed view that because Christ was in heaven, he could not be elsewhere, and that if so, it would be the end of the world! He believed strongly that Christ was present everywhere through faith and that the believer could be conscious of this. This was not the same as maintaining that the right ritual actions make him corporally present in bread and wine.

As one might expect, Strasbourg liturgy is verbose in the extreme. This was a danger of many Reformed rites, which is why Cranmer's virtues shine so bright in contrast. It is due to the desire to make worship intelligible, to explain everything so that it may be understood. This is a worthy motive, but it may be an affliction, evident today among those who cannot leave explanation to rubrics, or in some instances sermons, and who fail to realise that worship is not simply a mental activity and that liturgy has a symphonic, or poetic quality. It should itself carry the worshippers along into the heavenly places. The reaction against the mystery and secret of the Mass has gone too far.

From Schwarz's Mass onwards, as Bucer's influence increased, there was an increasing development in a Reformed direction at Strasbourg. Maxwell summarises what was happening even before Bucer became dominant:

> A choice begins to appear in the prayers; the Apostles' Creed is given as an alternative to the Nicene, the Aaronic blessing may be said instead of the Roman blessing; psalms and hymns in German metre appear, providing the people with opportunities to participate in the service; such phrases as, 'Lord's Supper', 'Minister', 'Holy Table' are beginning to replace 'Mass', 'priest', 'Altar', though there is a good deal of interchanging for some time; the Latin titles for parts of the service are gradually replaced by German titles; the Epistles and Gospels are no longer selected according to the old lectionaries, but are read in course and at greater length; sermons are regularly preached, sometimes one on each lection; the ceremonial is much simplified, and the elevation discarded; and the worship is now conducted from behind the Holy Table, which has been moved forward to provide room for the celebrant . . . (Maxwell, 1945, p. 91)

There was an atmosphere of excitement, not least over the ministry of the Word. The people looked forward to the exposition and discussed it eagerly.

Bucer describes a much simpler service than the Mass of Schwarz, typical of Strasbourg in the 1530s. There is exhortation to confession of sin, followed by the minister making this on behalf of the whole congregation, praying for pardon and pronouncing absolution. This is followed by the singing of short psalms and hymns, a reading from the apostolic writings and a brief exposition. There is more singing, possibly a metrical version of the Commandments, the Gospel reading and the sermon proper. This is followed by the Apostles' Creed sung in metre and the general intercession. Then as introduction to the ministry of the Sacrament, the minister, with Bucerian prolixity, 'admonishes those who wish to observe the Lord's Supper with him that they are to do so in memory of Christ, to die for their sins, and bear their cross willingly and be strengthened in faith for what must come to pass when we contemplate with believing hearts what measureless grace and goodness Christ has shown to us in that for us he offered up to his Father his life and blood upon the Cross'. The New Testament institution narrative is read, not as consecratory but as a warrant, and the minister distributes the bread and the cup, 'having partaken of them also himself'. There is a concluding hymn of praise, a short prayer and the blessing.

The revised rite of 1537–9 is the basis of the Calvinist and Scottish rites and therefore of great historic importance.

There are three confessions of which the minister may choose one, lengthening it or shortening it as time or opportunity affords. The second was translated into French by Calvin and in an enlarged English version was used by John Knox in his rite of 1556:

> Almighty God and eternal Father, we confess and acknowledge that we, alas, were conceived and born in sin and are therefore inclined to all evil and slow to all good; that we continually transgress thy holy commandments, and more and more corrupt ourselves. But we repent us of the same and beseech thy grace and help. Wherefore most merciful and most gracious God and Father, show thy mercy upon us, through thy Son our Lord Jesus

> Christ. Grant to us and increase in us thy Holy Spirit, that we, acknowledging from the bottom of our hearts our sin and unrighteousness, may come to be repentant and sorry for it, die to it wholly and please thee entirely by a new life blessed of God. Amen.

This is followed by the 'Comfortable Word' of 1 Timothy 1:15, or perhaps others such as John 3:16 or 3:35–6, Acts 10:43, or 1 John 2:1–2. Then comes the absolution by the minister, whose role throughout is priestly:

> Let each make confession in his heart with St Paul in truth ['that I am chief' in some editions], and believe in Christ. So in his Name do I pronounce forgiveness unto you for all your sins and I declare you to be loosed of them in earth so that ye may be loosed of them also in heaven and in all eternity. Amen.

There is then a psalm or hymn instead of the introit, sometimes followed by *Kyries* and the *Gloria in Excelsis*. A short prayer for the right hearing of the Word of God, that it may bear fruit in our lives, precedes the Gospel reading and the sermon. The Gospels are read in course, not discontinuous extracts, and the minister chooses as much as is necessary for his exposition. The reading and sermon at the Lord's Supper must always be from the Gospels; other books of the Bible may be expounded at other services.

The action of the Supper is explained immediately after the sermon usually in four points, summarised as follows:

- We reflect upon the total corruption of our body and blood, our whole nature. Of themselves, as Paul says, they could never share in the Kingdom of God.
- The Word became flesh so that there might be a holy flesh and blood, a divine man, through whom our flesh and blood could be restored and sanctified. This happens as we truly eat and drink of Christ's body and blood.
- The Lord truly gives us himself under visible things. His word says 'Take eat . . . drink ye all of this' and we must accept with simple faith that this is his very self under external signs, but ordained that he may live in us increasingly and we in him.

- In this action we keep the Lord's memory and festival with true devotion and thankfulness praising him with our whole life for his incarnation and death and for this blessed communion, through which we receive his whole self, true God and man for our eternal life both here and hereafter.

The Apostles' Creed in the German metrical version, or a psalm or hymn is sung after the sermon and then there is an extended version of the *Orate fratres* ('Pray, brethren') which concludes the Offertory of the Roman Mass. The Canon follows in three forms. Calvin made the last the basis of his great prayer. The *Sursum Corda* is incorporated as a prayer in the Preface. Intercessions follow, as in the Mass, but enlarged, for kings and governors, pastors and people and for 'men in general', especially the estranged and those chastened by affliction. The intercession is intensely evangelical and compassionate that 'the poor wandering sheep' may be gathered in and suffering be seen as the providence of God and may turn the hearts of its victims to him.

There is then in effect the Prayer of Consecration. It acknowledges our depravity, but contains an oblation, 'that we may yield ourselves with our whole hearts and a true faith to our Redeemer and Saviour'. He not only offered his body and blood to God on the cross for our sin, but gives it to us for food and drink to eternal life. This twofold offering of Christ to the Father on Calvary and to us in the Sacrament is a powerful concept. The prayer asks that we 'with our whole eager desire and true devotion' may receive Christ's goodness and gift, that we may 'truly be partakers of the true and eternal Testament, the Covenant of grace' in confidence that God will not impute to us our sins and that we may live as his dear children, at all times rendering praise and thanks to God, magnifying his holy name 'in all our words and works'. The prayer ends with the request that we may celebrate and keep the glorious and blessed memory of Christ and show forth his death so that we may grow and increase in faith and all goodness.

The prayer is wordy and lacks elegance, but is passionately evangelical. There is a link between it and the nineteenth-century story of the Scottish Hebraist 'Rabbi' Duncan, who offered the bread of communion to a woman, who in her tears would have refused it: 'Take it woman; it was aye broken for sinners.' This is the distinctive Reformed emphasis. The Sacrament is not a miraculous spectacle which brings us to our knees in adoration, so that there is no necessity for us actually to receive the consecrated species. It is our welcome as sinners to the Lord's table where we may feed on him for our salvation.

The prayer leads into the Lord's Prayer and after some further exhortation and explanation the words of institution are read immediately before communion. They are not consecratory but a 'cultus narrative' or authority for the action. Consecration is effected by prayer and its intention. The narrative concludes with the summons 'Believe in the Lord and give eternal praise and thanks to him.' Before distribution the minister says 'Meditate upon, believe, and show forth, that Christ the Lord has died for you.'

Communion was received standing or kneeling, the people going forward to the holy table, where the presiding minister stood at the north end to distribute the bread and the assistant at the south to administer the cup. At Strasbourg hymns were sung during Communion; at Geneva, in a practice followed by John Knox, passages from Scripture were read.

The service concludes with a prayer 'that this memorial of our salvation may never more depart from our hearts', one out of a choice of three thanksgivings, and the Aaronic blessing.

John Calvin was exiled to Strasbourg from 1538 to 1541. He taught theology and ministered to a group of fellow French exiles, who were already there. It was partly because of his sacramental teaching that he had been banished from Geneva. His aim was to try and recover the worship of the early Church. He was much impressed by the liturgy just described, of which he obtained a French translation which he rendered into a more literary style. He made few changes. He introduced a metrical Decalogue after the absolution, placed the Lord's Prayer in a long paraphrase after the intercessions, though repeated it in its scriptural form after the prayer of consecration. Before the Aaronic blessing, he included the *Nunc Dimittis* in a metrical version.

When he returned to Geneva, Calvin used his Strasbourg form but adapted to satisfy the insistence of the magistrates on a simple rite. The absolution was omitted, as were the Lord's Prayer after the consecration, and the *Nunc Dimittis,* while the words of institution were read as warrant before the consecration.

Calvin wished for Communion every Lord's Day. To communicate but once a year was 'certainly an invention of the devil'. It was a dispute over this which had led to his banishment to Strasbourg and he never succeeded in having his wish fulfilled on his return to Geneva; Communion was confined to Christmas, Easter, Pentecost and Harvest. This he deplored as contrary to the New Testament. He believed that the Eucharist (a term which he used) was there, the norm of Christian worship. As a compromise the service on the majority of non-Communion Sundays was given a eucharistic shape as at Strasbourg. It is a 'dry Mass', the order retained, but the consecration and Communion omitted. The prophetic word was preached from the pulpit, for not more than half-an-hour according to Calvin, which was short for those days, but the focus of worship was the holy table.

It is important to observe that the essential elements of the Christian liturgy were retained. It was the Mass in its bare simplicity deprived of accretions and any hint that the once-for-all sacrifice of Christ was repeated and reaching its climax in Communion. It took place in a building devoid of statues and pictures and colour and with the minimum of ceremonial. It may be thought to be dull in comparison to medieval or Orthodox splendour. It did, however, offer the Christ who had offered himself to the Father for our salvation. The people were given a part through singing. The proclamation of the Word, through Scripture, newly translated and fresh to their ears, was not interrupted through ceremonial or visual distractions. They could listen and concentrate. And preaching could excite and deeply move human hearts. It could be dull, and doubtless became more so as the centuries wore on and familiarity made it trite, but there is much testimony to its emotional power, of congregations moved to tears of joy as well penitence. In our own time there are instances of Scottish theologians who could not restrain their feelings in the pulpit or out of it at the wonders of redeeming grace, which in these rites is offered in Word and Sacrament. This indissoluble union is vital to Calvinistic worship. Calvin revived and preserved this more than any other of the continental Reformers (cf. Maxwell; Whale in N. Micklem, ed., pp. 154–71).

CHAPTER 5

THE CHURCH OF ENGLAND LITURGY

The English liturgy owes its particular power and historical endurance to the genius of one man, Thomas Cranmer (1489–1556), who was Archbishop of Canterbury from 1533. Its development follows his own from papal obedience and transubstantiation, through Lutheranism to an increasing eucharistic affinity with more radical Protestantism. He was by nature a cautious scholar, who read everything, almost always with a pen in his hand, but made up his own mind amid a multitude of contemporary influences. He had a remarkably retentive memory for phrases he had read in various liturgies and a fine ear for rhythms. For many years he had to bend to the oscillations of Henry VIII, who was an amateur theologian of uncertain temperament who could not wholly escape his Catholic origins, while having to keep a constant eye on political expediency and complex international relations.

The undoubted friendship between Henry and his archbishop is one of the most fascinating in history. Henry died clutching Cranmer's hand, but it was not until afterwards that the archbishop felt free to introduce an English liturgy. Hitherto he had gone no farther in public that the litany of 1544. Still a processional as in pre-Reformation times, this was a summons to national prayer in a threatening international situation, with Catholics and Protestants at war, and with the rise and demand for autonomy of nation States making the religious issue far from straightforward. There was already a ferocious war with Scotland and Henry VIII wanted his people to summon divine aid as he prepared for conflict with France. Cranmer said that his litany was devised 'to the intent . . . that your hearts and lips may go together in prayer'.

The litany endured for centuries, though by 1547 it had ceased to be a processional, being said 'between the porch and the altar' (Joel 2:17) on Sundays, Wednesdays and Fridays. Anglo-Catholics restored it as a processional.

The litany encapsulates what some would regard as the essence of Anglican liturgy, if not of Anglicanism itself. Litany is one of the earliest forms of Christian prayer and is found in all Eastern liturgies from the *Apostolic Constitutions* onwards. It was extremely common in the medieval West and Cranmer had the Sarum litany before him, as well as the office for the Visitation of the Sick, *Commendatio animae* (the 'Commendation of Souls'), and Luther's litany, which he found in Walter Marshall's *Primer* of 1535: 'Behind both Luther and Cranmer may be discerned the Solemn Prayers of Good Friday' (Cuming, 1982, p. 35). The Sarum litany had become an invocation of saints. The list of these Cranmer pruned in 1544; by 1549, they had disappeared completely. This litany is penitential. It was said that Cranmer had prepared other litanies for use on festive occasions, and he himself admitted as much in a letter to Henry VIII, but these have not survived (see Cuming, 1982, pp. 35–8).

In 1548, the bishops issued *The Order of the Communion,* to be inserted in English into the Roman rite after the communion of the priest. It is a preparation for communion of the laity. It is closely modelled on the *Deliberatio* ('A Simple and Religious Consultation') of Hermann von Wied, the reforming Archbishop-Elector of Cologne, who was much influenced by Martin Bucer, and also by the Order for Brandenburg and Nuremburg of 1533. Hermann aroused much controversy. His own cathedral chapter was opposed to him, and the *Antididagma* of 1544 was a Latin translation of a German work published to attack his views. Cranmer had a copy of this as well as of the *Deliberatio* and it may have given him some phrases. Hermann was excommunicated and deposed in 1546. Hermann's is an order for the Lord's Supper which Cranmer did not follow precisely, but he used material from Hermann's preparation which was intended for the Saturday night before Communion, although it was never used as such in England.

The English Order begins with an exhortation, which reappears in the 1552 *Order of Holy Communion.* Those who intend to take communion are warned that if any be of unrepentant evil life he must withdraw in pain of all iniquity being fulfilled in him and he be brought to total destruction. There is then the invitation with its demand for repentance and commitment and to being 'in love and charity with your neighbours' and the intention to lead a new life, which O. C. Quick said in fidelity to the New Testament should be *the* new life. There follows a general confession, said not all together but by one of the intending communicants, or one of the ministers, or the priest in the name of all. This form owes much to Hermann and Bucer. The priestly absolution begins from Hermann but concludes with the Sarum absolution from prime and compline. This is reinforced by the 'Comfortable Words', which in Hermann *precede* the absolution. Hermann has five texts which he regards as alternatives. They are 'So God loved the world'; 'This is a true saying'; 'If any man sin'; 'The Father loves the Son and has given all things into his hand' (John 3:35); and 'To him all the prophets bear witness that every one who believes in him receives forgiveness of sins through his name' (Acts 10:43). Cranmer has four texts - three from Hermann – but expects all to be read every time. He prefaces them with 'Come unto me . . .', taken possibly from Zwingli's Latin Mass, where, as we have seen, it follows the words of institution before Communion. 'It is true that Zwingli's text concludes "*et ego requiem vobis praestabo*" ("and I will give you rest") but on his title page he quotes it in [Cranmer's] form, "*et ego reficiam vos*" ("and I will refresh you")' (Cuming, 1983, p. 81).

This leads to the Prayer of Humble Access, which seems to be Cranmer's own. The familiar title probably derives from the Scottish Liturgy of 1637, where it is called 'the Collect of Humble Access', though it is not in the collect form. Most liturgies contain at some point prayers expressing our utter unworthiness. This prayer is scriptural with its echoes of the story of the Syro-Phoenician woman and of John 6. Aquinas's doctrine of concomitance, that the whole Christ is present in each element, seems to be denied in the prayer that 'our sinful bodies may be made clean by his body and our souls washed through his most precious blood', though Bishop Dowden quotes parallels to Cranmer's language in Aquinas, as also in Ambrose, both of whom were cited by English Reformers, and in Anselm. He maintains that the last would not have regarded the Prayer of Humble Access as incompatible with the doctrine of concomitance. The words of administration in the *Order of Communion* say over the bread 'The body of our Lord Jesus Christ, which was given for thee, preserve thy body unto everlasting life' and over the wine 'The blood of our Lord Jesus Christ, which was shed for thee, preserve thy soul unto everlasting life' (Dowden, 1908, pp. 317–43). The phrase about our dwelling in Christ and he in us is a favourite of Bucer's.

The Prayer Book of 1549, the first of two under Edward VI, retains the Canon of the Mass, but although it has commended itself to Anglo-Catholics, pained by what they felt to be the mutilations and inadequacies of 1552/1662, there can be no doubt of its Protestantism. Headed 'The Supper of the Lorde and the Holy Communion' it adds to the title 'commonly called the masse', to make clear to people that this is the equivalent of the service which so dominated the Church they had known. It follows the accustomed order, with the Collect for Purity, the introit psalm, probably sung as the priest was saying the Lord's Prayer and the collect, and the threefold *Kyries* but in English. Then there is the *Gloria in Excelsis*. After the Collect of the Day there is to be said one of two collects for the King. The Epistle follows and the Gospel, 'immediately', with no gradual in between and afterwards the Nicene Creed and the sermon or homily. If this has not exhorted the people to the worthy receiving of the body and blood of Christ, a statement is provided, which may be read once a month in cathedrals or where there is a daily Communion, and omitted on weekdays in parish churches. A model exhortation is added when on Sundays and holy days, people seem reluctant to communicate. This is urged upon them as a solemn duty, but they must come as penitents and in love and charity with all the world, having made restitution of wrongs done. Those with troubled consciences may make a private confession to the priest, though there should be no mutual offence between them and those satisfied with a general confession.

The Offertory follows. This is a collection of money for the poor, while the requisite number from a scriptural anthology of twenty sentences is sung. The communicants proceed to the choir, the men on one side, the women on the other. The priest takes sufficient quantities of bread and wine for the numbers present adding 'a little pure and clean water' to the chalice. He then begins the Canon which, unlike most Reformers, Cranmer retains, but with a difference. By this time Cranmer had abandoned belief in the sacrifice of the Mass and held that the true Christian sacrifice was that of praise and thanksgiving and the offering of ourselves. 'The true purpose of a Canon therefore was to make the memorial of Christ's passion and death, and to conjoin with the memorial the offering of the Scriptural sacrifice as Cranmer understood it.' Cranmer's Canon is 'not so much an equivalent of the Latin Canon as a substitute for it' (Ratcliff, p. 193).

The *Sursum Corda* and the Preface are translations from the Latin, but the Proper Prefaces for Christmas Day and Whitsunday are from the *King's Book*, properly entitled *A Necessary Doctrine and Erudition for any Christian Man*, published in 1543 and marking a Catholic reaction after Henry's flirtation with Lutheranism, represented by the so-called *Bishops' Book* six years earlier. Its principal author may have been John Redman, Lady Margaret's Professor and first Master of Trinity College, Cambridge (Collinson, pp. 89–90). It gives many phrases to the Prayer Books (Cuming, 1983, pp. 108f.) After the *Sanctus*, the Canon proper begins with a prayer 'for the whole estate of Christ's Church', not confined to this world. This ends with a thanksgiving for 'the wonderful grace and virtue declared in all thy saints from the beginning of the world. And chiefly in the most glorious and blessed virgin Mary, mother of thy son Jesus Christ our Lord and God, and in the holy Patriarchs, Prophets, Apostles and Martyrs . . . ' There is a commendation of the departed and a prayer that they and us may be seated at the right hand of Christ at the day of the general resurrection.

There is an abrupt transition to the Prayer of Consecration. The intercessions have no connection with what follows and could stand as an independent prayer as happened in 1552. There is no prayer for the acceptance of the eucharistic offering, under cover of which are the intercessory prayers, nor that 'it may become to us the body and blood of your dearly beloved Son Jesus Christ our Lord' which, in the Mass, links it directly with the consecration. The making of the sign of the cross over the bread and wine and manual acts and words of institution are introduced by the militantly Protestant phrase about Christ's death on the cross, 'who made there (by his one oblation of himself once offered) a full, perfect, and sufficient sacrifice, oblation and satisfaction for the sins of the whole world'. There is an epiclesis, 'with thy holy spirit and word, vouchsafe to bless and sanctify these thy gifts and creatures of bread and wine, that they may be unto us the body and blood of thy most dearly beloved son Jesus Christ.' The Latin institution narrative is replaced by an unadorned and scriptural account, a conflation of the New Testament passages, possibly suggested by the Church Order of Brandenburg. The prayer is to be said 'turning still to the altar, without any elevation, or shewing the Sacrament to the people'.

Anamnesis follows and prayer for the acceptance of 'this our Sacrifice of praise and thanksgiving' and the offering of ourselves, unworthy as we are to offer any Sacrifice. The angel of the Roman Mass appears, though in the plural, to bring our prayers 'up into thy holy Tabernacle [substituted for 'altar'] before the sight of thy divine majesty'. There is then the Lord's Prayer without the doxology but, as in the litany, with 'Deliver us from evil' as the response to 'And lead us not into temptation', all that is left of the embolism.

There follows the Peace and 'ye that do truly . . .', the confession, absolution and Comfortable Words and Prayer of Humble Access from the Order of Communion.

The words of delivery are different from those of the Order in that both body and blood are to 'preserve body and soul' unto everlasting life. The *Agnus Dei* is sung in English by the clerks, during communion. The post-communion consists of an anthology of scriptural passages followed by a greeting and thanksgiving, emphasising the '*spiritual* food of the most precious body and blood of thy Son our saviour Jesus Christ' (*emphasis added*) and the equally important consequence of the Sacrament that 'we be very members incorporate in thy mystical body which is the blessed company of all faithfull people'. The service ends with the Peace from Philippians 4:7 and the blessing.

Final rubrics prescribe omissions for workdays; only litany and ante-communion shall be said where there are none to communicate with the priest who shall wear a plain white alb or surplice with a cope; unleavened and plain bread, 'without any manner of print' but longer and thicker than the wafer for easy division; and the bread to be received from the priest in the mouth, so that it may not be taken home for superstitious purposes.

Cranmer almost certainly intended 1549 as a transitional rite to help conservatives to come to terms with the shock of the vernacular and Reformed doctrines, which affirmed the free grace of God not tied to any ordinances and denied transubstantiation. Stephen Gardiner, the Bishop of Winchester and Cranmer's antagonist over many years, declared that in his judgement 1549 was 'not distant from the catholic faith' and cited the position of the Prayer of Humble Access as giving credence to transubstantiation. On the other side, Bucer had reservations, spelled out in what came by his editor to be called the *Censura*, though he realised that this was an interim rite. John Hooper, the extremely radical and non-ritualistic Bishop of Gloucester disliked the 1549 book heartily.

The 1552 service is unequivocally Protestant. The service is now 'the Lord's Supper or Holy Communion'. There is no mention of the Mass. The Table, 'having a fair white linen cloth upon it', presumably with the elements too, stands 'in the body of the Church or in the Chancel', not at the East end (see picture in MacCulloch, p. 508). The priest stands on the north side and says the Lord's Prayer and the Collect for Purity which are followed by the Ten Commandments with responses, an innovation which may derive from the worship of a French refugee congregation, which the Duke of Somerset had set up in Glastonbury, 'although there the recitation and responses were in a metrical version'. Bishop Hooper, a firm friend of the 'Stranger' (i.e. refugee) congregations had anticipated this in his diocesan injunctions of 1551 (MacCulloch, pp. 505f.).

There follows the Collect of the Day and one of the two for the King, the Epistle, the Gospel, the Creed, the sermon, or one of the homilies. The Offertory is purely financial, for the poor, to the reading of one or more from the large selection of sentences. This, if there be any such alms, is offered for divine acceptance at the beginning of the Prayer for the Church, transferred from the 1549 Canon. It is now for 'the church militant here in earth', not for 'the whole estate of Christ's Church'. It concludes with the prayer for those in trouble. There is no mention of the departed. Nor is there any direction about the bread and wine, the quantities to be taken, when they are to be laid upon the table, or what happens should supplies run out.

There follow three exhortations: the first when people have become negligent about Holy Communion, pleading with them not to ignore God's gracious hospitality, or to be, as in the days of the Mass, spectators when Christ says 'Take ye and eat', 'Take and drink ye all of this'; the second to bid them to come after self-examination and in penitence, receiving, if necessary, ghostly counsel from the minister; the third as in 1549, with the warnings, even heightened from 1 Corinthians 11, about the dire consequences of receiving in a state of sin, or crime. There is then the 'Ye that do truly and earnestly repent of your sins . . .', with the necessity of being 'in love and charity with your neighbours', all that remains of the Peace, and the general confession and absolution from the Order of Communion transferred from the position after the Eucharistic Prayer, and concluding with the Comfortable Words, which are followed immediately by the *Sursum Corda,* the Preface with propers, as in 1549, for the seasons of Christmas, Easter, Ascension, Whitsun and Trinity Sunday. All is gathered up in the *Sanctus,* which no longer has with it the words 'Blessed is he that cometh in the name of the Lord'.

There is no Canon to follow; some think this a grievous mutilation, but this is to compare 1552 with other rites without realising its uniqueness. Someone once said that it was like criticising a game of cricket because it is not played with a hockey stick.

Other liturgies had not been blind to the Old Testament context of the *Sanctus.* It comes from Isaiah 6 and the prophet's reaction is 'humble access'. And so, having been joined for a moment to the perfect praises of heaven and glimpsed the court of God, the divine glory brings us to our knees. Adoration leads to penitence: 'We be not worthy so much as to gather up the crumbs under thy table.' And yet

God's nature is forever merciful and he will enable us so to eat and drink that we have union with Christ, a mutual indwelling. It is important that in this rite we no longer ask to receive in order to eat the flesh of Christ and drink his blood, 'in these holy mysteries'. And so to the great act of remembrance, in obedience to Christ's command, which is what for Cranmer by this stage the Communion is (Ratcliff, p. 196). There is no consecration of the elements, no epiclesis, no making of the sign of the cross over them. The institution narrative no longer says that Christ '*blessed and* gave thanks' before breaking the bread, removing any suggestion that he consecrated it before saying in effect grace before meat. The manual acts are removed. There is no 'amen' after the words over the cup. Communion follows straightaway. The words of delivery remove all mention of what Gardiner had half-mockingly construed as transubstantiation in 1549. There is no mention of the body and blood of Christ as in the *Order of Communion*, and in 1549, simply 'Take and eat this in remembrance that Christ died for thee and feed on him in thy heart by faith with thanksgiving' and 'Drink this in remembrance that Christ's blood was shed for thee and be thankful.' The Lord's Prayer, like the sacrifice of ourselves, follows communion. 'Give us this day our daily bread' has no sacramental reference, but it is when we have received Christ that we may call God 'Father'.

After the alternative prayers of oblation and thanksgiving, the *Gloria in Excelsis* is transferred from the beginning to the end of the service. This was on scriptural grounds. The Last Supper ended with a hymn of praise. Cranmer had used psalms and canticles in the offices preceding the Communion and he did not feel capable himself of writing a hymn, so he moved the *Gloria* from the beginning of the service to the end. Modern revisions will have none of this, but the twentieth-century liturgist, monk, and bishop W.H. Frere believed that this, which is uniquely Anglican, 'makes a more balanced service than the Latin one is, one which comes to a climax as no other rite does of an uplifting kind, and ends with a chorus of praise' (Arnold and Wyatt, eds, pp. 134f.). The modern liturgist is not only anxious to conform to the long Roman tradition, but to begin with praise and to leave the end 'open', the people not gazing Godward, but sent out into the world to engage in the liturgy of life.

Cranmer's detractors, obsessed with what they have regarded as his obsession with penitence, have thought that the pleas for mercy in the *Gloria* show his inability to escape from guilt even after the Sacrament. They should heed what the Russian Nicholas Cabasilas wrote in the fourteenth-century commentary on the Orthodox liturgy that a prayer for mercy is a prayer for the Kingdom of the God in whom mercy rules supreme (Cabasilas, pp. 47f.).

The rubrics at the end of the service include one for the provision of the bread, not unleavened, but such as is eaten every day with other meats, though 'the best and purest white bread that may conveniently be gotten. And if any of the bread or wine remain, the Curate shall have it to his own use.' This is a denial of any permanent effects of consecration. The elements of the Eucharist are like the water of baptism – an analogy which Cranmer pursued in his treatise of 1550, *A Defence of the True and Catholick Doctrine of the Sacrament of the Body and Blood of our Saviour Christ* – set apart for sacred use for a while, but then reverting to their ordinary condition with no supernatural properties.

There is also the 'black rubric'. Cranmer would not follow the extreme evangelicals and radicals who wanted communion to be received sitting, like the disciples at the Last Supper. Kneeling is for reverence and good order. It must not imply any adoration of the elements, for this is idolatry. They remain in their natural state, Christ's body and blood are in heaven. It is against the truth for Christ's natural body to be in more than one place at one time. Martin Bucer, though he was neither Roman Catholic nor Lutheran, would not have been happy with this.

The Elizabethan Act of Uniformity of 1559 made only one change in the 1552 service, in spite of the unease of some at the lack of consecration, countered by those who, like Bishop Jewel, asserted that consecration took place by the audible pronunciation of the words of institution over the elements. It conflated the words of delivery of 1549 and 1552 so that the communicant was offered the body and blood of Christ and not simply told to take, eat in remembrance and thankfulness. The 'black rubric' was omitted and there was an ambiguous direction that the minister should use 'such ornaments in church as were in use by the authority of Parliament in the second year of the reign of King Edward VI'.

There was still discontent, which the very minor alterations of the Hampton Court Conference of 1604 did nothing to dispel. The Puritans wanted a still more radical liturgy, and by the Commonwealth some were calling the Book of Common Prayer a 'brazen serpent'. Some Laudians felt with Jeremy Taylor that 'in the second liturgy . . . they did cast out something that might, with good profit have remained'. The table was restored to its position at the east end and railed in, though it was still a table.

Several bishops heightened the Prayer Book liturgy by setting it in elaborately furnished chapels and making some changes in the direction of 1549. John Overall of Lichfield (d. 1619) transferred the Prayer of Oblation from after communion to follow the words of institution which he and his kind used as consecratory. Lancelot Andrewes distinguished between alms and oblations, having the people bring their eucharistic offerings to the rails after the Creed while the celebrant read a new set of sentences. The alms were put into the 'poor man's chest' as the congregation returned to their seats after the *Gloria in Excelsis*, for which they had remained in the chancel after communion. Cranmer's sentences were read then.

The ill-fated Scottish Liturgy of 1637 represents the Laudian supremacy. The word 'Priest' or 'Minister', is replaced by 'Presbyter'. The Authorized Version of 1611 is used for the Scriptures and the Apocrypha is omitted as a result of the Hampton Court Conference. Fifteen Scottish saints are added to the Kalendar. The Collect for the King precedes the Collect of the Day. Six of Andrewes' sentences for the Offertory are included and ten of Cranmer's left out. The collection is to be presented and the elements offered 'upon the Lord's Table'.

The intercession is as in 1549, a prayer 'for the whole estate of Christ's Church' and the thanksgiving for the departed is restored, although it does not mention the Virgin, the patriarchs, apostles and martyrs. The great prayer is called the Consecration. The epicleis of 1549 and the manual acts are restored. The 'memorial or prayer of oblation' follows the words of institution with the 1549 anamnesis. The Lord's Prayer comes next with the doxology and then the Prayer of Humble Access. The words of delivery are as 1549. 'Amen' is to be said in response.

In view of all this and of high church feelings it is remarkable that the Prayer Book made mandatory by the 1662 Act of Uniformity was so little changed from 1552. John Cosin was the leading Church of England liturgist at the Savoy Conference. He returned from exile less enamoured of Rome than when he went and more understanding of the Presbyterian position. The name 'precision', says Cuming, 'fits him like a glove'. He believed that the Eucharist is the offering by us of Christ's once-for-all sacrifice (Cuming, 1983, pp. 126ff.). It is representation, which is very much the doctrine of Daniel Brevint's *The Christian Sacrifice and Sacrament* (1672), the principal source of the Wesley hymns on the Lord's Supper (1745). Cosin regarded the Prayer Book of 1549 as of the highest authority, more so than did his colleague and collaborator, Bishop Matthew Wren. Cosin began to enter suggestions for revision into a folio edition of the Prayer Book of 1619, now known as the Durham Book. Many of these derive from the Scottish Liturgy. They were too advanced to most of Cosin's contemporaries, though they have influenced liturgy in the Anglican communion (Cuming, 1961, pp. xiff.).

There are few alterations in the 1662 *Book of Common Prayer*, though they mostly would not have been approved by Cranmer and did not meet Presbyterian objections to the Prayer Book. There were tensions between the bishops, who would have preferred more in the manner of the Durham Book and the laity on the Privy Council and in the House of Commons. The Prayer for the Church Militant ends with a thanksgiving for the saints, though is not a prayer for them. The prayer which follows Humble Access is called the Prayer of Consecration and the priest 'standing before the table' has the bread and wine within reach of the manual acts. This prayer is concluded with 'amen'. The words of delivery are the conflation of 1559. Any unconsecrated bread and wine left over may be taken for the curate's own use, but any consecrated must be reverently consumed by the priest and any communicants he invites after the blessing. If the consecrated elements are used up during the distribution and more are required, there must be reconsecration by repeating the words of institution over fresh supplies. The Black Rubric is restored.

There is no doubt that a principal reason why 1552 remained basically unaltered at the Restoration was that it had already, not least through its memorable prose, endeared itself to worshippers. Proscribed under the Commonwealth and legally replaced by the Westminster Assembly's *Directory of Public Worship*, its use had continued unobtrusive and unadorned and it was loved the more through adverse circumstances and in its bare simplicity. After a century, it had become 'part of a rhythm of worship, piety, practice that had earthed itself into the Englishman's consciousness and had sunk deep roots in popular culture' (MacCulloch, p. 628).

Initiation

The Reformers reduced the sacraments to the two which they believed were instituted by Christ, though some, like Richard Baxter, admitted the five as 'sacramental ordinances'. The Anabaptists, so opposed by the majority, believed infant baptism to be in error but the principal Reformers retained it, though the conflict with the radicals was bitter. 'In the light of this disagreeable experience', writes John Bossy, 'it dawned upon them that all kinds of things by which they set great store – the Christian instruction of children, the integrity of the Christian household, the identity of the Church and civil community – hung upon the traditional practice of infant baptism' (Bossy, p. 115).

Luther, at first, thought that the pre-Reformation rite of baptism was the one unspoiled ordinance free for all. He later, under the influence of the doctrine of justification by faith, emphasised that what mattered most was the faith of the person to be baptised. Hence the unworthiness of the officiant could not invalidate the sacrament, but grace was not, as had been believed, irrespective of faith, 'the submission of the old self and the emersion of the new self'. He defended infant baptism because faith could be vicarious, the faith of those presenting the infant and the faith of the Church, while the child might come to faith later. But, somewhat contradictorily, Luther asserted that everything depends on God's word and command, the objectivity of the sacrament he had ordained.

Luther did not at first change drastically the Magdeburg Order of Baptism of 1497. He translated it into German so that it be understood. He felt that the additional ceremonies and embellishments, signing with the cross, salt, the effeta, oil, chrism, christening robe and candle were secondary. Exorcism, driving out the devil, was essential. After the giving of salt, he introduced the flood prayer, which we shall quote later in Cranmer's 1552 version. It adopts medieval typology and sees the flood and the crossing of the Red Sea as types of baptism. He includes the blessing of the children from Mark before the spittle and the effeta and the renunciations and the profession of faith. He does not make any distinction between males and females in baptism. The child is dipped in the font, anointed while the godparents hold him there, a cap is placed on his head to signify the white robe, and lifted from the font, he is given a candle, 'this burning torch'. As in the Latin rite, this evokes the parable of the wise and foolish virgins': the wise had their lamps burning to greet the bridegroom. Luther's second order, which had wide use, abandoned the external ceremonies except the sign of the cross.

Bucer at Strasbourg found the priests somewhat impatient of the ceremonies with which baptism had become cluttered and swept them away as enchantments except for the baptism itself. Baptism is the sign of the second birth of John 3; it is also being buried and rising with Christ as in Romans 6. The Gospel of the little children being brought to Jesus is read. Baptism should be administered as shortly as possible so that simple people may understand the bare act. The order at Strasbourg after 1537 was more verbose but devoid of all external ceremonies.

Zwingli at first thought that true baptism was inward and spiritual and the outward rite not necessary; infant baptism was indefensible. But he came to believe that the children of

Christian parents should not be forbidden baptism for they should not be excluded from salvation. His simple rite had a flood prayer, the reading of the blessing of the children, and the chrism, which by now is not anointing but simply clothing with a white robe.

For Calvin, baptism should take place after the sermon, with the father of the child present. After a lengthy explanation stressing the analogy with circumcision and the Lord's blessing of the children, but making much of our natural state of misery and our need to be born again, there is a prayer which asks that the sanctification of baptism may lead to the child's knowledge and glorifying of God at the age of understanding and throughout life. After the Lord's Prayer the Apostles' Creed is said, the summary of the doctrine in which the parents must instruct the child. Their duties to ensure that he reveres Scripture and keeps the two great commandments are given prominence before the simple ceremony with water. 'Chrism, candle and other such pomps' are not of God's ordinance. They may confuse people into thinking that they are the authentic sacramental acts.

At Cologne, John Gropper (1503–59), a mediating Catholic who later opposed Hermann von Wied, gave a lengthy rationale of the Catholic ceremonies in the *Enchiridion* (1538). His wish was that they should not be abandoned but understood. Hermann's *Consultation* was much influenced by the Lutherans, Melancthon and Bucer. It has very full explanations and exhortations and disposes of all ceremonies save water baptism. The *Consultation* did not survive in Cologne but a copy found its way into Cranmer's library at Lambeth where it kept company with Gropper's opposing *Antididagma* which defended the Catholic rite and ceremonies on scriptural grounds, some of them rather dubious since it supposed among other things pseudo-Dionysius to be Paul's convert.

In England, with baptism as with the Eucharist, reformation was slow. The *Rationale of Ceremonial* in the early 1540s upheld the ceremonies of the Sarum rite. The *Bishops' Book* of 1537 insisted on the necessity of baptism for salvation. It was a strong refutation of Anabaptists on the grounds that infants were born in sin and this must be remitted speedily by baptism else should they die they would be deprived of eternal salvation. 'Infants and children dying in their infancy shall undoubtedly be saved thereby, and else not.' The book asserts that neither for children nor adults must there be re-baptism. The so-called *King's Book* of 1543 was even more conservative, reaffirming that there were seven sacraments. As in the *Bishops' Book*, 'repent' in Acts 2 is rendered 'do penance'. Yet while declaring undoubted salvation through baptism for those who die in infancy, it omits the words 'and else not'. It shows Protestant influences in that it says that 'baptism may well be called a covenant between God and us' of which we must keep our part by serving and obeying him and forsaking all sin. The statement concludes with the Pauline teaching that in baptism we die with Christ and are raised together with him, which is to say that we are incorporated into his mystical body and live the new life of grace and the Spirit.

Meanwhile Tyndale had attacked the 'dumb ceremonies' of baptism and that priests played 'popinjay' with Latin expressions so that baptism was called in some places 'volowing' because of the Latin response which the godparents were supposed to make on behalf of the infant, '*volo*', 'I wish', to the question 'Dost thou wish to be baptised'? Cranmer doughtily defended infant baptism on the familiar analogy of circumcision and in the belief that infants 'pertain to God', evidenced by Christ's receiving children and teaching that they were of the Kingdom of Heaven.

He wished for baptism to be public and 'when the most number of people come together', so that they might renew their own baptism. But if this is not possible 'children ought at all times to be baptised', either at the church or else at home.

The 1549 rite of baptism is set in the context of the offices, not the Eucharist and, as with Sarum, begins at the church door with a brief exhortation, drastically abbreviated from Hermann's *Consultation*, and the flood prayer. A cross is made upon the child's forehead and breast. After a prayer which combines Sarum and Luther's second order, there is an exorcism much briefer than Sarum but using some of its words as well as Luther's. The blessing of the children by Jesus is read from Mark's Gospel and briefly expounded, followed by the Lord's Prayer and the Apostles' Creed with a prayer that the Holy Spirit be given to the children, who are led to the font where they – or adults on their behalf – forsake the devil and profess Christian faith for themselves, with the questions from Sarum to which, in their Latin form, Tyndale had objected. There is a threefold dipping ensuring that the child's whole body is touched by water, and the giving of the chrism, the white robe.

There is a final anointing, the unction of the Holy Spirit. Martin Bucer in the *Censura,* his comments on the 1549 Prayer Book, was opposed to the initial ceremonies taking place at the church door. The infants to be baptised should be brought straight into the midst of the people of God, who should be able to hear all that is said. In the 1552 rite, the service begins at the font, with a slightly revised form of the opening prayer of 1549. There is no signing with the cross. Next is the flood prayer also revised:

> Almighty and everlasting God which of thy great mercy didst save Noah and his family in the ark from perishing by water, and also didst safely lead the children of Israel, thy people, through the Red Sea, figuring thereby thy holy baptism, and by the baptism of thy well beloved Son, Jesus Christ, didst sanctify the flood Jordan and all other water to the mystical washing away of sin: we beseech thee for thy infinite mercies that thou wilt mercifully look upon these children, sanctify them and wash them with thy Holy Ghost, that they being delivered from thy wrath may be received into the ark of Christ's church, and being stedfast in faith, joyful through hope and rooted in charity, may so pass the waves of this troublesome world, that finally they may come to the land of everlasting life, there to reign with thee, world without end: through Jesus Christ our Lord. Amen.

Bucer had been disregarded here. In the *Censura* he states that the baptism of the cross accomplished the work of Christ much more fully than the baptism in Jordan, and 'although water is used to confer it in baptism, the washing away of sins is not the function of water but of Christ the Lord'. In the next prayer too, Cranmer retains the phrase that the children are 'coming to thy holy baptism' whereas Bucer would have preferred 'brought to thy holy baptism'. There is no exorcism.

The Gospel from Mark 10 is read and as in 1549 briefly applied. The Lord's Prayer and the Creed are omitted at this point, repetition of the Creed being superfluous since it is recited by the priest as an enquiry as to the godparents' faith; and there is no need for the child or children to be led into the church, being already at the font. The questions addressed to the children in 1549 are in 1552 addressed to the godparents in response to Bucer's criticisms. There follows a series of short prayers for the burial of the old Adam and the final prayer only for the 1549 blessing of the font, so that, again as Bucer wished, the water is not consecrated, but grace and fidelity are asked for those baptised in it. The child's name is used for the first time at the baptism – in 1549 and medieval rites it was used at the church door. Hence the association of baptism with naming, which has obscured its essential meaning. The sign of the cross, transferred from the 1549 beginning of the service at the church door, is made upon the child's forehead as he/she is received 'into the congregation of Christ's flock', and words from 1549, which have become part of the English heritage through this rite, 'that he shall not be ashamed to confess the faith of Christ crucified and manfully to fight under his banner against all sin, the world and the devil, and to continue Christ's faithful soldier and servant unto his life's end'. This signing resulted in the Puritan criticism that the ignorant would mistake this for the act of baptism. It has never been possible to avoid surrounding baptism with additional ceremonies. The water never seems to be sufficient. The vesting with the white robe and the anointing with Christ were however abolished as Bucer has recommended. The Lord's Prayer is said after baptism and there is a final prayer, new to this service, which thanks God that the infant has been regenerated through the Holy Spirit and incorporated into the holy congregation. The prayer goes on to ask that the child 'being buried with Christ in his death, may crucify the old man, and utterly abolish the whole body of sin, that as he is made partaker of the death of thy Son, so he may be partaker of his resurrection, so that finally with the residue of thy holy congregation he may be inheritor of thy everlasting kingdom'. There is a final exhortation to the godparents. They shall 'call upon' the baptised to hear sermons: 'and chiefly ye shall provide that they may learn the Creed, the Lord's Prayer and the Ten Commandments in the English tongue and all other things which a Christian man ought to know to his soul's health.' As soon as they have learned the three prescribed texts they shall be brought to the bishop to be confirmed.

Faustus of Riez in the fifth century had applied the term 'Confirmation' to those ceremonies which constituted a completion of baptism. The scriptural warrant was Acts 8:14–17. Samaritans had been baptised but did not receive the Holy Spirit until Paul and John from Jerusalem, apostles believed to be bishops, went and laid hands on them. This may have been an exceptional case, but was regarded as the rule and reinforced by decretals of the seventh century falsely supposed to be of the third or fourth. Baptism is like the enrolling of a soldier in the army; Confirmation equips him for war. 'Therefore the Holy Spirit who comes down upon the waters of baptism with his saving descent confers in the font all that is needed for innocence, in confirmation he provides an increase in grace.'

Some Catholics in the fifteenth century had suspected the authenticity of the decretals. Wycliffe thought that Confirmation was 'introduced at the prompting of the devil', that people should the more accept 'the dignity and authority' of bishops. There was a realisation that those baptised as infants needed instruction in the faith and some opportunity to accept it for themselves and be received into the congregation by laying-on of hands with prayer for strength to persevere. Erasmus felt that puberty in boys was the age for public profession 'with solemn ceremonies fitting, pure, serious and magnificent', which have greater authority if performed by bishops.

Luther was puzzled by the Roman Catholic Church making a sacrament out of the laying-on of hands. According to the accounts in Acts it was not necessary to the reception of the Spirit. Was anything the apostles did a sacrament? If so, why did the Romanists not make a sacrament of preaching? Episcopal Confirmation has no foundation in Scripture, though Luther agreed that the children should be examined *by the pastors,* who may then lay on hands and confirm them. He compared Confirmation to the ceremony of blessing baptismal water but produced no German rite. He believed the confession of faith should allow admittance to first communion. Bucer at Strasbourg felt that there was a need for a ceremony at the age when Anabaptists would administer baptism. There was a rite used about the year 1550, after Bucer's departure which undoubtedly embodies his convictions. It is largely an affectionate examination and instruction of the children that they continue to learn Christian doctrine, shun the Roman Church, and, above all, that they faithfully 'act and live' in accordance with membership in the Church and its teaching. Obedience and respect of elders is the right learning attitude, and submission to their discipline and punishment should the baptised children do wrong and commit sin. The congregation is then bidden to receive them and watch over them and themselves. After a collect, the priest stretches his hand over the children and says the Prayer of Confirmation.

Bucer found scriptural warrant for Confirmation in the Lord's blessing of the children and seems to have regarded this as a third sacrament; but in his Catechism of 1543, he denied that Jesus had ordered the use of the laying-on of hands in Confirmation, although he thought this was a practice which the Church should continue as it had proved a means of blessing.

Hermann von Wied did not regard Confirmation as 'of absolute necessity', but believed that it had its use, though should not be given before a child was seven and able to make sacramental confession. The *Enchridion* of Cologne, though the work of Gropper who came to oppose him, had Hermann's approval. Confirmation was the gift of the Spirit who had been bestowed in baptism, descending not as a dove but with the fiery tongues of Pentecost to strengthen those who have passed through the baptismal waters, as Israel through the Red Sea, and were now in the wilderness of this world. Chrism is the matter of the sacrament taught by early Fathers as received from the apostles. A mixture of oil representing 'the richness of grace, the splendour of faith and the warmth of charity' and balsam. The sweetness of the Spirit which gives us 'the good odour of Christ', signifies the internal unction of the Holy Spirit. It was not needed in the days of the New Testament when the gift of the Spirit was attested by 'temporal and visible miracle', speaking with tongues and the like. Now, as Augustine said, the divine charity is poured into the hearts of Christians and chrism is the outward sign of this. The sign of the cross on the forehead, the place of modesty, admonishes the candidates to open and courageous confession of Christ. The blow on the cheek after Confirmation is a reminder that sufferings and insults are bound to come and that to him who strikes on the right cheek the left must be offered also. Henceforth the confirmed are sent as the Father sent Christ. Acts 8:17 makes clear that Confirmation must be administered by the bishop, the successor of the apostles. Hermann in his *Consultation* thought that by his time, dioceses were too large for bishops to examine candidates adequately and ensure that they had been properly prepared, which was the practical reason for the bishop's monopoly. Confirmation should be done by visitors after the most careful preparation by the parish priest, the results of which are seen in a lengthy interrogation which the *Consultation* takes from Bucer. No children must be brought for Confirmation unless the parish priest is satisfied that they 'know the sum of religion and truly believe in Christ'. But it is recognised that some of a true faith may not be able to express themselves well or remember forms of words, whereas some less sincere may be adept at glib responses. The parish priest must be able to discern these matters and the service must include a warning that the congregation 'humbly pray for these children'. This prayer is the long collect from Bucer, after which 'the pastor' (presumably a visitor) lays on hands and confirms with the prayer from Strasbourg (Bucer). All this was fiercely attacked in the *Antididagma*.

In England, Henry VIII defended the traditional doctrine of Confirmation against Luther in 1521, but by 1536 he ordered the issuing of the Ten Articles which, among much else, stated that children should not be brought to the bishop for Confirmation before they had reached the age of discretion, that no ceremonies should be allowed which were not 'clearly expressed in Scripture' and that hallowed oil was no better than the Pope's grease or butter. There was much debate in which Cranmer took a radical view that

Confirmation was not instituted by Christ and that instances of it in Scripture were acts and deeds of the apostles done by a special gift needed at the time which does not now remain with their successors. But Cranmer did not follow Calvin and Zwingli in abandoning the rite. The English Church retained the name. The 1549 Order implied that it should be a means of edification administered to those who had reached 'the years of discretion', or are 'of perfect age', able to say at least the Creed, the Commandments and the Lord's Prayer and answer questions of the short catechism, and who are ready to discern the Lord's body in the Sacrament. Some may do this before they reach 'the perfect age'. Others may be later but to delay Confirmation is not to deprive anyone of eternal salvation. Baptism is the sacrament which ensures that. Confirmation is necessary for admission to Communion. This goes against the custom of the Eastern Church, in which baptised infants are eligible, and the Western from the third century to the twelfth.

The 1549 Order opens with a prayer for the sevenfold gifts of the Spirit which derives from the sixth-century Gelasian Sacramentary and is, of course, in Sarum. There was then the signing with the cross on the forehead and the laying-on of hands. Chrism has gone. There is a final prayer, a new composition, for the children.

The 1552 Order in the opening prayers asks that the Holy Spirit strengthen God's servants, not be sent down from heaven upon them. It omits the signing of the cross on the forehead. It is much more a service of edification which admits to Communion than an objective sacramental act by which the Holy Spirit is conveyed. John Cosin complained that the concluding prayer after the hand-laying could be said by any minister and was not specifically episcopal (cf. Fisher, *passim*).

In the seventeenth century some bishops were careless about Confirmation. Richard Baxter described how a bishop would confirm by tapping the candidates on the head as he walked up the church path. But the devout Anglican felt as did the nineteenth-century Cambridge theologian F. J. A. Hort, who wrote to a lady who had joined the Church of England from the Society of Friends: 'Baptism chiefly concerns us as to what we *are*, Confirmation as to what we *do*'. It gives us special help for the new tasks of manhood or womanhood. 'It is an assurance of active "gifts of grace", varied helps from the One Spirit, a spirit of "wisdom" and "strength", of "holy fear", meeting all our own efforts and giving them power from on high. Confirmation reminds us strongly that Baptism is not so much a single event, accomplished once for all, as the beginning of a life which calls for daily rekindling and renewal' (A. F. Hort, ed., II pp. 81f.).

CHAPTER 6

THE PURITANS AND THEIR SUCCESSORS

Who exactly were the Puritans, is a question which is not easily resolved, and it is bedevilled by the popular notion of the Puritan as an austere and censorious killjoy implacably opposed to the arts and, in religion, to the compromise represented by the Church of England. Some would restrict the name to those who, until 1640, wanted to reform the English Church further from within. They were mostly Calvinists and from James I's time, and especially during the ascendancy of Charles I and Archbishop Laud some left England for Holland or the American colonies. There was always a possibility that opposition to the established Church would lead some to separatism. After the outbreak of the Civil Wars, there was a proliferation of sectarianism, and Puritanism divided into two main streams, the Presbyterian and the Independent, although there was an embarrassing number of more radical allegiances, of which the non-liturgical Quakers were the most enduring and influential. Some of the Independents were Anabaptists, whom the leaders of the Reformation and Cranmer had always resisted. The name Puritan may be old-fashioned, if not an anachronism after 1640, but although ecclesiologies differed and some passed from moderation to radicalism, there was a common spirituality, founded on personal encounter with the living God, through Scripture and also personal experience of the Holy Spirit, not always without agonising struggles, which governed style of life and political attitudes.

In worship, Puritans objected to the *Book of Common Prayer*. *An Admonition to Parliament* of 1572 described the Prayer Book as 'an unperfect book culled and picked out of that popish dunghill, the mass-book, full of all abominations'. Cranmer's defenders believed that his work had been interrupted and that 1552 was a transition on the way to a more complete reform. The Puritans disliked the brief extracts from Scripture read as lessons ('pistling and gospelling'), the ping-pong of responses, the brevity of the collects. Prayer should be lengthy as in Scripture, either read from a book, or extempore, offered by the minister alone on behalf of the people, whose one response should be 'amen'. Communion should not be received kneeling, which was, they believed, contrary to the ancient tradition of the Church as described by Chrysostom as well as to the posture of the Upper Room, although on this last they were mistaken since the disciples in fact were reclining, not sitting. There was a further difference, since many Independents felt that the elements should be taken to the people in their seats, whereas the Presbyterians thought that the communicants should come to the table and sit there. There was argument about a single or double consecration, or as the Independents preferred, sanctification. Should the bread be blessed and distributed before the wine? For the priest to give the elements into hands or mouth when the Scripture injunction was 'Take, eat!' was incorrect; and communicants should eat and drink all together, as the Gospel implies, not individually. The words of delivery should be straight from Scripture. And there should be no accretions and appurtenances, such as the *Gloria,* and the Creed, no singing of introits, no vestments or wafers. There should be a sterner examination of recipients, 'fencing of tables' so that only those seriously in the Christian way should communicate. Insistence upon a minimum attendance of three times a year was an insult to the ordinance. Easter was particularly inappropriate as a Communion season, since the Lord's Supper is a proclamation of Christ's death, not his resurrection (Davies, 1948, pp. 57ff.).

It is John Bunyan, the Baptist/Independent, who condemns adherents of the Prayer Book with scathing sarcasm. They have:

> . . . both the *Manner and Matter* of their Prayers at their finger ends; setting such a Prayer for such a day and that twenty years

> before it comes. One for *Christmas* and another for *Easter* and six dayes after that. They have also bounded how many syllables must be said in every one of them at their public Exercises. For each Saints day also, they have them ready for generations yet unborn to say. They can also tell you when you shall kneel, when you should stand, when you should abide in your seats, when you should go up to the Chancel, and what you should do when you come there. All which the Apostles came short of not being able to compose so profound a matter . . . (Bunyan, *Miscellaneous Works* II, pp. 247–8)

Even so, some Puritans used the *Book of Common Prayer* but made alterations to satisfy their more Reformed principles. In 1646, John Geree delineated 'The Character of an old English Puritane' and wrote among much else that:

> He esteemed that manner of prayer best, where by the gift of God, expressions were varied according to present wants and occasions. Yet he did not account set forms unlawful. Therefore in that circumstance of the Church he did not wholly reject the liturgy, but the corruption of it . . . The Lord's Supper he accounted part of his soul's food: to which he laboured to keep an appetite. He esteemed it an ordinance of nearest communion with Christ, so requiring most exact preparation.

By that time the Prayer Book had been proscribed and *A Directory for the Public Worship of God* had become the authorised liturgy by Act of Parliament in 1645. This attempts to reach a compromise between Presbyterians and Independents, a service of the Genevan type with a combination of set forms and free prayer and one completely free, with even the Lord's Prayer rejected because it was believed to have been given as a model or pattern, not as a fixed form of words. There was lengthy, sometimes bitter argument over many details. The *Directory* is really a collection of rubrics, or suggestions, which may be turned into set forms, or give guidance for extempore prayer. It presupposes a sabbatarian Lord's Day devoted entirely to solemn public meetings of the congregation, to private prayer, devotional exercises and works of mercy. Public worship must take precedence over all else. It should be done decently and in order; but without those bowings towards the East which a Convocation Canon of 1640 had commended as 'good and behoveful'. The sermon is the main act of worship, preceded by a long prayer. There is a prayer after the sermon, a thanksgiving which also may make the heads of the sermon petitions. Where there is a Sacrament, it follows this with an exhortation, the words of institution from Scripture and a prayer of thanksgiving for the sanctification of the elements. The bread is broken, that is, cut up for distribution by the minister. Bread and cup must be consecrated successively before distribution. This is accompanied by the words said to the communicants as a whole:

> According to the holy institution, command and example of our blessed Saviour Jesus Christ, I take this Bread and having given thanks, I break it and give it unto you. Take ye, eat ye; this is the Body of Christ which is broken for you. Do this in remembrance of him. According to the institution, command and example of our Lord Jesus Christ, I take this Cup and give it unto you. This Cup is the New Testament in the Blood of Christ, which is shed for the remission of the sins of many. Drink ye all of it.

The words of institution are more than a part of the preaching and a warrant for the ordinance, coming immediately before the Eucharistic Prayer; 'they were made an integral part of the setting apart or sanctifying the elements' as the Cambridge Puritan, William Perkins, had taught in his exposition of the second, the blessing, of the fourfold actions of the Eucharist (Spinks, 1984, p. 42).

There was no double consecration. The Thanksgiving is divided into three parts. The first two parts comprise confession and thanksgiving for redemption in Christ, and for the means of grace, and the confession of the name of Jesus. This follows closely *The Forme of Prayers* of 1556, better known as Knox's Genevan Service Book and Calvinist in ethos. The first paragraph seems to have been the source of 'A General Thanksgiving' by Edwin Reynolds, a former Puritan and by then the Bishop of Norwich, in the 1662 *Book of Common Prayer.* The third part is a petition for consecration or sanctification. Bryan Spinks questions the insistence of

W. D. Maxwell and Horton Davies, that this is an epiclesis, that is an invocation of the Holy Spirit to change the elements into the body and blood of Christ, which was missing from the *Forme of Prayers* and from the *Book of Common Prayer.* But the *Directory* prays that the Spirit may effectually work in us. The petition continues to ask God, 'and so to sanctifie these Elements both of Bread and Wine and he blesses his own Ordinance, that we may receive by faith the Body and Blood of Christ' (Maxwell, 1931, p. 135; Spinks, 1984, pp. 44f.).

The explicit petition for consecration does not presuppose Scottish influence as some have thought. It reflects the thought of English Puritans such as William Fulke, Dudley Fenner and William Perkins, as well as the Dutch liturgy of Dahleen, which would be known to some (Spinks, 1984, pp. 45f.).

Administration seems to have been in silence, contrary to Catholic tradition and deplored by Maxwell (1931, pp. 139f.). The reading of Scripture had been proposed but was resisted by Independents. There may have been the singing of a psalm after the administration. It was the scriptural authority of Matthew 26:30 and Mark 14:26 which led Nonconformists at the end of the seventeenth century to follow Cranmer's example in his transfer of the *Gloria in Excelsis* and compose hymns for the end of the Sacrament. Joseph Stennett, the Baptist's was the first collection in 1697. In the eighteenth century they were followed by Watts – 'When I survey the wondrous Cross' is a Communion hymn – and by Doddridge and the Wesleys, whose hymns were sung during the administration at their crowded Eucharists.

The service was to be without colour or adornments, with no participation of the people other than in the metrical psalms and 'amen', no provision for seasons or festivals and a dependence on the minister which could result in appalling dullness if he were not a person of charisma (Ratcliff, pp. 225–34). This tradition has persisted, though is rather against the modern demand for participation of the people which is more than listening, and singing and saying 'amen'. It underlies the writings on prayer and worship of the Congregationalist theologian, P. T. Forsyth (1848–1921). Ministers stand before God and the people as do none of their flock. He says that 'Public prayer should be in the main liturgical with room for free prayer.' As much as E. C. Ratcliff, Forsyth believes that prayer should end in heaven: 'The true amen is when prayer expires in its own liturgical fulness. It should yield up its spirit like Christ on the Cross, saying "It is finished"' (quoted by G. S. Wakefield in Hart ed., pp. 67 ff.).

Recent scholarship has maintained that the liturgies of Nonconformity play a much larger part in Bunyan's *Pilgrim's Progress* than is usually acknowledged. 'In his depiction of pastoral settings, church membership rites, communal meals and solemn entries into the Heavenly City, Bunyan freely varies details, metaphors and structures of worship in a variety of liturgical modes. In the process, writing is portrayed as a liturgical act, or it shares with the liturgy an identical purpose, "the improvement of time" through instruction and participation in Christ's redemptive sacrifice' (Ken Simpson in *The Recorder*, A Publication of the International John Bunyan Society, Winter 1996, pp. 9f.). Alexander M. Forbes argues that Christian's progress through the Interpreter's House follows the order of worship established in the *Directory*. 'A "Prayer of Approach" precedes readings from the Old and New Testaments and a sermon and blessing follow' (*The Recorder*, Winter 1996, p. 9). The liturgy which Richard Baxter drew up for the Savoy Conference of 1661 in the vain hope that it would replace the Prayer Book liturgy is in some ways less Protestant than Cranmer. Baxter regarded the Prayer Book as 'a true worship though imperfect'. He felt it insufficiently scriptural and he used far more texts from his prodigious knowledge of the Bible, although he retains the Prayer Book order of mattins, litany and ante-Communion, the canticles, the creeds and the psalms, though in a metrical version. He assumes extempore options for the prescribed prayers.

With regard to the Eucharist, there may be an Offertory or presentation of the elements before the Eucharistic Prayer, or they may be laid on the table beforehand. There is a fraction as there was not in the then Prayer Book, and a libation, the 'shewing forth of Christ's death' with the words 'Behold the Lamb of God which taketh away the sins of the world' which could seem very daring indeed. Baxter's Presbyterian colleagues 'removed a few lines, where the word Offering was used', implying that they feared possible suggestions of the sacrifice of the Mass. Baxter insists that the action is appropriately called a sacrifice. It is as much a sacrifice as that of our bodies, our alms and our prayers. 'Certainly', wrote E. C. Ratcliff, 'Baxter's eucharistic and liturgical ideas approach more closely to the historic western tradition than the ideas expressed in the Communion service of the contemporary Prayer Book' (Ratcliff, p. 237).

Baxter's liturgy was in effect stillborn. He himself did not use it. The *Directory* continued to have influence throughout the eighteenth century, though Independents did not go in for printed orders and we rely on worshippers' accounts for knowledge of their procedures (Spinks, 1984, pp. 72ff.). Isaac Watts' *A Guide to Prayer* in its examples may give some idea of what he would pray at the worship which preceded the Eucharist and sufficed on most Sundays, such as a lengthy thanksgiving for God's choice of 'a certain number of the race of Adam' to be given into the hands of Christ before all worlds and to be his covenant people. This is a mercy not shown to suffering, fallen angels who perish. There is praise for God's justice and grace, his work of terror and compassion, reconciling sinners to himself by the punishment of his Son, for the triumphs of the gospel of grace in our lives and in the nation, for our being rational human beings born of religious parents, for our preservation through unforeseen dangers and that we were not cut off in a state of nature but should have the blessings of this life and the means of grace brought to us before we began to know God (Watts *Works*, iv, p. 125; see Spinks, 1984, pp. 74f.). Doddridge, like Watts, believed in comprehensive petition:

> Forget not the public – but pray for them with seriousness – Plead for Heathens, Jews, Mahometans, Papists, and Persecuted Protestants – Pray for your own country with cordial love and esteem – Remember that praying for the King is part of the condition on which our toleration is granted. Forget not magistrates and ministers. (Doddridge *Works* v, p. 469; Spinks, 1984, p. 74)

Communion was restricted to once a month at most – Doddridge observed that it had been more frequent in the early Church. It was administered after the morning worship, thus sundering Word and Sacrament, a separation which persisted until our own time. For Anglican Evangelicals, the Eucharist usually followed Morning Prayer, often no more than once a month, a custom which Bishop E. A. Knox of Manchester applauded in the twentieth century since it divided the nominal from the really intense Christians and illustrated the poignancy of Doddridge's hymn, printed in the Prayer Book:

> Why are its dainties all in vain
> Before unwilling hearts displayed?
> Was not for them the Victim slain?
> Are they forbid the children's bread?
> (Nuttall, 1967, p. 154)

Philip Doddridge (1702–51) was one of the most attractive of all divines, moderate, magnanimous, ecumenical, with joy in the Lord, which could be conveyed at its most rapturous in the Sacrament, 'joy unspeakable and full of glory'. Yet he regarded it as but one means of grace, as is revealed in an anecdote he tells in a letter to Isaac Watts: 'When one of the company said, "What if Dr. Watts should come down to Northampton!" another replied, with remarkable warmth, "the very sight of him would be as good as an ordinance to me"' (Nuttall, 1967, p. 166 n. 3). Is this the beginning of what has been pejoratively called 'the cult of personality' instanced in the next century by the numinous silences which attended Spurgeon's appearances at the beginning of his services? It cannot be dismissed in a cliché. Doddridge refers to the 'real absence' of Christ in the Eucharist, a view which tallies with Zwingli's and others' beliefs, which so alarmed Bucer, that Christ is in heaven and were he to descend in the Sacrament on earth, it would be the *parousia*. But Doddridge also spoke of Christ 'crucified and set forth before me' in the ordinance, though this refers to the Sacrament as a showing forth of his once-for-all and perpetually effective death, not to the descent of his heavenly body upon the consecrated elements, even though he wrote a hymn of the saints on earth and those above joined in the common accord of the body of Christ.

Watts and Doddridge adhered to a double consecration of bread and wine as well as both a fraction and libation. Watts's Second Catechism followed the tradition which interprets the broken bread as signifying the body of Christ wounded or broken on the cross, ignoring the Johannine quotation about the unblemished lamb, 'not a bone of him shall be broken'; the wine poured out into the cup signifies the blood of Christ poured out in his death to take away our sins.

Doddridge would engage in brief devotional meditations at the fraction and libation, reminding the congregation of the love of Christ and the need publicly to declare by receiving the cup that one is Christ's for ever; or that the breaking of the bread is an act of the remembrance of Christ. It is strange that we should need a memorial, yet we may forget him even at his table, who remembers us in heaven itself. The cup is the cup of blessing, indeed of a variety of blessings, pardon and strength and grace and the foretaste of heaven.

The nineteenth century saw an abundance of liturgical texts in Congregationalism, but since the Churches were independent, there was no authorised liturgy. *A New Directory* was produced by a group of ministers in 1812. It was solely a service of the Word, based on the 1645 service, but with the long prayer divided into two and more singing. Dr Spinks has described five other rites, which sought to enrich worship, latterly with some provision for children. What is remarkable is the increasing influence of the *Book of Common Prayer,* which could not but represent the antithesis of Independent worship. We have noted Puritan criticisms and it could hardly be beloved as the imposition of the State and an instrument of persecution. Yet English life could not escape the power of the Prayer Book, its phrases ploughed even into common speech – witness Hardy's rustics – and quoted even more than the Authorised Version of the Bible. In the eighteenth century, the Countess of Huntingdon's Connexion used it and exercised some influence on the Independent Churches. The Countess had to secede from the Church of England in 1781, when her appointment of a chaplain to Spa Fields Chapel, Clerkenwell, was challenged by the incumbent, whose sole authority in the parish was upheld. The Connexion which consisted, Wesley said rather dismissively, of 'genteel Methodists'' separated from Wesleyanism on grounds of Calvinist theology. It became in effect Congregationalist. The Prayer Book was retained in but four Churches by the twentieth century.

When revisions of worship were needed in Independent Churches, the Prayer Book could not be ignored. The Prayer of Humble Access often makes its appearance, sometimes with emendation of its close, to avoid what some, forgetting John 6, have regarded as 'Christian cannibalism'. Dr Spinks lists nine service books between 1847 and 1897, which are Free Church adaptations of Morning and Evening Prayer, with some borrowings also from the Prayer Book Communion Service. But there was little interest in the Eucharist, which it was thereby implied was a quiet devotional service for those whose spirituality required it. Memorialism and Zwinglianism prevailed. Any hint of Roman beliefs was repudiated, with opposition growing through the rise of Anglo-Catholicism. R. W. Dale attacked what he thought was the prevailing attitude to the Sacrament in many churches, a service for edification and self-improvement, with a memory of historical events and an expression of faith and fellowship. Almost seventy years later, the Cambridge historian and layman Bernard Lord Manning, could describe churches in which the bread and wine were treated as tiresome adjuncts to a 'spiritual' service. There was no fraction, no libation, no thanksgiving, or invocation of the Holy Spirit preceding the distribution (Manning, 1939 pp. 66ff.). At the very end of the nineteenth century, under the influence of the temperance movement, unfermented wine began to be used in some churches and, in consequence, individual cups or glasses as a hygienic precaution in the absence of alcohol. This seriously damaged the corporate nature of the act. It made it less 'communion'.

A very Independent production which had wide influence was the *Devotional Services for Public Worship* (1886–1901) of Dr John Hunter. Much of this was due to his undoubted gift for composing prayers. He did not introduce a eucharistic order until the third edition in 1886; the Eucharist was essentially a 'poetic symbol'. In its origins it was a social meal and Hunter was sympathetic to non-sacramental

Christians. He wrote powerfully of the commemoration of Christ and the thanksgiving for all the blessings which have come to us through him, and thanksgiving too for the Holy Communion, 'the sign of our communion with God our Father and Jesus Christ his Son and a help of its realisation – the sign of our communion with all disciples of Christ, with the Church of all ages and lands, and with the Church triumphant, especially with our dear and holy dead, in a Love from which neither life nor death, things present nor things to come can separate us' (Hunter, p. 59; Spinks, 1984, p. 112).

Hunter's theology was more of immanence than incarnation. There is indebtedness to James Martineau, the Unitarian's *Common Prayers for Christian Worship* (1861), and Hunter is rather shy of the doctrine of the Trinity. Only the Collect for Purity is taken from the Anglican service, in his 1886 Order, but the Prayer Book has greater prominence as revisions proceed. In 1892, the Prayer of Humble Access is an option with the words about eating the flesh and drinking the blood replaced by 'that in hunger and thirst after righteousness we may be filled with Jesus Christ'. The relation of the bread and wine to Christ's body and blood is avoided throughout Hunter's services.

Hunter had one single Eucharistic Prayer of Consecration. The prayer is memorialist and exemplarist:

> Help us to yield ourselves to the influence of this hour of holy memories and immortal hopes . . . We would remember Christ – the gracious beauty of his life, his obedience unto death, the charity of his Cross, and his victory over the world's sin and sorrow. We would remember all that we owe to him . . . impress and quicken our hearts with the memory of our Master and Saviour.

There is prayer for forgiveness of our forgetfulness of Christ in our fear and anxiety, in our weariness and indolence in God's service. 'Help us to enter into the spirit of this service that we may go out into the world the better to remember Christ amid the care and strife and sorrow of our common days.'

In 1892 there was added among other things the invitation 'Come to this sacred table not because you must but because you may', which is later used in official services of Congregationalism. In 1895, a second liturgy based on that of the Scottish Episcopal Church was included. This, with its relation to 1637 and Cranmer's first liturgy of 1549, conveyed a much higher doctrine than that of the other order.

Until 1892 the words of delivery had been Martineau's:

> Take eat this in remembrance of Christ.
> Drink this in remembrance of Christ.

After this they became:

> Let us eat of this bread in remembrance of Christ:
> and may the life which was in him be in us also.
> Let us drink of this cup in remembrance of Christ:
> and may the spirit in which he died be our spirit.

Dr W. E. Orchard could not bring himself to use these words, or indeed Hunter's rite, which he inherited at King's Weigh House, London in 1914, though he used his other services. Orchard is an extreme example, perhaps an aberration, of where Independency could lead. He had a deep and intense devotion to Christ, he was, above all, a man of prayer and in the 1930s he had some influence in spirituality on Leslie Weatherhead. But his inclinations, though he travelled by way of Presbyterianism, Liberalism and R. J. Campbell's 'new theology', were towards Rome, where he arrived in 1933.

He fairly soon adopted eucharistic vestments, lights and incense at King's Weigh House, and later Benediction or Exposition of the Blessed Sacrament. He devised two eucharistic orders. A 'simple' service was a concession to those who wanted to remain in the Free Church tradition, with individual cups and no consecration, the elements regarded as symbols. But there was plenty for meditation for those so inclined, with the scriptural warrant and rubrics – for there were no set prayers – suggesting self-examination, confession, silent invocation of the Holy Spirit, the fraction, adoration and thanksgiving. After communion, the prayers could plead the sacrifice of Christ and offer the oblation of oneself, followed by the collection for the poor in its traditional Congregationalist place. There was then a reading of texts from the 'high priestly' prayer of John 17 which could lead to remembrance of the saints and the departed, the living and the unity of the Church. A hymn was introduced by Matthew 26:30 and the benediction was John 14:27: 'Peace I leave with you; my peace I give unto you. Not as the world gives give I unto you. Let not your hearts be troubled neither let them be afraid.'

The service near to Orchard's heart could be used for a low celebration without music, a festal occasion, fully choral with the *Kyries* omitted and the *Gloria in Excelsis* included, or as a penitential rite or requiem, with *Kyries* and no *Gloria*. It was mostly taken from the *Book of Common Prayer* and the Roman Mass. There was some skilful blending. Dr Spinks says, 'Orchard here presented a rite in which the Liturgy of the Word and Sacrament was restored in unity in which the Eucharist was linked to a liturgical calendar, and in which a rich variety of Western classical forms with some Eastern elements, were reintroduced into the Congregational liturgical tradition' (1984, p. 130).

The Eucharistic Prayer was very scriptural, with use of St John's Gospel to underline the unity of the Word of God in the Old Testament with the Word made flesh. It has the classic shape and elements of the anaphora.

Orchard was governed by the doctrinal allure of the sacrificial aspect of the Eucharist and belief in the real presence. He included, for instance, the Roman Offertory prayers, versicles and responses, which emphasised sacrifice and altar, and the prayer in which 'the Bread of everlasting life and the cup of salvation' were offered to God. There was an epiclesis and the institution narrative had the words 'This is my body which is broken for you' and 'This is my blood of the New Covenant which is shed for you and for many unto remission of sins' in heavy Gothic script. This was accentuated by the revision of 1926. Orchard's romanising tendencies and ceremonial meant that a fine liturgy would be ignored by Congregationalism as a whole. It was not until 1920 that a Service Book was published for the whole Congregational Union. For decades there was a feeling among some Congregationalists that the advantages of liturgy outweighed its defects. The *Book of Congregational*

Worship is slender. The production of a uniform order was difficult because of the variety of incompatible sacramental views which Congregationalists held. P. T. Forsyth, for instance, believed that memorialism was a worse heresy than transubstantiation. The Sacrament is an *opus operatum*, something done, an act of the Church created by the eternal act of Christ. On the other hand, A. E. Garvie was not sure that Christ ever meant the ordinance to be a sacred mystery, simply that he should be remembered at every common meal. Some even thought that the symbols should every now and then be changed, so that sometimes the congregation might sit and look at a picture. Liberalism gained hold, encouraged by the 1907 'new theology' of R. J. Campbell and others. Immanence replaced incarnation and the resurrection was a subjective experience. Sacramentalism was due to an alliance between Christianity and the mystery cults, while higher criticism of the institution narratives cast doubts on the intention of Jesus as interpreted by Catholicism. Was the command for repetition authentic? (Spinks, 1984, pp. 137ff.).

The *Book of Congregational Worship* is unadventurous apart from its use of the prayer from the *Didache* about the bread scattered over the mountains, by then very much in vogue, and the Gelasian collect, 'O God of unchangeable power and eternal might'; it does not go beyond the *Book of Common Prayer*, though the service concludes with the reading from John 13 of the washing of the disciples' feet a happy conjunction.

A Manual for Ministers had two services of Holy Communion. The first was a liberal revision of 1920 with no *Sursum Corda*, Preface or *Sanctus*, and the Prayer Book 'Ye that do truly . . .' was replaced by the longer and more 'memorialist' invitation of Hunter. The Prayer of Commemoration and Thanksgiving was not prescribed but left entirely to the discretion of the minister with no guidance as to content. The Prayer of Humble Access has its conclusion about eating Christ's flesh and drinking his blood replaced by the petition from Ephesians 3:17–19. There was no connection of the Lord's presence with the elements and no breaking of the bread.

The second order was the work of the liberal modernist Harry Bulcock, representing even more radical views. 'The

Supper is a fellowship meal, at which God is present as at any gathering of Christians; the bread and wine are incidental to the rite' (Spinks, 1984, p. 150).

Unitarians

Unitarianism has been an increasingly eclectic and varying form of Independence. There has been a strong 'Free Christian' emphasis, but also one that is more theistic and rationalist. It has been a minority allegiance, though not solely of an intellectual elite, and it has had working-class congregations and adherents. It has stood for intellectual and ethical integrity and liberty of conscience, although it has not been free of internal controversies, or of those whom one of its women adherents, Lucy Atkins, described in the mid-nineteenth century as 'good haters'.

It began with the theology and influence of Faustus Socinus, an Italian, who worked largely in late sixteenth-century Poland and whose teachings reached England via Holland. He was a biblicist and questioned the doctrine of the Trinity because it was not found in Scripture. Thus he could not accept Christ's pre-existence or divinity. Those who, in William Chillingworth's famous phrase, declared that 'the Bible only is the religion of Protestants' could, like Chillingworth, be on the verge of Socinianism. Socinus also denied the atoning sacrifice of Christ. His sacramental teaching was near to that of Zwingli. Sacraments were not a *sine qua non* of salvation.

The fiercest foe of Socinianism was Calvinism. It found more hospitality among the Arminians of the English Church such as the Great Tew circle around Lord Falkland in the 1630s. Embarrassing as it is to Catholic Anglicans, there has always been a 'liberal' tendency in the English Church, a desire for comprehensiveness. Archbishop Laud was accused of Socinian sympathies and, provided one accepted episcopal order and dignified and chastely ceremonious worship, for which he relished the imposition of cruel penalties on his opponents, he supported theological tolerance.

Many Socinians preferred to be called simply Christian, a desire which persisted in the nineteenth century, but the term 'Unitarian' was first used in 1687, under James II's Declaration of Indulgence, in an unlicensed book by Stephen Nye, *A Brief History of the Unitarians called also Socinians. In Four Letters written to a Friend.* Two years later, Papists and anti-Trinitarians were both excluded from the tolerance of 'the Glorious Revolution', but there remained sympathetic tendencies in the English Church. Archbishop Tillotson wished they were rid of the Athanasian Creed. There was considerable publication of Unitarian tracts in the 1690s and many attempts to refine the doctrine of the Trinity to make it acceptable to Unitarians, the most influential of whom denied any wish for separation from the Church and were willing to accept its forms of worship, because religion was not worshipping God by themselves. Presumably they would join in the authorised corporate orders and offices, with mental reservations at certain points. By the end of the century the Unitarians appear to have been absorbed into the English Church, seeking to reform it from within, though there were some who felt separation to be the honest course. (Trowell, pp. 77–101). The 'Age of Reason' and such works as that of Locke's disciple John Toland, *Christianity not Mysterious,* were conducive to Unitarianism.

The Lord's Supper was probably too Christo-centric to be regarded as binding upon worshippers, though for those who were in the Church of England, the Prayer Book, used by Unitarian clergymen, 'familiarized the minds of worshippers with addresses and petitions to the three persons of the Trinity. Whatever the parson said or left unsaid from the pulpit could not sink into the mind as did the prayers from the reading desk and the responses from the pews repeated Sunday by Sunday.' (McLachlan, p. 334).

It was different in Presbyterian meeting-houses, where there was no Prayer Book and the metrical psalms dominated worship; praise, prayer and petition were thus addressed to the one Almighty God. This may account for the replacement of Presbyterianism in England by Unitarianism, (McLachlan, p. 334). In 1773, Theophilus Lindsey left the Church of England and founded the first Unitarian Church. The worship of Christ was unthinkable to him, as it was to Joseph Priestley, the versatile and creative thinker, and father of the modern science of chemistry and of psychosomatic humanism, which denied the existence of the soul apart from the body; Priestley was also a determinist, believing that every action was governed by previous experience and the motives that arose from it. Lindsey in 1774 prepared a *Revision of the Liturgy* deriving from Samuel Clarke's private revision of the Prayer Book. There were always Unitarians who favoured ordered and formal worship, non-Trinitarian versions of the Prayer Book, and in the mid and late nineteenth century they built imposing Victorian Gothic churches which, in some of the districts of Greater Manchester, for instance, are the most imposing in the communities, easily mistaken for the parish churches. James Martineau had his Liverpool church rebuilt while he was on a lengthy sabbatical in Germany in 1847–8. It was Gothic not octagonal, with carvings, stained glass, choir stalls and a high altar. The last two were never used, but were there for 'atmosphere'.

Martineau was a Unitarian who became opposed to Priestley's theology. He was influenced by the Romantic movement and Samuel Taylor Coleridge, and gave more place to feeling, being regarded as an English Schleiermacher. He criticised those who thought of prayer 'as an act of disciplinary prudence not of Christian piety' and took 'the air of heaven for the sake of exercise rather than in love of the light and quest of the immensity of God'. Martineau denied Priestley's determinism and opposed those who would loosen their hold on Christ in their desire for immediate communion with the Supreme Being. Like Ruskin he taught a meditation which by use of the imagination would be present as in the body at every event in the life of Christ. He came increasingly to distrust sectarianism and believed that Unitarianism was 'not a Church but a theology held by people of various ecclesiastical affiliations'. He compiled two hymnbooks, the first in 1831 while he was a young minister still in Dublin, entitled *A Collection of Hymns for Christian Worship*. In the early 1840s, he produced *Hymns for the Christian Church and Home*. He cast his net wider than previous Unitarian hymnbooks, including, for instance, Isaac Watts and Reginald Heber.

His chief contribution to Christian worship was his *Common Prayers for Christian Worship*. Like John Hunter who, as we have seen, borrowed from him, Martineau had an outstanding gift for the composition of prayers. As Horton Davies has written, 'In unforgettable cadences he expressed a blend of Biblical faith, the insights of the day derived from the comparative study of religions, and from the love of nature and a conviction of the basic unity of mankind emanating from German and American versions of Transcendentalism' (Davies, 1965, p. 414). The book was widely used in the Free Churches and its prayers included in the services of John Hunter and W. E. Orchard, as well as in the Methodist book *Divine Worship* (1935).

The Sacrament of the Lord's Supper was not central to Unitarian worship. In some churches it was hardly administered at all, as being incompatible with a denial of Christ's divinity, as we have already mentioned. Ralph Waldo Emerson in the United States resigned as a minister because he believed administration of the Sacrament to be inappropriate. Provision was made for it in the *Orders of Worship for Use in Unitarian and Free Christian Congregations* of 1932. The outline is as follows:

Sentences of invitation
The Lord's Prayer
Collect for Purity
Summary of Commandments
Prayer of approach
Scripture lesson
Address or homily
Words of institution
Delivery of bread
Delivery of wine
Silent thanksgiving concluding with the *Gloria*
Post-communion prayer
Hymn (optional)
Blessing

Horton Davies, while admitting that the service must be judged on Unitarian principles and is 'a moving tribute to Christ and a solemn pledge to follow his leadership', criticises it as excessively subjective, more concerned with the participants than with God. He cites the words of the homily:

'Today whatever our perplexities or difficulties, we still acknowledge the truth and beauty of the Christian principle.'

Unitarianism had its Orchard in the Revd J. M. Lloyd Thomas, Minister of the Old Meeting Unitarian Church in Birmingham. He was devoted to Richard Baxter and edited his autobiography. He founded the Society of Free Catholics in which he was associated with Orchard. He wished to combine the ecumenical Puritanism of Baxter with the modernism of Loisy and Sabatier and Catholic worship. He was a Trinitarian who exercised the freedom which he believed Unitarianism made possible. In some ways he was in the succession of Martineau. Orchard's *Divine Service* was a product of the movement, but Lloyd Thomas's contribution – and he never changed his allegiance as minister of Old Meeting – was the *Free Church Book of Common Prayer* (1929), an amazingly comprehensive compendium, which included prayers ancient and modern, pre-and post-Reformation, and, although used as a liturgy only in Old Meeting, it was a source book for many ministers. It even included a service in which Christian theists could join, for unity was its object. It was fifty years before its time, while the Society itself, as Horton Davies said, 'contained too heterogeneous a collection of individuals', mostly suspected by their denominations, not least by those worshippers fearful of the Jesuitical infiltrations of Rome and desirous of simple services with a minimum of ceremonial. It did, however, add to the resources of Free Church worship, make responsive prayers gradually acceptable, encourage reverence, and help to regain a sacramental consciousness (Davies, 1965, pp. 359–69; 416f.). The revival of the sacramental tradition in the Free Churches was, however, due more to their discovery of Reformed churchmanship. Geneva, not Rome, was its inspiration.

CHAPTER 7

PRESBYTERIANISM AND METHODISM

Presbyterianism

The Directory of 1644–5 had satisfied the Presbyterians. In England, they were destined to decline in spite of the fact that they were the largest of the Nonconformist bodies at the end of the century, and the bitterest opponents of Socinianism and supporters of the Westminster Directory in the middle years. Their commitment to the ideal of a national Church and their hierarchical structure as well as their opposition to the Independent and Baptist insistence on religious experience as the criterion of church membership, meant that the 'Happy Union' of 'United Brethren' in 1691, marked by the administration of a common fund, could not survive. Since the Presbyterian desire for a national Church on their principles could not be realised because of the establishment of the Church of England, they became virtually Independent congregations in some places, and as their Calvinism was moderated they became susceptible to Unitarian ideas, so that by the nineteenth century English Presbyterianism was extinct, to be reborn through Scottish immigrants.

The first Scottish Reformers commended the 1552 *Book of Common Prayer* and it was used in many Scottish parishes. But John Knox's enthusiasm for the Genevan service against the Anglican carried the day from 1560. What became known as the *Book of Common Order* or, more popularly, 'John Knox's Genevan Service Book', had as its original title *The Forme of Prayers and Ministration of the Sacraments &c used in the English Congregation at Geneva and approved by the famous and godly learned man John Calvin*. A Latin version for the study of those unable to read English was called *Ratio et forma publice orandi Deum &c.*

It was not a slavish version of Calvin's rite. There are new intercessions, both in the Order for Sunday Morning Worship and the Lord's Supper, while the Consecration Prayer of the latter is original. The influence of the *Book of Common Prayer* may be detected in the pre-communion exhortation. The Order of the Lord's Supper is as follows:

Confession of Sins
(A lengthy prayer based on Daniel 9 was omitted in favour of a shorter alternative in 1562)
Prayer for Pardon
Metrical psalm in unison
Prayer for Illumination (extempore)
Scripture reading
(A chapter from a Gospel being read consecutively)
Sermon
Possible collection of alms
Prayer for the whole estate of Christ's Church
(This included a prayer for the city of Geneva, 'our miserable countrie of England', then under Marian persecution)
The Lord's Prayer
The Apostles' Creed in the prose version
Offertory: preparation or presentation of elements while a metrical psalm is sung
The Manner of the Lord's Supper
(Words of institution, 1 Corinthians 11:17–27, possibly in a translation from Calvin)
Exhortation, much from the *Book of Common Prayer* and Calvin.
Thanksgiving, including adoration prompted by our creation and redemption; anamnesis and doxology
Fraction and delivery to the people, seated at the table, 'who distribute and divide the same among themselves'; likewise the Cup During communion the Passion story is read
Thanksgiving for communion and prayer that its memory may remain with us to assist our growth in grace and good works

Metrical Psalm 103
Aaronic or Apostolic Blessing.

As W. D. Maxwell points out, this rite, truly Catholic in most respects, lacks an epiclesis (Maxwell, 1965, p. 124). The *Forme of Prayers* was the standard for eighty years until the *Westminster Directory*. Over the next century, the liturgy fell out of use. The original text envisages monthly Communion, but the custom in Scotland became less frequent due at first to shortage of ministers. The reading of Scripture from the Cromwellian period until the mid-nineteenth century was neglected in spite of directives. It has been said that 'towards the close of the eighteenth century, the public services of the Church of Scotland had become probably the baldest and rudest in Christendom' (Maxwell, 1965, p. 134). The sermon dominated. This could be very powerful and deeply emotional, the preacher himself not infrequently in tears. The period from 1850 to 1950 was a great age of Scottish preaching, as it was in England. Communion seasons might be but once or twice a year at this time, but they lasted possibly for a whole week. The Sacrament was preceded by the most intense preparation which Michael Ramsey thought shamed the Parish Communion of our own time. The seasons concluded with devotional meditations. At Highland Communions, there was a 'question day'. 'The day was so called because questions that have arisen in the minds of "the men" in connection with doctrine and with experience are on that day set forth, debated out, and solved by much meditation and prayer; age, saintliness, doctrinal and experimental reading, and personal experience all making their contribution to the solution of the question in mind' (Whyte, p. 179).

It would now be objected that here, although the exercise fulfilled the need for the participation of those who attended, the emphasis was chiefly didactic. We must, however, beware of sweeping generalisations. A sermon, like some passages of St Paul, may lead its hearers far beyond convincing rational argument to the worship of heaven and there may be moments in corporate discussion when the company is 'lost in wonder, love and praise'. These are rare though, and discussion is sometimes reductionist and often inconclusive. A preceding Quaker silence does not always lead to the numinous.

The Church Service Society was founded in the Church of Scotland in 1864, as was a similar church worship association by ministers of the United Presbyterian Church in 1862. The former published *Euchologian* in 1867, followed by *Prayers for Divine Service.* These enriched worship by adding to its resources, though they assimilated Scottish worship to the Anglican Order of Morning Prayer rather than to 'the ancient Reformed Church norm of ante-communion' (Maxwell, 1965, p. 134). *The Book of Common Order* of the Church of Scotland in 1905 enjoined that the Lord's Prayer be said by minister and congregation at the close of the first prayer and the intercessions and thanksgiving were to precede the sermon. This had its dissentients as being a departure from primitive and Reformed usage and because it did not follow the Order of Holy Communion, 'which is the normal service of the Church'.

The ground was being prepared for the greatest achievement of Scottish liturgy, the product of the union in 1929 of the Church of Scotland and the United Free Church of Scotland which healed the disruption of 1843. This was *The Book of Common Order* (1940).

This is a most comprehensive book of services for all occasions which Anglicans found themselves using to supplement the Prayer Book where additional material was allowed or no provision was made. There is, for instance, an Order for the Burial of the Dead 'to be used in circumstances of deep distress'. It is the book of a national Church with a service for Remembrance Day and many additional prayers for the Christian Year, 'for occasional and special use', such as Church Anniversary or Harvest, and for special graces. There are services of Preparation of Holy Communion and Thanksgiving afterwards. Its chief glory is its first of four orders for the celebration of 'the Lord's Supper, or Holy Communion'.

To read the text is to engage in an act of great solemnity. It begins with a call to worship – no cheery 'good morning' or 'welcome' – and a psalm such as Psalm 43:3–5, or a hymn. Then there is a call to prayer in the words of Scripture which may be varied according to the Christian Year, the Collect for Purity and Confession of Sin and plea for forgiveness to 'newness of life' completed in the Collect for the Sixth Sunday after Trinity, 'O God who has prepared for them that love thee such good things as pass man's understanding'. After a canticle, psalm or hymn, there are three readings from Scripture, the Epistle and Gospel read consecutively after a psalm such as Psalm 116 in the prose version, or verses 13 to 19 of it in metre. They are introduced and concluded in the same way, 'Hear the word of God' and 'The Lord bless to us the reading of his holy word and to his name be glory and praise.' The Nicene Creed may follow, though it may be cast in the form of a prayer, or said after the bringing in of the elements. Intercessions come next, which are pastoral, inclusive and tender with an economy of words. There is a resplendent prayer for the communion of saints. A psalm or hymn, intimations, a prayer for illumination and the sermon follow. The last would have been better after the lections, but the service is faithfull to *The Book of Common Order* of 1905. The financial offerings are made during which the minister goes to the holy table. He gives an invitation in the words of Scripture – Matthew 11:28, 29; John 6:35, 37b; Matthew 5:6. The elements of bread and wine are brought into the church during the singing of a psalm, a paraphrase, or a hymn and laid on the holy table. The minister unveils the elements and says two offertory prayers.

The central act of the Eucharist begins with 'the Grace', the apostolic benediction, followed by the words of institution as in 1 Corinthians 11:23–26. The minister then follows the Lord's example in the name of the Trinity:

> As the Lord Jesus, the same night in which he was betrayed took bread, I take these elements of bread and wine, to be set apart from all common uses to this holy use and mystery; and as he gave thanks and blessed, let us draw near to God and present to him our praise and thanksgivings.

There is then the *Sursum Corda*, the Preface with thanksgiving for creation with seasonal propers, and the *Sanctus* with 'Blessed is he who cometh in the name of the Lord' and the Hosanna. There follows a thanksgiving for redemption with the quotation of John 3:16 and the moving words:

> Not as we ought but as we are able do we bless thee for his holy incarnation, for his perfect life on earth, for his precious sufferings and death upon the Cross, for his glorious resurrection and ascension, for his continual intercession and rule at thy right hand, for the promise of his coming again and for his gift of the Holy Spirit.

This leads to the anamnesis, oblation and epiclesis, the consecration and the offering of ourselves and brief intercessions as: 'in fellowship with all the faithful in heaven and on earth, we pray thee to fulfil in us and all men, the purpose of thy redeeming love'. There is a doxology and the Lord's Prayer. The words of institution are repeated with the manual acts. There is the *Agnus Dei* and the communion of the presiding minister. Communion of the people is given with the words 'Take ye, eat ye; this is the body of Christ which is broken for you: this do in remembrance of him'; and 'This cup is the new covenant in the blood of Christ, which is shed for many unto remission of sins; drink ye all of it'.

The Peace comes next, not as in Matthew 5:23 or the invitation of the Prayer Books as the condition of communion, but as a gift of the Lord in consequence of receiving him in the Sacrament. There are three possible thanksgivings, the first from the *Book of Common Prayer,* and a commemoration of the departed: 'bring us with them at the last to those things which eye hath not seen, nor ear heard, which thou hast prepared for them that love thee.' The service ends with a hymn or psalm and the benediction, 'The peace of God' as in the Anglican rite. 'As the elements are being removed from the Church, *Nunc Dimittis* or a paraphrase may be sung.'

In 1948, there appeared *Prayers for Parish Worship* by Colin F. Miller. This owed much to W. D. Maxwell and his thesis that Christian worship is a combination of the liturgy of the synagogue and the upper room. Later scholarship would revise what Miller says about the 'hours' and 'the offices' (see Chapter 11 below). He affirms the centrality of the Eucharist but interprets it in terms of the purgative, illuminative and unitive ways of mystical spirituality. The Christian way of worship is composed of 'ever widening concentric circles of devotion', so that the three stages may be represented in each part and in the course of the Christian Year for which Miller's orders are devised. There is a good deal of Roman and Eastern material, and Miller may well have been a latter-day Orchard or Lloyd Thomas in the Church of Scotland; certainly he was a man with a high church liturgical mission. Rich as it is, it is doubtful if the book had much influence. For one thing, it appeared on the eve of a much wider liturgical reform throughout the West.

The Book of Common Order and the writings of W. D. Maxwell had considerable influence on the neo-Genevans among English Congregationalists, although their movement was contemporary. They were identified with Mansfield College, Oxford, under the principalship of Nathaniel Micklem, who edited a fine symposium on *Christian Worship* with very distinguished scholars as contributors, including a Presbyterian and a Baptist, to commemorate the golden jubilee of the college in 1936. *A Book of Public Worship* was compiled for the use of English Congregationalists in 1948 by John Huxtable, John Marsh, Romilly Micklem and James Todd. It follows Maxwell closely and regards the central service of Christian worship as a union of Word and Sacrament, not Morning or Evening Prayer with sermon as much Anglican worship at that time implied. The first Order of Holy Communion is very similar to what we have summarised for the 1940 *Book of Common Order.* All the thanksgivings follows the *Sanctus* in a Prayer of Consecration, though the anamnesis is rather lacking. But there is epiclesis and oblation, though there is no intercession nor commemoration of the departed, these having been included in the preceding ministry of the Word.

The Methodists

Methodists are not historically dissenters nor Nonconformists, though they have been identified with the Free Churches in England since the end of the nineteenth century. They arose as a movement for holiness within the Church of England, inspired by two clergymen, the brothers John and Charles Wesley. At one time it almost seemed as though they could become a religious order with their discipline and rules. They became a Church because they had to separate from the established body for reasons in which sociology as well as ecclesiology played a part. They grew greatly in numbers, and divided with much acrimony in the nineteenth century into different branches and emphases. They were largely united in 1932.

Liturgy was not their prime concern though Wesley showed interest in ancient practices. He hoped that their worship would be sustained by the *Book of Common Prayer* either in the parish churches or their own meeting places. He wrote in September 1784:

> I believe that there is no liturgy in the world either in ancient or modern languages, which breathes more of a solid, scriptural rational Piety than the Common Prayer of the Church of England. And although the main of it was completed considerably more than two hundred years ago, yet is the language not only pure but strong and elegant in the highest degree.

He wrote that in a note appended to his revision of the Prayer Book, *The Sunday Service of the Methodists in North America*. He instances the following alterations:

> 1 Most of the holy-days so called are omitted as at present answering no valuable end.
> 2 The service of the Lord's Day, the length of which has often been complained of [it was then Mattins, Litany and Ante-Communion] considerably shortened.
> 3 Many Psalms are left out, and many parts of the others, as being highly improper for the mouths of a Christian congregation.

Some of Wesley's emendations are on the lines of the Puritan objections to the Prayer Book the previous century. He insisted, like the Puritans, that liturgical forms should be neither imposed nor mandated. He believed strongly in extempore prayer and would use it in the course of a service of set forms.

The Prayer Book for Wesley was not an ascetic regime, but an order of public worship which, for Methodists, was supplemented by preaching services at 5.00 am and 5.00 pm, which Wesley regarded as essential to Methodism's life. They were not liturgies, the emphasis being on the preaching, on the analogy which Wesley somewhat quaintly used of the University sermons, though the aim was to convert sinners and strengthen saints in the ways of perfect love. It was these services which at other times and mostly on Sundays became typical Methodist worship, characterised by hearty, sometimes harmonious, sometimes raucous singing. Methodists introduced the Covenant Service, taken from the Puritans, lovefeasts (*agapēs*) and watchnight services, which Wesley thought an equivalent of early Church vigils. Wesley believed in 'constant communion', even suggesting it should be daily and once indeed communicated himself on each of the twelve days of Christmas. The crowded Sacraments over which he presided – in some cases congregations numbered over a thousand – made Methodism at a time when Communion was often infrequent in the Church of England something of a sacramental revival. For these services the Wesleys published their best-selling 166 *Hymns on the Lord's Supper* in 1745. They are mostly paraphrases of the Caroline Anglican, Daniel Brevint's *The Christian Sacrament and Sacrifice,* with some echoes also of the fourth-century *Apostolic Constitutions* as we have noted. They have a high doctrine of eucharistic sacrifice and presence, which Anglo-Catholicism discovered in the 1860s and which has always been cherished by a few Methodists. But it is doubtful whether this intense sacramental devotion was reproduced in most early or later Methodists. For the former the crowded Eucharists were more like rallies of evangelical fellowship in which people were sometimes converted. The 1662 Communion Office was the Wesleyan and, from 1932, the Methodist norm until 1975. 'Our venerable Father's abridgment' had but little vogue anywhere, but in the 1936 *Book of Offices* 'the burden of them is intolerable' is removed from the confession of sin and 'you' is changed to 'us' in the absolution, and most unfortunately, in what 1662 calls the Prayer of Consecration, the Protestant affirmation in the chiasmus of 'a full, perfect and sufficient sacrifice, oblation and satisfaction' is reduced to 'a full perfect and sufficient sacrifice'. Hebrews 13:20, 21 is inserted before the final blessing. There is no provision for a sermon and the service was often an 'after-meeting' which succeeded the main preaching service.

That the sacramental life of Methodism declined after Wesley, was due to the exclusion of Methodists from the parish churches, the ambiguous status of Methodist preachers for some decades, and thereafter the shortage of the ordained compared with the number of chapels and revival of the Mass in Anglo-Catholicism which frightened evangelicals of all kinds. In the nineteenth-century galleried chapel in St Mawes, Cornwall, there is a large dominant rostrum for preaching and the table is hardly visible, somehow tucked beneath the rostrum as a part of it, so small and inconspicuous as to make one wonder whether there is room for the elements let alone their administration. Yet there may well have been more sacramental devotion than there appears. The 'after-meeting' was attended by the committed with great reverence.

In those Wesleyan Churches which retained it, Morning Prayer was often referred to as 'the liturgical service'. The breakaway bodies – Methodist New Connexion, Primitive Methodists, Bible Christians, United Methodist Free Churches – were, apart from the first, hostile to set forms. But this does not mean that they dishonoured the Sacraments, or did not observe them with devotion, though not more than monthly and never as the main Sunday service. The United Methodist Free Churches which broke away from Wesleyanism in 1850, believed in worship governed by the Holy Spirit but felt that 'there are certain special and solemn occasions in our Church life which ought not to be left entirely to the discretion of the ministers or other presiding brethren.' The Form for the Administration of the Lord's Supper has no responses, since they shared the Puritan objections to them. It does not show much dependence on other liturgies. It begins with a general thanksgiving for creation, redemption and especially the Sacrament, with a prayer for purity and the realisation of the presence of Christ and more faithful service in daily life. There is then the Lord's Prayer and the words of institution from Matthew, Luke and 1 Corinthians. This is followed by a long address which is a moving account of the meaning of the Sacrament, the one sacrifice, our glory in the cross, 'of which the broken bread and outpoured wine are chosen symbols' and of Christ's mysterious union with us by the power of his Spirit.

The Sacrament is the 'imperishable sign' of the communion of saints and the meal of 'brotherhood'. It ends with the consecration of our whole being and the promise of the Kingdom. There is much which is of the true content of a Eucharistic Prayer but it is exhortatory, addressed to the congregation not to God and with little emphasis on the elements. As we eat and drink we hear Christ's command to remembrance. After a hymn, the distribution follows, with the Prayer Book words over the bread and passages of Scripture concerning the atonement as it is being delivered. Similarly, the cup is taken round – the service book predates individual glasses – and after the Prayer Book words there are texts about the efficacy of Christ's blood. There is then the financial offering as sentences are read and a lengthy intercession concluding with Hebrews 13:20, 21 and the apostolic benediction.

The Primitive Methodist Order of the early 1900s is an abbreviation of 1662, beginning with the Prayer for the Church, going on to the exhortation and confession with the Comfortable Words as absolution. There is no *Sursum Corda*, nor *Sanctus* but immediately a prayer which is a conflation of the 1662 Consecration, the chiasmus included, but no words of institution, and a sentence from the Prayer of Humble Access and some phrases of the compilers. It is more a prayer for the right observance of 'the ordinance' than a consecration and one feels that behind it there lurks a fear of transubstantiation. These orders, like those contemporary in other non-episcopal Churches, are spoiled by the insistence on being not as the Romans, rather than a straightforward uninhibited desire to provide a eucharistic rite faithful to the New Testament and Christian tradition.

The New Connexion, the Bible Christians and the United Free Methodist Churches joined together to become the United Methodist Church in 1907 and merged with the Wesleyans and the Primitive Methodists in 1932. The 1936 *Book of Offices* recognised the need for a freer form of Communion than that of 1662 by providing an alternative order which, like the two rites just mentioned, did not necessarily mean that the Congregation would need service books, though it includes the *Sursum Corda*, to be followed by an extempore prayer, the post-communion Prayer of

Oblation from 1662, the commemoration of the departed from the end of the Prayer for the Church militant, a liberalised form of the Prayer of Humble Access, the words of institution and the distribution. Liturgically it is an unstructured muddle, again nervous of the bread and wine. It does, however, have two verses of Charles Wesley's Easter hymn after communion and before the *Gloria*, which means that the service is not totally concentrated on the Passion.

There were Methodists with the Catholic leanings of Orchard and Lloyd Thomas and who felt that the Wesleys' sacramental teaching was much neglected in their Church. They formed the Methodist Sacramental Fellowship in 1935. Its aims were to give Holy Communion a central place in Methodist worship and revive sacramental devotion, to reaffirm the historic creeds, to work and pray for Christian unity and to bind its members to a discipline of daily office, forms for which were provided. Its inspiration was a minister of some genius and remarkable influence, Theophilus S. Gregory, one of a long dynasty of preachers bearing his name. On the eve of the Fellowship's birth he became a Roman Catholic, which aroused grave suspicions. He retained his devotion and use of the Wesley hymns and served thereafter as editor of the *Dublin Review* and of the religious broadcasts on the BBC Third Programme. The fellowship needed to be rescued and this was done by strong representation of the laity and by the wisdom of its leaders, such as A. E. Whitham and J. Ernest Rattenbury. The latter's immensely able defence of the Fellowship at the 1938 Methodist Conference secured its existence within the Church. Rattenbury was a London Missioner whose style was that of a Methodist preacher and who, largely uncassocked, gave no impression of sacerdotalism. He wrote a renowned study of *The Eucharistic Hymns of John and Charles Wesley* in 1948. The Methodist connexional and itinerant system did not provide opportunity for the independence of an Orchard. Methodist services did not come to resemble the Mass though members of the Fellowship brought greater order and reverence into celebrations, performed the manual acts and occasional genuflections and gave such Catholic teaching as was compatible with the Methodist tradition. They were much assisted by the hymns.

Hymns

Methodism, it has been said, was 'born in song', but so was Christianity itself, as St Paul testifies and the Gospels and Epistles bear witness. Eusebius's fourth-century *History of the Church* speaks of 'all the psalms and hymns written from the beginning by faithful brethren which sing of Christ as the Word of God and address him as God' (Williamson, trs, p. 236). There may well have been hundreds of hymns in the first two centuries, free in structure, though modelled on the psalms, and some, perhaps, too free in doctrine. *Phos hilaron* ('joyous', 'gladdening', 'gladsome' light) was regarded as ancient in the fourth century. Ephraem Syrus (c. 306–73), 'that man of a broken heart' according to Wesley, who found him a kindred spirit, was 'the real father of Christian hymnography' (Martimort, p. 213). His metrical homilies 'with each verse having the same number of syllables and a set number of accents' became extremely popular, 'for when divided into stanzas, they allowed the congregation to participate by singing a refrain (*madrocho*) sometimes they took the form of acrostic poems (*sognite*).

Ephraem had his successors and the Eastern *kontakion* was a development of his hymnography, being composed of stanzas with the same number of syllables or the same rhythm. The congregation would sing a refrain. Later there was St John of Damascus, whose hymns are sung in English translations today. The various Eastern offices often gave a great space to hymns. There was a rapid growth in hymnody as the Church moved into large buildings with large congregations and increasing drama in worship, under the influence of the imperial court. They were connected with the new liturgical piety of the post-Constantinian era (Schmemann, 1975, pp. 127-32). In the West there was Hilary of Poitiers in the fourth century but Ambrose of Milan was the real founder of Latin hymnody. His hymns, intended subliminally to implant orthodoxy in the minds of Christian people, were adopted by Benedict and the Roman Church as a whole. Prudentius wrote hymns in the fifth century and they became an essential part of the office.

Congregational singing was one of the developments of the Reformation, witness the German chorales. It was also prominent among the sects such as the Amish Mennonites, who possessed a hymnbook, and it brought strength to the persecuted from Paul and Silas in prison to refugee groups and the ostracised whose hearts it uplifted and to whom it gave a sense of identity and divine support. Much of the hymnody of the persecuted was in the tradition of Bernard of Clairvaux and of an intense Jesus-piety. The German Pietists were no sect but a movement of mystical and evangelical religion in reaction to Lutheran Scholasticism. They owed something to the English Puritans. They were notable hymnodists, especially Paul Gerhardt (1617–76). John Wesley was much moved by the Moravian refugees singing during an Atlantic storm on the voyage to Georgia in 1735, while he cowered in fear. He translated many hymns of the German pietists and mystics. Some of the Puritans felt, with Augustine, that music might be a sensual distraction from worship, while others believed that hymn-singing should be totally spontaneous, of immediate inspiration and that a hymnbook was as improper for Christians as a prayer book. But, as we have seen, the singing of Jesus and his disciples at the end of the Last Supper gave scriptural precedent, and Communion hymns were being written by the end of the seventeenth century. At first confined to psalm paraphrases, hymns relieved Nonconformist verbosity from dullness; they also made it possible for people's response to be fuller and to show greater commitment than the unsung one-sentence replies to versicles. Isaac Watts was admired as a poet by Dr Johnson. He immolated his gifts for the sake of a plain style for ordinary worshippers, but wrote with power on the themes of creation, providence and redemption, and paraphrased the psalms with new metres. John Wesley regarded hymn-singing as a spiritual act and set down some directions in 1761, which it cannot be said have always been observed:

> That this Part of Divine Worship may be more acceptable to God, as well as the more profitable to yourself and others, be careful to observe the following Directions:
>
> 1 Learn *these tunes* before you learn any others; afterwards learn as many as you please.
> 2 Sing them *exactly* as they are printed here, without altering or

mending them at all; and if you have learned to sing them otherwise, unlearn it as soon as you can.

3 Sing *all*. See that you join with the congregation as frequently as you can. Let not a slight degree of weakness or weariness hinder you. If it is a cross to you, take it up and you will find a blessing.

4 Sing *lustily* and with good courage. Beware of singing as if you were half-dead, or half-asleep; but lift up your voice with strength. Be no more afraid of your voice now, nor more ashamed of its being heard, than when you sung the songs of Satan.

5 Sing *modestly*. Do not bawl so as to be heard above or distinct from the rest of the congregation, that you may not destroy the harmony; but strive to unite your voices together, so as to make one clear melodious sound.

6 Sing *in time*: whatever time is sung, be sure to keep with it. Do not run before nor stay behind it; but attend close to the leading voices, and move therewith as exactly as you can. And take care you sing not *too slow*. This drawling way naturally steals on all who are lazy; and it is high time to drive it out from among us, and sing all our tunes just as quick as we did at first.

7 Above all sing *spiritually*. Have an eye to God in every word you sing. Aim at pleasing *him* more than yourself, or any other creature. In order to do this attend strictly to the sense of what you sing and see that your *heart* is not carried away with the sound, but offered to God continually; so shall your singing be such as the Lord will approve of here, and reward when he cometh in the clouds of heaven.

The Wesleys published more than thirty hymnbooks in their lifetime. Most of the hymns were written by Charles Wesley. The definitive book was *A Collection of Hymns for the Use of the People Called Methodists* in 1780, which John Wesley termed 'A little body of experimental and practical divinity'. It is a conspectus of Methodist spirituality, consisting of 525 hymns. It begins with a section 'Exhorting and beseeching to return to God'. The pleasantness of religion and the attractiveness of God are described and also the warnings of reprobation. There is a section on formal and inward religion, followed by prayers for repentance, 'For mourners convinced of sin and brought to the birth' and convinced of and recovered from backsliding. The majority of hymns are for believers, rejoicing, fighting, praying, watching, working, suffering, groaning for full redemption, brought to birth, saved, interceding for the world. The collection concludes with hymns for the Society, which became the local Methodist Church.

Some of the hymns may be too subjective and personal for liturgy. Charles Wesley also wrote doctrinal hymns for the great festivals. He is daring on the incarnation:

> Beings source *begins to be*,
> And GOD himself is BORN.
>
> JESUS is our brother now
> And GOD is all our own.

The hymns are heavily scriptural. Sometimes every line has biblical reference and, occasionally, Wesley offers a better translation than the Authorised Version. When they are well chosen, the hymns assist the movement of liturgy. There are those suitable to each element of worship and excellent as graduals or to clinch the points of the sermon. They turned the teachings of Christianity and Methodism into song. And even the most personal ones are valuable in private devotion and it has been a time-honoured Methodist custom to use the hymnbook as a private prayer book.

The Olney hymns of John Newton and William Cowper (1779) seem to have been used in informal services and prayer meetings, where they would be expounded, rather than in the Prayer Book liturgy, although there was a late addition of short hymns for use after the sermon and the *Gloria Patri*. The contents are different from Wesley's collection. There are eight, less elaborate, sections:

1 Solemn Addresses to Sinners
2 Seeking, Pleading, Hoping
3 Conflict
4 Comfort
5 Dedication and Surrender
6 Cautions
7 Praise (focused upon Christ)
8 Short liturgical hymns

There is nothing like Wesley's forty-nine hymns on 'Groaning for Full Redemption' with their perfectionism which Newton found dangerous (Hindmarsh, pp. 257–88).

It must be recognised that not all Methodists have worshipped with hymns as Wesley desired. For some they have simply been an opportunity for a good sing and the tunes have meant more than the words. But it has been said of Caribbean Methodism that 'It was the hymns that were the wheels with which the Church moved through the liturgical year and it was the hymns, chiefly, which carried the chapel over into daily life' (Watty in Westerfield Tucker, ed., p. 257).

Throughout the world Methodists have been a singing people, but to some of them Charles Wesley has been a comparative stranger, too English, perhaps and not easily transported into indigenous culture. And he no longer has his traditional prominence in English Methodism today.

The Church of England did not judicially sanction hymns in the liturgy until 1792, but in the nineteenth century hymns became part of the life of all mainstream Churches. The Oxford Movement led to translations of ancient hymns, through the works of Isaac Williams, John Mason Neale and others. Many hymns were composed, not least by evangelicals, culminating in Moody and Sankey, while there were many women hymnwriters – Cecil Frances Alexander, Frances Havergal, Charlotte Elliott, Dora Greenwell among others – and in the great age of the expansion of Christianity there were many missionary hymns. The first of many Anglican collections was *Hymns Ancient and Modern* in 1860, of high church provenance, edited by the Revd Sir Henry Williams Baker, a Herefordshire incumbent, hymnwriter and composer of tunes himself. Some poems, not written as hymns, became favourites such as Newman's 'Lead kindly light'. A poet such as Robert Bridges wrote to improve the quality of hymns at the end of the century, basing many of his hymns on German Protestant and Pietistic sources. Eminent musicians like Ralph Vaughan Williams wrote tunes.

Initiation

The Puritans adhered to baptism as one of the only two

gospel sacraments. John Bunyan regarded it as a minor sacrament compared with the Lord's Supper. But he was disheartened by the controversies it provoked between Paedo-Baptists and Believers Baptists, of which he would be aware at Bedford Meeting where Christians were sundered by the controversy. He was fearful of 'a new law of commandments contained in ordinances'. The sacraments were made for us not we for them. The Supper only was a church ordinance, 'for the Church as a Church'. Baptism, he claimed, was 'not commended as a rule of strict obedience' and we have no clear, scriptural guidance as to the receiving or rejecting of believers unbaptised. This was not the general Puritan position. Baptism was instituted by Christ and of perpetual obligation, but they refused to consign the unbaptised to hell or limbo. William Gouge castigated the Roman attitude as 'a mercilesse sentence without any warrant of God's word'.

The majority contended for infant baptism in terms of the new covenant which would be narrower than the old if children were excluded, for children were circumcised. Baptism is the counterpart and fulfilment of circumcision. It is to be administered but once and is for all to whom the covenant belongs. All are as passive infants in the beginning of regeneration. Faith and repentance do not make the covenant of God. It does not depend on our understanding or ability to receive it, as Bernard Lord Manning was to say in the twentieth century. Baptism was the essential preliminary to partaking of the Lord's Supper. There is no magic in baptism and we must beware of sacramental superstition or idolatry. Our dependence must be on Christ not the sacrament, which is only a voluntary instrument which Christ is pleased to use.

The sign of the cross in baptism was deplored. It is an unlawful addition to the sacrament, not instituted by Christ, superimposing a reverence which should be confined to the solemn act with water itself. Ignorant people would think that the crossing was the sacrament.

The Puritans also opposed the Anglican requirement of godparents. The parents were responsible for the spiritual well-being of the child, a view which prevailed in non-Anglican Churches until our own time. The father should present the child, if at all possible. The Scottish Presbyterians asked the father to recite the Apostles' Creed as proof that he was a believer. The Independents objected to this and it was not included in the *Directory*. But both insisted that baptism was a sacrament of the divine convenant 'to you and to your children'.

This is why baptism should be administered in the congregation by an authorised minister. Private baptisms by private persons implied a magical doctrine. Emergency baptisms were not approved as smacking of the belief that the unbaptised would be damned. The sacrament should take place not in a hospital or bedroom by a nurse or relative, but in church by the minister.

In the mid-eighteenth century it was, however, the custom to hold independent baptisms in private houses rather than in churches. This made possible an intimacy and directness within the family; the other children could have the meaning explained to them. Its defect was that the church congregation could not accept responsibility with the parents, nor, as Puritans so often enjoined, 'improve' their own baptism by meditating on the rite, asking themselves how far they had advanced in the grace therein proclaimed.

Immersion was not regarded as essential. Doddridge's order which would not differ much from the Presbyterian was as follows:

Short introductory prayer
Discourse on a suitable text
Prayer of Confession and Petition for Grace for the parents
Interrogation of parents
Pronouncement of Triune Name and Baptism
Charge to parents
Prayer of Thanksgiving (for the family and its branches and for Christ's interest in the present generation)
The Blessing.

(Wakefield, 1957, pp. 39–42; Davies, 1948, pp. 216–21)

Some Puritans would have denied that baptism was of the *esse* of the Church and some were so determined to confine it to the children of believers that they hardly baptised at all.

There was a weakening of the hold of the sacraments on many Puritans, through denial of the sacerdotalism with which they were associated. Milton regarded them as 'not indispensable'. William Dell believed that Christ's baptism put an end to John's water baptism and Spirit baptism to creature baptism, though a Welsh Independent deprecated the vilifying of outward things and said that the sceptics should seek the Christ who is hidden through them (Nuttall, 1946, pp. 90–101).

Confirmation was excluded, though there might be some opportunity for those baptised as infants publicly to confess their faith and to be received into adult membership of the Church.

Methodists were vehement believers in infact baptism. John Wesley, who never abandoned the doctrine of baptismal regeneration, held the Anglican view that it should be done by an ordained minister to emphasise that it was a Church ordinance and not a magical act to be performed by anyone. For decades Methodists went to the Parish Church for baptism. Primitive Methodists allowed lay baptism.

Confirmation was neglected 'Decision for Christ' or testified Conversion was all-important. 'Recipients into Full membership' a dubious title, was increasingly introduced after the union of 1932 to be given the alternative title of Confirmation from 1960. Infant Baptism continued to be affirmed.

CHAPTER 8

POST-REFORMATION CATHOLIC DEVELOPMENTS

The Council of Trent (1545–65) suffered from two disadvantages. Although it achieved something of a Catholic Reformation it had its agenda theologically and especially liturgically too much dominated by the controversies with Protestantism; and the sources which might have resulted in a creative eucharistic renewal were only just being discovered. 'The first known edition e.g. of Justin Martyr was only issued in 1551, of the liturgy of *St James,* in 1560, of the *Apostolic Constitutions* in 1563.' Both Protestants and Catholics were unaware that they were arguing from the Western medieval tradition alone. 'The lack of historical perspective due to the medieval ignorance of history, was perhaps the greatest single contributory cause in the intellectual field of the sixteenth-century break-up of Western Christendom' (Dix, 1945, pp. 626f.).

The Reformers were better historical critics than the Catholics. Zwingli in *An Attack upon the Canon of the Mass* maintained that it was neither evangelical nor apostolic in origin but more recent, a compilation by different people at different times. He doubted whether Dionysius, the so-called Areopagite, was Paul's Mars Hill convert; his *De Ecclesiastica Hierarchia* was not evidence of the way the apostles celebrated Mass. The Catholics, on the other hand, had an army of scholars who proved to their own satisfaction, with the support of medieval authorities, that the Mass originated with Peter at Antioch and was also celebrated by James in Jerusalem and Mark in Alexandria. Thomas Maria Beccatelli argued that the Canon was later than the apostles, but none the less apostolically authentic, being the work of Gelasius,

Leo and Gregory. The majority insisted that in spite of later additions and minor modifications the Canon went back to the very beginnings of Christian faith and worship. The Tridentine debates have been comprehensively summarised by David N. Power in an essay on 'Tridentine Theologians and the Roman Canon' (Austin, ed., pp. 131–64). There were mediating theologians like Tapper and Gropper who tried to connect the propitiatory sacrifice of the Canon with the sacrifice of thanksgiving which was what the Reformers would allow. It would have helped them and the cause of reconciliation had they thought of the Canon as beginning with the Preface of the Eucharistic Prayer with its thanksgiving rather than with the *Te igitur* ('We therefore pray and beseech thee') after the *Sanctus*. The Tridentine Fathers were determined above all else to reaffirm the Mass as a propitiatory sacrifice like that of the cross. And, being unaware of the insights of modern scholarship, to them 'sacrifice' meant 'to slay'. They and their successors, therefore, were much preoccupied with the questions how and at what point Christ is slain in the Mass. One theory maintained that the slaying was 'mystical' in that the death of the Christ, who was really present through transubstantiation was re-presented in the double consecration of bread and wine, the separation of his body and blood being the external appearance of death, the sign of the total sacrifice of his whole self.

Another theory postulated a 'real' sacrifice. Slaying means destruction and this takes place through the change in the elements. Cardinal Bellarmine (d. 1621) saw it as happening in communion, largely, of course, confined to the priest. The body and blood are destroyed because they are consumed. It is interesting that traces of this view are found in the 'terrible prayer' of Simone Weil, the young Jewish philosopher of the 1930s and 40s, haunted by the Mass, who asked that she might be a complete paralytic, will, sensibility, intelligence, love stripped away, 'devoured by God, transformed into Christ's substance, and given for food to afflicted men, whose body and soul lack every kind of nourishment'. She used the language of eating and drinking in connection with friendship. In loving our friends 'we are like cannibals'. She learned that 'only in connection with the language of eucharistic sacrifice was it possible to talk of eating and drinking someone' (Loades in Sykes, ed., pp. 247, 257–8).

The Mass, according to Trent, is an unbloody sacrifice in contrast to Calvary. It makes the one sacrifice accessible and available both for the living and the dead. The communion of the priest, in private, is sufficient. The Latin language both safeguards the mystery and makes it universal. It is entirely preoccupied with the sacrifice of Christ through his death.

'The devotion of the faithful was directed far more toward the veneration of the sacrament than the co-offering of the sacrifice. In fact, it was at this time that the Communion of the faithful became more and more disjoined from the Mass as a devotion in its own right' (Jungman, 1976, p. 87). The Mass became increasingly theatre and attracted, along with baroque architecture, the most glorious music, so that attendance was almost like going to a concert. The congregation were spectators and hearers, which does not mean that they might not engage in a spiritual participation which transcended the physical and caught them up into the heavenly places. It was a musical experience very different from Protestant hymn-singing which was similarly transcendent and indulgent. It was less communal than that and perhaps lifting to a different heaven.

But the liturgical movement began with Dom Prosper Guéranger (1850–75) at the Abbey of Solesmes, which he refounded in 1833. In 1851 he was one of the first to use the term. He protested against the elaborations of music, which might be secular and arouse a sensuality very far from what he understood as a truly Christian reaction. He revived Gregorian chant in all its chastity, though since he was almost an archaeological medievalist, he did not understand eucharistic origins and patristic doctrine. He deplored the eucharistic reforms of Jube, parish priest of Asnères near Paris in the seventeenth century. Jube made the Mass a corporate act, using the high altar only on Sundays and festivals, placing the linen cloth on it just before Mass and leaving it bare of cross or lights other than the processional cross or tapers that were set in place at the beginning. He made the texts of the confession and the *Kyries*, the *Gloria* and the creed congregational, restored the Offertory procession and included gifts other than bread and wine and never began the Canon until the *Sanctus* had ended, when he said it aloud in order to be heard. He anticipated many later reforms (Bouyer, pp. 53f.). Guéranger was undoubtedly unfair to the liturgical reforms of Port Royal and the Jansenists in the seventeenth century. He did not appreciate that their aims were not dissimilar from his. The grounds of his harsh criticism were valid though misapplied. He was opposed to liturgical nationalism, elitism and individualism. He reacted against 'a sentimental and anthropocentric egotism'. 'He taught very clearly that the eucharistic liturgy was both the praise of God and the means for being incorporated into a human community, the Church.' Liturgical prayer was social action. The restoration of common worship could restore the weakening social fabric of European life. He was no dry-as-dust antiquarian but a Romantic, influenced by that movement, and radiant with the poetry of the sacraments. Paradoxically this made him at once an ultramontane (that is, a believer in the universal jurisdiction of the Pope, 'beyond the mountain', the alps), convinced of the necessity of the worldwide Church under papal authority and, through his influence in the Benedictine order and French parishes, a begetter of the triumph of the liturgical movement at the Second Vatican Council (Franklin, pp. 60–77).

The *Book of Common Prayer* of 1662 held sway in the Church of England, though there were many projects for revision, many in the eighteenth century in a Unitarian direction, combining Arianism with enthusiasm for the *Apostolic Constitutions*, which some believed were genuinely apostolic. The rather ineffectual non-jurors were aware of its deficiencies compared with Eastern Orthodox rites. At first they tended to prefer 1549, but became aware that it was as medieval as the Roman Mass and sought to correct it by their patristic knowledge. They wanted to add the mixed chalice, the epiclesis, the Prayer of Oblation transferred to the Canon, and prayers for the departed. Their 1718 Communion Office, devised shortly before they became extinct, follows 1549, but has its Offertory Prayer from *St Basil*, the Consecration from *St James* and the Oblation and Invocation from the *Apostolic Constitutions*. This influenced episcopal liturgies in Scotland (Cuming, 1982, pp. 128–46).

The nineteenth century saw a great interest in liturgy, some of it fired by fear and controversy. The Tractarians were, at first, anxious to restore the full use of the Prayer Book in which they found a frozen Catholicism waiting, if a modern metaphor be allowed, to be brought out of the refrigerator of centuries. Newman in his Anglican days said of those seeking to explore new ways of worship and spirituality:

> If they would but follow the Church, come together in prayer on Sundays and saints' days, nay every day; honour the rubric by keeping to it obediently, and conforming with their families to the *spirit* of the Prayerbook, I say, that on the whole they would practically do vastly more good than by trying new religious plans, founding new religious societies, or striking out new religious views. (Chadwick, p. 142)

As a Roman Catholic, Newman said that one reason why he would not return to the Church of England was because of the dreariness of Anglican worship compared to the Mass in which all joined, old and young. It must not be forgotten that the altar was often obscured by the three-decker pulpit from which the parson and clerk conducted the service and shared the responses. Thomas Hardy in 'Afternoon Service at Mellstock' looks back nostalgically to the church worship he had known as a boy:

> On afternoons of drowsy calm
> We stood in the panelled pew,
> Singing one-voice a Tate-and-Brady psalm
> To the tune of 'Cambridge New'.

That was how worship was.

This is one reason why Anglo-Catholicism emerged from the Oxford Movement. 'Ritualism' was a combination of three factors: response to the new militancy of Rome consequent upon Catholic emancipation and the restoration of the hierarchy; belief that although the papacy was a departure from ecclesiastical truth, the Mass enshrined it and the Anglican liturgy was impoverished through inadequacies of doctrine and lack of ceremonial; and concern to bring colour and light into the lives of the poor in the slums of the industrial revolution. Christian worship should not be for an elite establishment of the prosperous but for those whom Christ came most to seek and save. Theologians such as Herbert Kelly of the Society of the Sacred Mission and Frank Weston, Bishop of Zanzibar, were less concerned to bring the street to the Mass as the Mass to the street. It was not enough to remain at the altar or in devotion before the reserved Sacrament. The Church must go out into the highways and hedges and celebrate the neglected sacrament of the Fourth Gospel, the washing of the feet of the poor and undesirables. In some ways it was inconsistent that this should go with a high clericalism – rather than high churchmanship – which barred the laity from the sanctuary, except as communicants. It was also unfortunate that they sought to adopt Roman worship in its Tridentine medievalism, without benefit of the scholarship which was to bring about liturgical revolution. There grew up the habit of farsing the English rite with the Latin, that is, interpolating in a low voice the Consecration Prayer of the Mass into the Prayer Book anaphora, which W. H. Frere condemned because it made the Roman liturgy, 'which is in fact the least satisfactory of all the ancient liturgies . . .' the one standard to which it is desirable as far as possible to conform':

> This is an unhappy state of things; and unless this tendency is to increase, steps must be taken to remove, as well as may be, the defect in our rite from which it has arisen. Once let the English Canon resume something of its original form, and the farsing of it with the Latin Canon will become not only unattractive but even impossible. (Frere, pp. 194f.)

Frere's practical suggestions were for the Prayer of Humble Access to follow the Comfortable Words and the Prayer of Oblation, and the Lord's Prayer to be before communion. He also held that the consecration of the elements was the whole Eucharistic Prayer, not simply the words of institution as in Western tradition, and that this required an epiclesis to make the prayer fully trinitarian. This last, not agreed or thought to be needed by many of those involved in the Anglican liturgical revision of the 1910s and 1920s, complicated the process of revision. Frere also believed that a trinitarian structure of the anaphora demanded that the epiclesis come after the words of institution as in the Eastern rites and not before.

The battle was between Anglo-Catholics who wanted a liturgy much enriched by ceremonial and extra services of a Marian and sanctorale (a calendar of saints' days) nature nearer to the Roman, the evangelicals who wished to reaffirm the Prayer Book, and the central churchmen, who realised the need for change and produced the 'Grey Book', 'a remarkable combination of sound liturgical craftsmanship, modernist theology, and high-flown liberal sentiment' (Cuming, 1982, p. 169). There was also Frere's 'Orange Book' which attempted to harmonise the 'Grey Book' and the Anglo-Catholics' 'Green Book'.

The ill-fated Prayer Book of 1927/8 has the commandments of the Lord Jesus as an alternative to the ten except on at least one Sunday in the month. The *Kyries* in English or Greek are also an option. The Collect for the Sovereign is omitted. The people are to stand for the Gospel. The intercession is 'for the whole state of Christ's Church', it introduces prayers for 'all nations, missionaries, and places of learning' and asks that the faithful departed may be granted 'everlasting life and peace'. There is a briefer alternative confession and absolution from compline for weekdays. The mixed chalice is allowed. The Prayer of Humble Access follows the Comfortable Words, as in the 1548 devotions. The greeting precedes the *Sursum Corda*. The Preface is brief, though there may be Propers. 'Blessed is he that cometh in the name of the Lord' is printed as an anthem at the end of the service but may be said or sung after the *Sanctus*. The consecration shows some slight changes from 1662, the manual acts are mandatory during the words of institution, followed by the anamnesis from 1549 slightly rearranged, the epiclesis from the same source with a phrase from the Catechism, and the oblation in Prayer Book words with a concluding doxology. Then there is the Lord's Prayer and the Peace. There is no rubric about this being passed through the congregation. After communion is the thanksgiving from the *Book of Common Prayer* and the *Gloria in Excelsis* with the final blessing.

The book has an improved Kalendar, with St Mary Magdalen and the Transfiguration added to the Red Letter days. But it satisfied few, largely because both Anglo-Catholics and Evangelicals were unwilling to compromise.

CHAPTER 9

THE LITURGICAL MOVEMENT

In 1912 W. H. Frere wrote that there were indications from all quarters that people were living in an age of liturgical ferment:

> We are in the swirl of one of those movements which strangely develop themselves, one hardly knows whence, and propagate themselves throughout the civilized world, one hardly knows how and lead to immense transformation. This is the significance of the present moment in the world of worship, and it is well that we in England should realize that we are sharing in a world-wide movement, and not merely being agitated by local unrest. (Arnold and Wyatt, eds, p. 77)

This movement would proceed throughout the century. It was the product of two developments: the liturgical movement and ecumenism. We have noted the first stirrings of the former in the Roman Catholic Church at the Abbey of Solesmes. The Benedictine Order, in particular, would play an influential part, but Fr Louis Bouyer regards as the real starting point a conference at Malines in Belgium in 1909 and the work of Dom Lambert Beauduin. He had been a parish priest in Liège before taking Benedictine vows. The conference had been preceded by the leadership of Pius X, his *Motu Proprio* on sacred music, and his efforts to make Christians communicants, with the Mass not something primarily to be seen or heard but shared by individual participation in community.

Dom Lambert quoted often a sentence from the *Motu Proprio*:

> Our deepest wish is that the true Christian spirit should once again flourish in every way and establish itself among the faithful; and to that end it is necessary first of all to provide for the sanctity and dignity of the temple where the faithful meet together precisely in order to find that spirit in its primary and indispensable source, that is . . . the active participation in the most holy and sacred mysteries and in the solemn and common prayer of the Church.

Dom Lambert interpreted this to mean that the Missal should become the Prayer Book in private as well as in the congregation and should be translated into the vernacular for this purpose, with Latin and the language of the people in parallel columns. He wanted the Gregorian chant to be fostered and for choirs to make annual retreats at Benedictine abbeys (Bouyer, pp. 58ff.).

The movement was also inspired by scholarship due to the discovery of ancient liturgies such as the *Didache* and the *Apostolic Tradition* of Hippolytus. This delivered liturgical studies from preoccupation with Reformation controversies and the medieval categories in which they were conducted. It enabled criticism both of the Roman Mass and the *Book of Common Prayer* with reference to ancient liturgies and the historic constituents of the thanksgiving.

The cornerstone of the liturgical movement is the reaffirmation of the Eucharist as the central act of Christian worship and the source of the Church's life, from which all prayer, devotion, witness and evangelisation flows. This was the aim of the Anglican parish and people movement and of Fr Gabriel Hebert's books, *Liturgy and Society* and *The Parish Communion*. Its consequence has been that over the years, the Parish Communion has become the principal service of the Lord's Day in the majority of English parishes. 'Eucharist', the third oldest name for the service, has become the one in ecumenical use. It singles out thanksgiving as the governing purpose of the service and is less identified with low church than 'Lord's Supper', though that does emphasise Christ's action, invitation and hospitality. Also 'Eucharist' has associations less likely to provoke hostility than 'Mass'. The liturgical movement insists that it is a service of Word and Sacrament, but with short lections and sermons the Word may not occupy much time.

In the Church of England this has resulted in some impoverishment in the diminution of the offices, which in the *Book of Common Prayer* are services of the Word, as we see below. Sermons in the Church of England have become fewer and shorter; in the Church of Rome they have increased. There is, of course, an art in the short sermon and there has been some good writing on preaching in the liturgy from such biblical scholars as R. H. Fuller. Although it is not now regarded as improper to consecrate and partake of communion in the evening, Sunday worship in the United Kingdom has become increasingly confined to the mornings. Evening congregations have declined. What used to be deplored as 'the continental Sunday' is universal and it has also become a day of shopping and business. The parish and people movement was also criticised for undue emphasis upon the Offertory, the cruets at the back of the church being brought in procession to the altar. Much was said and written about the offering of bread and wine being not only of the fruits of nature but of human industry. There was danger of Pelagianism here for the essence of the Eucharist is not our offering but Christ's and the Offertory is the bringing of our gifts, gratefully received but stained by sin into the realm of redemption (Mascall, pp. 173ff.).

The other characteristic of the liturgical movement is, as we have seen, participation of the whole congregation. They are the celebrants not the minister alone, who presides. It has been suggested that he – or she – is more like the producer of a play than the chief actor. Responses have multiplied, lay voices are more often heard in lessons and prayers, and liturgical dance has been introduced in some places, so that the whole person is involved, while the visual is not regarded as a sensual distraction. Eargate is not the only way into the divine presence.

Some of this, as we have seen, was not new to the Calvinist tradition, where the norm of worship was, historically, Word and Sacrament, though this had become much ignored. On the other hand, there was the distrust of the visual, which pervades Scripture and Judaism. A common feature of new liturgies is the use of the second person plural in address to God. This was much resisted in the 1960s and after. The then Dean of Bristol, the Very Revd D. E. W. Harrison of the

Church of England Liturgical Commission and first Chairman of the Joint Liturgical Group argued for the traditional singular as appropriate to a unique relationship, as did Professor Charles Cranfield of Durham in United Reformed Church discussions. He argued that the singular affirms the oneness of God as well as the 'I–Thou' relationship (Spinks, 1984, p. 241). But 'you' has prevailed and more easily than seemed possible, though some Churches have rites in both forms and there is often in prayers either read or extempore a confusion of both, which people do not seem to mind, if indeed they notice it. The nadir is the song 'For you alone are my heart's desire and I long to worship thee'. 'Thee' has been amended to 'you', though it was still sung in a broadcast in 1996.

Ecumenism

The increasing communication of separated Churches with one another had inevitable liturgical repercussions. The World Council of Churches published a symposium in 1951, somewhat delayed, on *Ways of Worship*, presenting the differences between the Churches, but also showing fundamental agreements which are sometimes masked by different rituals. Before that the United Church of South India had produced its liturgy, used for the first time in 1950. Some felt that this represented an Anglican takeover, but at that time the principal non-Roman liturgical scholars were mostly Anglicans and there had appeared, already in 1920, the *Bombay Liturgy*, a remarkably rich rite, with orthodox affinities and provision for lavish burning of incense. It is divided into six sections: the prayers before the service, in which the bread and wine, mixed with a little pure water, may be set upon the altar and blessed, followed by a prayer for purity and the acceptance of 'this our pure sacrifice'; the Prayer of the Catechumens, who are dismissed when it is done, includes a litany and the ministry of the Word with three lessons; the Prayers of the Faithful, confession and absolution, not declaratory, prayer for the worthiness of the worshippers, the Nicene Creed, the Peace, the lavabo and the removal of the veil from the elements with a prayer said privately by the priest; the anaphora, which is lengthy but interspersed with congregational amens and responses and with a prostration of the people for the epiclesis, which follows the words of institution and an anamnesis and is the supreme moment of consecration ending with a doxology and followed by intercessions before the fraction and the Lord's Prayer with embolism and further prayers for worthiness and an elevation of the gifts before communion, with the words of delivery, 'The Body of Christ, the Bread of Life', 'The Blood of Christ, the Chalice of Life'; post-communion thanksgivings and a dismissal; brief prayers after the service. This liturgy is full of adoration and praise (Wigan, p. 113).

The *Liturgy of the Church of South India* owes much to Dom Gregory Dix's *The Shape of the Liturgy* (1945) and its advocacy of a fourfold shape corresponding to the actions of Jesus at the Last Supper. It has a preliminary preparation with the institution narrative of 1 Corinthians 11, the Ten Commandments, or the Lord's summary and an exhortation. The Eucharist itself begins with the placing of the Bible on the table or on a lectern, a 'little entrance' in Orthodox terminology. The presbyter may stand behind the table facing the people. After the Collect for Purity there is the *Gloria in Excelsis* or an alternative based on Revelation 5:12 with responses. There is confession, Comfortable Words and absolution in the second person. In the Ministry of the Word there are three lessons. The sermon is followed by the Nicene or Apostles' Creed and intercession with alternative litanies, the second modelled on the opening litany of the Orthodox liturgy. After this there is opportunity for any who wish to leave to do so. These must include any who are excommunicate or under discipline. The breaking of bread begins with texts of joy and the bringing of the Offertory, somewhat parallel to the Orthodox 'great entrance', though without its awesome associations of Christ's incarnation and Passion. The Father is humbly asked to accept the gifts, which are of his own and to use them to his glory. Before the anaphora is a brief petition, from a Mozarabic source, that Jesus, the good High Priest, may be known in the breaking of the bread. The anaphora itself, like the Bombay liturgy, has responses, the *Benedictus qui venit*, after the *Sanctus*, altered to 'Blessed be he that hath come and is to come in the name of the Lord. Hosanna in the highest', as in Syrian liturgies and said by presbyter and people. After the words of institution is a response from Bombay, 'Amen. Thy death, O Lord, we commemorate, thy Resurrection we confess, and thy second coming we await. Glory be to thee O Christ.' The Lord's Prayer follows and the Prayer of Humble Access with concomitance replacing the division of bread and wine, body and soul. The communion is to be by 'tables' as the Methodist custom. A spoon may be used for communion because of Indian taboos about drinking from a common cup and Anglican dislike of individual glasses. The Oblation is after communion as in the Prayer Book and the blessing is also that of 1662.

This liturgy has been praised as celebratory, corporate and flexible, a solemnity with intervals of silence. Its Syrian echoes bring it into the Middle East if not exactly to India. Yet there are those who feel that however good its intentions it is the importation of imperialists, and not indigenous, not Indian. To create an indigenous Indian liturgy is a very difficult task, as is true everywhere. Such an attempt like the 'Indian Mass' may be too Brahmanist and detached from the realities of Indian poverty, while many Indian Christians are conservative and want a liturgy which gives them a distinct identity different from the prevailing culture. An alternative liturgy of 1985 'is an impressive attempt to respond liturgically to the realities of Indian life and faith', but it has not been successfully incorporated into congregational worship. There is a parallel between the intense expressions of love in the Wesley hymns and the *bhakti* or 'love devotion' of the Indian religious heritage, but the passion for God found in the Hindu *Hymns of the Alvars* translated in 1929 by the Methodist missionary Stirling Hooper, has not influenced Christian worship as it might have done (Eric Lott in Westerfield-Tucker, ed., pp. 53–66).

In 1963 in the United Kingdom, Archbishop Michael Ramsey agreed to take the initiative in the formation of a Joint Liturgical Group to devise ecumenical projects and share information about the revision of services. The group has been in existence ever since and includes Roman Catholics, first as observers and for many years as full members. It has not escaped criticism, too didactic, for one thing, and there has been a feeling that the Church of England has been less than wholehearted in spite of the inclusion of a succession of leading Anglican liturgists, all of whom have worked with great amity and loyalty. The first Secretary was Dr R. C .D. Jasper, Chairman of the Anglican Liturgical Commission, who himself felt that his communion did not co-operate with the group as it ought. There has been an impression of Anglican self-sufficiency and superiority in liturgical matters, though one must not fail to reckon with the need in liturgy and in all else to hold together different theologies which results in Anglican self-preoccupation. But the Church of England adopted many of the group's early proposals, which have had great effect on British worship. The Christian Year has been organised around the great festivals of Christmas, Easter and Pentecost with the omission of obscurer Sundays such as Septuagesima. The pre-Christmas period begins nine Sundays before, the themes being the preparation for the coming of Christ in the Old Testament, with John the Baptist and the Annunciation on the last two Sundays of Advent, which is no longer the beginning of the Christian Year, as only in the West. Epiphany is a season of the manifestation of God in Christ, with emphasis on Christ's baptism, not simply the coming of the wise men and its last Sunday, the numbering of which depends on the date of Easter, is followed by nine Sundays before Easter, which are concerned with the work of Christ as teacher, healer, friend of sinners, and then in Lent, the temptation and sufferings of Christ, including the Transfiguration. The lectionary has a two-year cycle. Sundays after Trinity as in the Anglican Kalendar have been replaced by Sundays after Pentecost as with Rome.

After more than twenty years, this has been shown to need revision. Anglicans have enriched the period between All Saints and Candlemas with *The Promise of His Glory.* It offers an alternative lectionary and a wealth of material, some of it for services of light, appropriate, it is felt, in wintertime. And there are signs that some of the traditional Anglican observances may be restored – creation after Epiphany as with the old Septuagesima and Sundays after Trinity not Pentecost, perhaps due to the revival of trinitarianism in theology in the United Kingdom.

The Joint Liturgical Group produced a series of Holy Week services, in 1970, which were widely used until the publication of the Church of England's *Lent, Holy Week and Easter* (1984–6). In 1978, the group published a Eucharistic Canon for use on ecumenical occasions. It is doubtful if it has been often used for this purpose, but it is found, as may be expected since the late J. M. Todd, the Congregationalist, was its principal author, as one of two additional modern Eucharistic Prayers in the United Reformed Church *Book of Services*, 1980. (The other is by the Dutch Roman Catholic priest and poet, Huub Oosterhuis.) In the Preface the acts of God are proclaimed as far as possible in terms of present activity rather than as past events. The *Sanctus* is taken from the *Te Deum*, a move which is supported by the theory of some scholars that this hymn was originally a Preface, *Sanctus* and *post-Sanctus* for the Mass of an Easter Vigil. The institution is 1 Corinthians 11. There is no epiclesis over the bread and wine. The fire of the Spirit is to be kindled in us. The group published a symposium in 1972, *Initiation and Eucharist*, which questioned Dix's fourfold shape of the Eucharist corresponding to the actions of Christ in the upper room: 'he took', offering; 'he gave thanks', Eucharistic Prayer; 'he broke', fraction; 'he gave to them', distribution. As well as the Churches of South India, this has influenced many revised rites since the 1960s. The group felt it to be artificial. At the Last Supper there was a sevenfold, if not a ninefold, shape, as is observed in the Eucharists of the Baptists and the Churches of Christ. But the Eucharist is not a repetition of the Last Supper and the two basic actions are the blessing and the giving. Jesus took bread and wine in order to give thanks; he broke the bread in order to share it. These are mere necessities, in spite of the symbolic meaning read out of the breaking of the bread, while there is a distinction between the presentation of the eucharistic gifts and, maybe, the financial offerings along with them, the Church's provision, and the 'taking' and setting apart by the President. What matters, supremely, in the service is thanksgiving and communion.

There is no mandatory place for the words of institution. They may be read as a warrant before the thanksgiving, included in the thanksgiving, or occur immediately before communion. Basic to the thanksgiving and its progression are:

> The proclamation and recital of the mighty acts of God in creation and redemption.
> The *anamnesis* (memorial) with the bread and wine of the crucified and risen Lord 'until he come'.
> The petition that by the power of the Holy Spirit what we do may be united to the perfect sacrifice of Christ as so accepted by God, that in communion with our Lord we may receive the benefits of his passion and victory. (Jasper, ed., 1972, pp. 25, 27)

The work of the Joint Liturgical Group on the Daily Office will be dealt with below. It has considered a good many other subjects – preaching, hymns, children's worship, and of course, initiation – as well as devising forms of service for ecumenical projects, such as the induction of new ministers and an ecumenical marriage service. It has also produced a four-year lectionary, allocating one Gospel to each year; but this, though adopted by the Methodist Church and others, is not likely to survive. The *Revised Common Lectionary,* the work of the Consultation on Common Texts in the United States and Canada, with which the Joint Liturgical Group is associated, may well supercede it. This lectionary is based on the Roman *Lectionary for Mass* of 1969, a three-year cycle focused on the Gospels of Matthew, Mark and Luke in turn, with John, which is seen as a theological exposition of the paschal mystery rather than a chronological account of the Lord's life, used during the major seasons of the Christian Year. There is considerable criticism, particularly on the part of biblical scholars, that the lectionary passages are too short and do not do justice to their contexts. The excuse for this is the need not to extend the Eucharist beyond a reasonable time, but compilers may have paid too much attention to half-truths about attention span and to a feeling that long lections are due to the desire of clergy and readers to hear their own voices. The *Revised Common Lectionary* has lengthened many readings for the Sundays after Pentecost with an option that in a service solely of the Word they may be lengthened further.

The English Language Liturgical Consultation is an

international Joint Liturgical Group concerned with the liturgy in English. It succeeded the International Consultation on English Texts (1968–75), after an interval, in 1985. In 1990, it published a revision of its predecessors' *Prayers We Have in Common,* English translations of the texts found in most liturgies, the *Gloria,* the Lord's Prayer, the creeds. The title of the revision is *Praying Together.* The Consultation has given its attention to an ecumenical Eucharistic Prayer and in 1992 published four samples, with an introduction summarising the agreed elements in the prayer: the dialogue; the Preface with thanksgiving for creation and with opportunity for praise for individual gifts; the *Sanctus,* with the admission that the *Benedictus qui venit* from Psalm 118:26 and Matthew 21:9 will be omitted by some because they find in it implications of a certain theology of eucharistic presence; the post-*Sanctus,* which may include the narrative of institution, and/or thanksgiving for salvation history in the New Testament, for God's continuing action in the present and for bread and wine; the words of institution which may not always be included in the prayer but read beforehand or before communion as a warrant; the anamnesis, or remembrance of Christ, his dying and rising, the paschal mystery into which we are drawn through baptism, possibly also particular recall of Christ's sacrifice, which gives opportunity, somewhat dangerous some feel, for the re-presentation of it, though not the repetition; the epiclesis, invocation of the Holy Spirit upon the people or the elements, or both, sometimes divided, the latter here, the former before the narrative; there may be commemorations and intercessions, some confining the latter to the ministry of the Word; doxology.

In 1982 the Faith and Order Commission of the World Council of Churches agreed on a report on *Baptism, Eucharist and Ministry,* on which a vast number of Churches commented. It is a remarkable document agreed by the most representative body that could be assembled. It was accompanied by a liturgy which enshrines its eucharistic doctrine and is a sample of what all Churches might accept. It contains elements from all the main liturgies and from some traditions not represented in the World Council of Churches. It has not, to my knowledge, been much used; it was more for illustration than performance, but its anaphora is very much in harmony with the principles later enunciated by ELLC. The intercessions are not included but come at the end of the ministry of the Word.

Since Charlemagne, the tradition in the West has been for one Eucharistic Prayer, with seasonal and particular variations. This has now changed and across the Churches there is a plethora of anaphoras. In the major revisions from the Second Vatican Council, the major denominations have offered several Eucharistic Prayers, apart from the Methodists who in 1975 kept to one on the grounds that Methodists might more easily become acclimatised to the new service if they were not confused by alternatives. It may be argued, with the *Book of Common Prayer* in mind, that one prayer constantly repeated becomes part of the very life of worshippers. They come to know its phrases and expressions and these sustain them throughout their lives and even in the hour of death. This is a very serious argument for one prayer; but have modern liturgists Cranmer's gift? Are they able to construct forms that may be recalled in all times and circumstances? In any case are not all recent prayers temporary, to be discarded after a decade or two? Security in liturgy may be no more attainable in our time than security in life. And is there not an outburst of almost poetic creativity in the composition of anaphoras, bearing in mind both the inheritance of the past and the new understanding of liturgy and the changes in language? Some of the new anaphoras are very fine.

The first of four prayers from the English Language Commission is that of the Uniting Church of Australia and is also used by Anglicans. It emphasises creation and human responsibility for the care of the earth, sets the *Sanctus* in the whole cosmos, gives specific thanks for bread and wine, includes 'the outpouring of the Spirit' in the anamnesis and prays for unity and renewal by the Holy Spirit, though it does not invoke the Spirit upon the elements.

The second prayer has Roman Catholic origins and is also printed in the Church of England *Patterns for Worship* (1989). It is the most poetic of the anaphoras, with echoes of St John of the Cross and there are symbolic pictures drawn from biblical, patristic and contemporary images. Its language is rich and resonant. There are optional and seasonal insertions and an acclamation, 'To you be glory and praise for ever!', which may be said by the whole congregation after each part of the prayer. It also pleads the once for all sacrifice and concludes the double epiclesis with the prayer over the bread and wine, 'Show them to be for us the body and blood of your dear Son'.

This is a moving anaphora of exquisite tenderness and full of Scripture. Those who feel that a Eucharistic Prayer should be bare and expressionless, left to work its miracle without human artistry or, what is for them, the diversion of beautiful language, will not approve of it. Metropolitan Anthony Bloom, explaining to Dom Aidan Kavanagh his impersonal and impassive celebration of the liturgy, said that left to itself, without any attempt to present it 'beautifully', it should hit you like a locomotive.

The third prayer is brief, being taken from the Boston University School of Theology where the whole rite with homily must not last more than thirty minutes. It is trinitarian but 'politically correct' in that it avoids addressing God as 'Father, Son and Holy Spirit'. The Spirit of the loving God is asked to 'touch us and these gifts of bread and wine' which some have found strange. Political correctness has its points, such as 'making women visible' but it can go to extremes which are post-Christian. Is it possible to have a Christian liturgy which does not call God 'Father', a concept so central to the religion of Jesus, or which abandons language of the Kingdom which some so strongly abominate? The whole question of liturgical language in a world context and the continuing age of Auschwitz demands intense study and discussion. To what extent does one yield to the sensitivities of groups and individuals, which may result in objections to what have been regarded as foundation categories of faith and undermine the essential Gospel?

The fourth prayer is a paean of adoration and praise with little trace of humble access, though it recognises that we 'were estranged and ensnared by death' and that our 'praise and petitions' are to be received, 'as Jesus received the cry of the needy'. A subjective doctrine of atonement seems to underlie the prayer. God calls to us through the life and death of Jesus. We remember 'his life for others, and his death and resurrection which renewed the face of the earth', but there is no sense of the awesome sacrifice for sin, of the cost of redemption and of the agonies of the world and distress of nations. There is an exuberant optimism about it and a touch of receptionism.

The Roman Catholics

The new Roman Missal consequent upon Vatican II provides four Eucharistic Prayers. The first is the Roman Canon, the second an adaptation of the prayer of the *Apostolic Tradition* of Hippolytus, the third is a prayer, presumably composed in the 1960s, which is very much of traditional faith and theology, and the fourth is based on the liturgy of St Basil. The last three have an epiclesis over the elements before the words of institution. Revision has concentrated on better renderings of the Latin in which all the prayers were first written and on inclusive language, particularly in Prayer IV which was deemed far too 'sexist' and was least used partly on that account. '*Clerus*', translated as 'clergy' in the earlier versions, is given a broader meaning to conform to contemporary understandings of ministry, so that in Prayer II it means 'all who are called to your service', in Prayer III it is made concrete, 'bishops, priests and deacons', and in Prayer IV 'our priests and deacons and all who minister in our church'. In Prayer III God is no longer asked to 'see the Victim whose death has reconciled us to yourself', but to see in the Church's offering 'the sacrifice by which you reconciled us to yourself'. This is both closer to the Latin and turns one's mind away from the tortured and crucified body to the great act of divine self-giving which took place in Christ's offering of himself.

Rome, of course, has many Masses other than those of Sunday. There are, for instance, Masses of Reconciliation and Masses with Children, and 1970 provided a rite for the latter which is full of joy with sung responses, remembering Christ's life and ministry and love for children and proclaiming his death, the giving of his life for us. One thinks this is better than the family services and all-age worship, with their didactic emphasis and gimmicks, that are prevalent elsewhere.

Transubstantiation remains the official doctrine of the Roman Church. It is basically an affirmation of the real presence of the whole Christ in the Sacrament expressed in the Aristotelian terms which were all the Scholastic and Tridentine had at their disposal. It was, among other things, a corrective to the intense sensuality into which some popular medieval devotion to belief in the real presence fell. Much modern thought has gone into its republication. This even includes the work of a Calvinist theologian F. J. Leenhardt, who wanted to retain the term 'transubstantiation' because he insisted that if we believe Jesus when he said of the bread 'This is my body' meaning his whole self and whole activity past, present and to come, 'faith will acknowledge that this bread . . . no longer has the same substance.' It is the truly present body of the Lord. 'Transignification' replaces 'transubstantiation' as a modern term for some Catholic theologians, change of sign for change of substance. Others think of transubstantiation as a poetic metaphor. Goethe wrote to his beloved, 'For me, you are transubstantiated into all objects.' For some people a gift from a dearly loved person may be their presence and their very self, and their presence may be more real than that of the person sitting beside them. Edward Schillebeeckx, however, feels that these views, despite the light they shed, lack 'metaphysical density'. It is important 'to know whether Christ is merely giving me in the Eucharist a present in which I can taste his love, or whether he is giving me himself as sacramental nourishment'. Transubstantiation is the orthodox teaching of the Church, not what pleases individual Christians, 'but what God postulates in Christ as the reality of salvation and thus defines as a mystery of faith'. Grace comes from heaven, not vertically like rain, but horizontally through our human relationships and the things which lie about us in the world, its orientation is towards the secular. 'The secular world is intrinsically involved in Christ's gift of himself in the Eucharist.' Transubstantiation has two dimensions, '*change of being* of bread and wine (in which Christ's glorified body is really offered through the Holy Spirit), but *within the terrestrial, but now* (through this change of being) *sacramental form* of bread and wine, which remain subject in this secular world, to the terrestrial laws of corporealty . . .'. Schillebeeckx quotes 'The Pastoral Constitution on the Church in the Modern World' from Vatican II:

> The Lord left behind a pledge of this hope and strength for life's journey in the sacrament of faith where natural elements are changed into his glorified Body and Blood, providing a meal of brotherly solidarity and a foretaste of the heavenly banquet. (Schillebeeckx, 1977, pp. 155f., 159, 82–3, 151)

Dom Odo Casel, who died after singing the *Exultet* at Maria Laach at Easter 1948, was a student of the mystery religions and applied some of the insights thus gained to the Eucharist. The most fruitful is that of the 'making present' not only of Christ but of the whole work of redemption. It may be compared to the well-known statement of the Congregationalist, C. H. Dodd, that at each Eucharist 'we are there, at the night in which he was betrayed, at Golgotha, before the empty tomb on Easter Day, and in the upper room where he appeared and we are at the moment of his coming with angels and archangels and all the company of heaven, in the twinkling of an eye, at the last trump' (Dodd, 1938, pp. 234f.). But this may not give to the consecrated bread and wine the supernatural significance of Tridentine theology for which they are there on the table and central to the whole service not simply as bread and wine but as the body and blood of Christ.

Twentieth-century Roman Catholics have made much of the presence of both Christ and the Church in the Sacrament. 'This is my body', said Jesus. 'You are the body of Christ', said Paul. 'We ourselves lie on the paten', said Augustine. This is why Roman Catholics now assert that eucharistic celebration requires the presence of a believing community. Masses said by the priest alone (usually with server) have fallen into disfavour; hence concelebration.

The Church of England

The most signal development in Church of England liturgy in the past half-century has been the emergence of liturgical experts among evangelicals. Liturgy is no longer the preserve of Catholics; and evangelicals have advanced far beyond defence of the Prayer Book. Colin Buchanan is the outstanding but by no means the only example. He must be credited with an immense achievement in promoting the study of liturgy through the Grove booklets and other publications such as his two volumes of *Modern Anglican Liturgies*.

Church of England endeavours in revision resulted in the *Alternative Service Book*, the result of almost twenty years' labour and experiment (see Jasper and Bradshaw, 1986; Cuming, 1982, pp. 208–29). It is unlikely that more prolonged and thorough consultation has been achieved anywhere else before the authorisation of new services (Cuming, 1982, p. 209), though this omitted the Joint Liturgical Group, which was told of the proposals without its opinion being asked, whereas the Methodists and the United Reformed Church presented their services for discussion and advice. On the other hand, as we have seen, the JLG calendar and eucharistic lectionary were largely accepted by the English Church, as were the revised offices of Morning and Evening Prayer.

The *Alternative Service Book* has two eucharistic rites, Rite A in the 'you' form of address to God, and the ICET (International Consultation on English Texts) texts and Rite B which retains 'thou' and is more traditional. A has four Eucharistic Prayers, B two, with no acclamations, the congregational proclamation of the mystery of faith. There is also 'the Order following the pattern of the Book of Common Prayer' and a 'Eucharistic Prayer for Use with the Sick', not much shortened.

The first Eucharistic Prayer of the *Alternative Service Book* is that which, after much debate, was offered in Series Three of the experimental Eucharists. There had been great controversy over a phrase in the anamnesis, 'Having in remembrance his saving passion, his resurrection from the dead, and his glorious ascension into heaven, and looking for the coming of his kingdom, *we offer unto thee this bread and this cup*'. This comes from the *Apostolic Tradition* of Hippolytus, though the substitution of 'this bread' for 'the bread' is from the *Apostolic Constitutions*. The compromise was to say 'we celebrate with this bread and this cup', which neutralised the objections of the evangelicals and Prayer Book loyalists who were opposed to any suggestion of offering Christ in the Eucharist. As in the 1552 and 1662 Prayer Books, the oblation of ourselves follows communion in the rites of 1980, which avoids what Dix condemned as the Pelagianism of offering ourselves before we have received Christ. The epiclesis in all four prayers follows the *Sanctus* before the institution narrative, not in the eastern position preferred in 1928. In the fourth prayer, the Spirit is invoked on those who receive the eucharistic gifts not on the gifts themselves. The third prayer, which has become the most loved, is like the second Roman prayer modelled on that of Hippolytus. New comprehensive orders will appear in 2000.

The Episcopal Church of Scotland

The Eucharist of the Episcopal Church of Scotland has been admired by Anglican liturgists ever since the rite of 1637, which was so unfortunate in its timing. W. H. Frere had close association with Dr Maclean, Bishop of Moray, Ross and Caithness. The Scottish Communion Office of 1929 is basically that of 1637. The title 'presbyter' is used instead of priest or minister. For the Prayer of Consecration he is to stand 'at such a part of the holy table as he may with the most ease and decency use both his hands'. The 1929 rite transfers the epiclesis, which in 1637 comes before the words of institution, to follow the anamnesis. The prayer for acceptance of 'this our sacrifice of praise and thanksgiving' and the humble offering of ourselves, both in the language of the *Book of Common Prayer* with its sense of the worshippers' unworthiness, end the Canon. The prayer 'for the whole estate of Christ's Church' follows, with commendation of the departed and petition that we may follow the example of the saints and rise with them to receive the divine accolade. The Lord's Prayer and the fraction come next. There are then the table prayers, confession, Comfortable Words, 'the collect' of humble access as in 1549, with the *Agnus Dei* before communion. The words of delivery are those of 1549. After communion there is the thanksgiving of 1549 and subsequent *Book of Common Prayer* and the *Gloria in Excelsis.* In 1970 this last was moved to the Catholic position after the confession and absolution. There is now an Old Testament lesson. The anaphora is unaltered but the intercessions now conclude the ministry of the Word. The Prayer of Humble Access in its Cranmerian form follows the Peace. The thanksgiving after communion is brief.

The liturgy of 1982 is in the 'you' form. The Peace may come at the beginning, or after the confession and absolution, as these are not said at the start but follow the intercessions for which a set form is not given, merely headings provided. The first new anaphora is of beautiful clarity and some memorable passages such as:

In Christ your Son our life and yours
Are brought together in a wonderful exchange.
He made his home among us
That we might forever dwell in you.

The sacrifice is skilfully introduced in the anamnesis:

Made one with you, we offer you these gifts
and with them ourselves,
a single, holy, living sacrifice.

The second anaphora is of anticipation. God is still drawing the universe to its fulfilment:

Dawn and evening celebrate your glory
Till time shall be no more

In Christ your Son
the life of heaven and earth were joined
sealing the promise of a new creation,
given yet still to come.

The actions of Jesus at the Last Supper are joined with his vision of the feast of the Kingdom. The eschatology of the Eucharist is proclaimed in this prayer as in few others.

The theme of the third prayer is 'Returning to God'. It majors on the reconciling work of Christ to which he dedicated himself as he broke bread. The third prayer is of the resurrection and life in the Spirit and the joy of the Easter garden, that

> he whom they had loved and lost
> was with them now in every place
> for ever.

The fifth prayer is the shortest. It is a prayer of light and joy:

> You give us your Spirit
> so that we can look at the world with your eyes
>
> One day we will be with you in heaven
> but already we laugh with the saints and angels
> and sing their song.

The fraction follows the Eucharistic Prayers, done either in silence or with the words:

> The living bread is broken for the life of the world
> Lord unite us in this sign.

Then there is the Lord's Prayer. The Prayer of Humble Access has disappeared. The *Agnus Dei* is called 'the Communion Song'. The post-communion prayers include 'Father we give you thanks and praise' from the *Alternative Service Book.*

The Church of Scotland

There was much creative liturgy emanating from the Iona Community founded by George Macleod in 1938 to revive the ancient missionary endeavour of Christianity, combining rule of life and retreat for spiritual renewal with work among the unemployed and destitute in disadvantaged areas. Macleod himself was a believer in the centrality of the Eucharist, a gifted composer of prayers and his work has been continued notably by John Bell.

The latest *Book of Common Order* was published in 1994. It had been generally agreed that its model should be that of

1940. Its language is inclusive as far as possible, masculine titles for God, even though scriptural, are used sparingly, but biblical and classical texts are not altered. The feminine is often preferred to the masculine when one pronoun is used, for instance for those being baptised. Prayers are in the 'you' form. There is material for every conceivable occasion. The book is spaciously and beautifully produced.

There are no less than five forms and orders for Holy Communion. The first order begins with the bringing in of the Bible and then follows the pattern of most contemporary rites with the Collect for Purity and confession and absolution somewhat shorter than in 1940 with alternative declaratory absolutions rather than pardon comprehended in the penitential prayer. The Collect for the Sixth Sunday after Trinity is retained in the 'you' form followed by the collect of the day and the *Gloria in Excelsis* and the ministry of the Word with the sermon after the readings, the Nicene Creed, the intimations, the intercessions, the invitation, the offering and what is called in Orthodox terminology 'the Great Entrance', when the offerings of money and the bread and wine are brought to the communion table. The grace is said and the elements are unveiled with the option of prayers, one evoking the new and living way consecrated in Christ's blood that we may obtain mercy and offer a pure sacrifice in righteousness, the other presenting the bread and wine. The institution narrative is read from 1 Corinthians 11, there is a taking of the bread and wine and the thanksgiving follows. There are three possibilities. The first is classical with a Preface thanking God for both his original and new creation and a thanksgiving for Christ after the *Sanctus* with the anamnesis, and epiclesis on both people and elements. An oblation and doxology end the prayer.

The second thanksgiving is from the Genevan Service Book; the third is an adaptation of an English Language Liturgical Commission prayer. The Lord's Prayer, the breaking of bread, the *Agnus Dei* in its modern form ('Jesus, Lamb of God') precede communion. It is permitted to speak of the Body of Christ broken, as in many liturgies, though the word is not in the Revised English Bible and there are objections from John 19:36, as we have seen. The elements may be taken to the people in their seats or they may gather round the holy table. The Peace is given – and may be shared – after communion. There is a final thanksgiving and before the blessing the fourth-century Syrian prayer that our senses and members, our souls and bodies may be saved from abuse and serve the Lord with joy and gladness.

The second order is Celtic in inspiration. The prayers have a freshness, simplicity and directness. There is a statement of belief as an alternative to – in this service – the Apostles' Creed, which is laudatory with a celebration of creation, as is also prominent in the thanksgiving:

> You made the sun and stars above our heads
> the earth beneath our feet.
> Your word brought forth
> the rocks and streams
> the surging seas,
> the wild winds and the mild.
>
> You fashioned life in all its myriad forms
> and shaped from clay
> the wonder of the human frame.

Some may wonder if this recognises sufficiently those aspects of nature which have led some to speak of a fallen universe, of the cruelty and waste, destructive gales, Fabre's wasps and the malarial mosquito. Is there not too much of what a bereaved and saddened Wordsworth called 'the consecration and the poet's dream'? Perhaps Hopkins's 'The Wreck of the Deutschland' should be read in subsequent meditation. It leads, however, to God's coming himself in Christ, to the Passion and the transforming of nature and human abuse of it:

> You made the tree of death the tree of life
> the empty grave a sign of glorious hope.

The thanksgiving ends with the oblation but also with a petition that we may be gathered into God's Kingdom with the faithful of all ages. The intercessions follow communion, in a rite which is much shorter than the first, but warm and tender with this final blessing:

The blessing of God be yours,
the blessing of the beloved Son be yours,
the blessing of the perfect Spirit be yours,
the blessing of the Three
be poured out upon you,
serenely and generously,
today and for ever.

The third is a short order for use at a second service, the fourth is when children communicate beginning with 'the Great Entrance'. The language is simplified as far as possible, although the great concepts of the Gospel cannot be diminished. Jesus gave his life, rose from death and lives to pray for us for ever. He 'has made us friends with you and with one another'. The intercessions again follow the communion. This moves away from the fashion of the 1960s and 1970s that once communion has been received the congregation should be sent out into the world to engage in the liturgy of life as quickly as possible. The tendency is now for the consequences of communion to be demonstrated in the congregation. These intercessions seek to enter into children's lives, but also to remember young people and the old. They are succinct.

The fifth order is for use in hospital or for the sick. No rites so powerfully combine solemnity with evangelical compassion as do these of the Kirk.

The Baptists

All the major denominations have ordered their new rites according to Dix and to the patristic structure of the Eucharistic Prayer, which gives a homogeneity to all Eucharists at the expense of distinctiveness. It does, however, point to that unity at the Lord's table so sadly fractured throughout Church history, and helps towards a common understanding which may lead to the day when all Christian people are gathered there. And it illustrates what has been recognised for some decades, that differences and varieties of churchmanship are much more likely to be within denominations than between them, though there are still distinctions in the way liturgy is done, in ceremonial, 'gesture, vesture and posture', and in atmosphere, though there is much more warmth and informality in Anglican worship than has been regarded as characteristic.

Among the Free Churches of Great Britain, the Baptists have not been least in liturgical expertise, and Neville Clark and Stephen Winward were prominent in the generation now passing; the former's *Call to Worship* (1960) mediated the Catholic tradition to Free Churches, while the latter with Ernest A. Payne, produced *Order and Prayers for Church Worship* (1962) and, on his own, a book of responsive prayers. Both were prominent members of the Joint Liturgical Group, Clark with a large share in the lectionaries, Winward introducing the first edition of the Daily Office. They are not without successors.

In 1991, the Baptist Union issued *Patterns and Prayers for Christian Worship*. This, compatible with the Baptist belief in freedom of worship, is a book of guidance, though it contains many forms. 'It will link Baptists with the world Church.' It enshrines the belief, in Barth's words, that worship ought to be 'the most momentous, the most urgent, the most glorious action' that can ever take place.

There are three patterns of the Lord's Supper, each making it inseparable from the Word, which needs to be broken as well as the Bread. 'The Breaking of Bread', an early title for the Lord's Supper, 'will have a different significance for different people. It may be seen as the necessary preparation for sharing, a sign of the violent cost of our salvation, or the completeness of Christ's self-offering and the complete self-offering to which we are called.' Corresponding is the 'lifting up' of the cup: 'elevation' is not used, since there is no hint of adoration of the consecrated elements. This is appropriate even when there are individual glasses, 'as it links what is happening to the account of the Lord's Supper'.

The first pattern begins with words of invitation in two forms, both aware of those who come weary of sin and doubt, conscious of weakness, seeking to renounce sin. In the Supper, as we recall his death, we meet the risen Christ. The Supper 'is for those who know him a little and long to know him more', a phrase which echoes a passage in Michael Ramsey's *Sacred and Secular* (1965). The preparation suggests a prayer of confession without supplying a form, and gives opportunity for the reception of new members and news. Words from the Gospels precede the institution narrative which is either from 1 Corinthians or Matthew. The thanksgiving is extempore, but guidance is given earlier as to what it should include:

> The Prayer of Thanksgiving centres on those mighty acts of God whereby our redemption was accomplished. It is a recalling of the Passion when our Lord was lifted up in suffering and glory and a looking forward in hope to the final victory of love. It is a thanksgiving for the bread and wine which are symbols of the grace of our Lord Jesus Christ. The prayer calls upon the Holy Spirit, that by his presence in their hearts the people may enter into the meaning of the bread and wine, draw near to the risen Christ, and receive him afresh. It concludes with a fitting response of love, gratitude, and reconsecration.

There is then the breaking of the bread and the sharing of the wine which are distributed by the deacons, who are served after the people. The words of Jesus 'This is my body . . .' are said when all have received. Similarly after the distribution of the wine, 'This cup is the new covenant in my blood . . .'. The Lord's Prayer is said and various prayers may end the service.

The second pattern begins with the Prayer Book words, modernised, 'If you truly and earnestly repent of your sins', followed by the invitation, two forms of which begin with Hunter's words which some find questionable, 'Come to this table, not because you must, but because you may.' There is stress on coming in weakness, while the third option concludes, 'Consecrate yourselves afresh to God and pray for strength to do and bear his holy will.' There is then provision for a passage from Scripture and some Gospel words. The preparation begins with the Collect for Purity or the 1975 Methodist version of the Prayer of Humble Access. There is then the Peace, prefaced by the words from the *Didache* about the bread scattered over the hills. The words of institution are read from 1 Corinthians and, though the thanksgiving may be extempore, two forms are given, the first rehearsing the events and gifts of the Gospel with a prayer for the Holy

Spirit, the second, the *Sursum Corda*, followed by extempore or open prayer and concluding with the *Sanctus*. The bread is lifted and broken with the words of Jesus. It is distributed either with 1 Corinthians 10:16, 17 or 'Take this in remembrance that Christ died for you and feed on him in your heart by faith with thanksgiving.' The cup is raised in full view of the congregation to the words either of Psalm 116:12–14, or 1 Corinthians 11:25, or 'Drink this and remember that Christ's blood was shed for you and be thankful.' After communion there are alternative words of acclamation from the Roman source or the thanksgiving and oblation from the ASB or the prayer from Rite A, 'Father we give you thanks and praise that when we were still far off you met us in your Son and brought us home', or a prayer composed for the purpose. There are final words of commissioning, dismissal and blessing, the alternative from Romans 1:9–17.

The third pattern is more informal and participatory. The thanksgiving may be composed of one-sentence prayers from members of the congregation, but these must be for God's mighty acts in Christ. The bread is given to the servers, and the congregation serve one another with the words 'This is the body of Christ broken for you.' A modern version of the Lord's Prayer may be said and the wine is served in a similar way to the bread with the words 'This is Christ's blood shed for you.' The words as bread and wine are distributed are very direct and realistic. Songs or choruses may be sung at various points in the service and there is a final emphasis on the fellowship of believers; there is no speedy dismissal as became for a while the fashion and still is in some rites, but the Peace, after communion it should be noted, the reception of new members, the sharing of news, and prayers of healing and intercession, together with words of testimony and encouragement. Communion is not the consummation of worship but the high point from which there is descent to the concerns of Christians who have received Christ. The final hymn is of triumph; the Grace is shared.

Hymnody is as important for Baptists as for other Churches who overcame initial Puritan reluctance, and *Baptist Praise and Worship* was issued in 1991. With *Patterns and Prayers for Christian Worship* it succeeds the *Baptist Hymnal* of 1962. In many respects it is very ecumenical with charismatic choruses as well as traditional hymns and material from Taizé and the Iona Community. It is in liturgical form with sections on: the call to worship; proclaiming the Gospel (which includes the Christian Year); celebrating the Gospel (including the Sacrament); and living the Gospel. There are hymns in Welsh, which especially through William Williams (Pantycelyn) and Ann Griffiths made a notable contribution. There is greater awareness of the brokenness of human life and the warring state of the world than in 1962 and a return to more inward and spiritual religion (cf. Paul Ballard in *Studia Liturgica* 1993).

The United Reformed Church

The Congregationalists travelled a long way liturgically from the late 1930s and the liberal memorialism of *A Manual for Ministers* to their 1970 *An Order for Public Worship.* The story is told in detail in Brian D. Spinks *Freedom or Order?* (1982). The work of the Genevan school represented by *A Book of Public Worship* (1948) is reinforced by the liturgical movement, ecumenical co-operation and the burgeoning of liturgical scholarship. The name of J. M. Todd is enshrined in liturgical history, but he had colleagues, not least the Revd Stuart Gibbons, who had studied under E. C. Ratcliff. *An Order for Public Worship* is remarkably Catholic. Three of the anaphoras end with the *Sanctus,* which Ratcliff thought was the original ending of the *Apostolic Tradition* of Hippolytus. The most interesting of the prayers is VI, which was the work of Gibbons redrafted in part from his original. This lacked an epiclesis. Gibbons argued that this was not required because in the New Testament the Holy Spirit is poured out on people not things and an epiclesis obscures the truth that the elements are consecrated by thanksgiving for the sacrifice of Christ which they symbolise. An epiclesis on the congregation suggests that the Holy Spirit has not been active already in the worship and the Eucharistic Prayer. Gibbons's original prayer like Prayer VI in the Order is largely made up of scriptural texts, but it is redolent of the sacrifice of Christ. The words of institution are in the prayer because they are Christ's offering of himself. The cup of the new covenant, especially, establishes his impending death as a sacrifice, which is not only the expression of his own obedience but the means whereby Christians participate in the new covenant foretold by Jeremiah, enter into Christ's death and his obedience. The prayer ends in heaven as Ratcliff thought a Eucharistic prayer should.

Service books are rarely found in the hands of Congregationalists and the worshippers and even the deacons have often been more knowledgeable about the method of distribution than about the order and text of the liturgy. Also, Oxford University Press delayed the publication of the Order and it had little time to become known before the birth of the United Reformed Church in 1972. The union of the Congregationalists and English Presbyterians demanded a new service book. Some ministers were even unaware of the Order's existence.

Meanwhile in 1967, Caryl Micklem had edited *Contemporary Prayers for Public Worship*, the work of a group of younger ministers. There was a desire to escape from the traditional language of liturgy and also a 1960s questioning of the image of God which this language, often of supplication and subservience, implied. There were six Eucharistic Prayers, three of which ended with the *Sanctus*. The prayers were a brave attempt to interpret the traditional elements of the anaphora in terms compatible with modern understanding. They may have lost some of the original meaning in the effort, with the epiclesis reduced to a thanksgiving that the Holy Spirit has part in the action, and the anamnesis to a remembrance of the work of Christ, rather than a making present. There were other unpublished local rites devised by ministers, each of which has some valuable insights (Spinks, 1982, pp. 225–31).

The United Reformed Church issued *A Book of Order for Worship* in 1974. It was the fruit of considerable co-operation between the two separated denominations and their ecumenical involvement, particularly in the Joint Liturgical Group. J. M. Todd acknowledged that it followed closely the Group's *Initiation and Eucharist* in the structure of the Eucharist (he had a great share in both productions). The group's advice was sought, particularly that of the Anglican Dr Jasper and the Baptists Winward and Clark.

There is a very full account of the 1974 and 1980 liturgies in Bryan D. Spinks's *Freedom or Order?* The services are printed in both the 'you' and 'thou' forms as in the experimental Methodist Sunday Service of 1968. The contemporary form used the ICET texts for the ecumenically common prayers, though there was some unhappiness with the attachment of 'Lord' to the 'Holy, Holy, Holy' of Scripture.

The United Reformed Church has a very clear doctrine of eucharistic sacrifice and presence. In the two anaphoras of *A Book of Order for Worship,* the one in the traditional 'thou' form, the other in the 'you', 'we celebrate his perfect sacrifice on the Cross', the word 'celebrate', with its precedent in Cyprian, avoids the dangers of 'offer'. The Anglican Series Three was an influence here. *Perfect* sacrifice is preferred to *eternal* sacrifice of the Scottish *Book of Common Order,* as more accurate and more defensible. The perfect sacrifice has eternal significance, but to describe it by that epithet may be ambiguous. In the first prayer the bread and wine are 'set before' God as 'the thank-offering of [his] people'. It is in fact an ellipsis for 'to offer the bread and the cup' as in Hippolytus, which caused such dispute in the Church of England. This is omitted in the modern prayer, where we 'eat and drink at [Christ's] command'. Todd insisted that in both 'we are expressing our share in that sacrificial action by which we are united to Christ in his perfect self-offering to the Father'. In both prayers the epiclesis, following the anamnesis, is to make the gifts the body and blood of Christ, although the traditional prayer specifically asks for the Spirit to sanctify 'both us and these thy gifts'. After this, God is asked to 'accept our sacrifice of praise', which includes the recalling of Christ's once-for-all sacrifice and our setting apart of bread and wine.

The 1974 Eucharist was incorporated in 1980 into *A Book of Services.* The Eucharist is presented as the normal pattern of Sunday worship. The modern rite is included with a few variations, together with the JLG anaphora and the prayer from a Dutch Roman Catholic source as we have mentioned. The 1974 service is the first joint compilation of English

Congregationalists and Presbyterians since the *Westminster Directory* of 1645.

The Congregationalists made a signal contribution to hymnody in the mid-twentieth century, through the writings of the Cambridge historian Bernard Lord Manning, in the 1930s and especially the immense work of the late Dr Erik Routley. In 1951 *Congregational Praise* was published. A supplement, *New Church Praise,* which included a revision of the 1974 modern eucharistic rite, appeared in 1975. There was a new hymnbook *Rejoice and Sing* in 1991. This recognises the fact that neither Congregationalists nor English Presbyterians were used to prayer books in the pews and has a first section of congregational responses and the common texts of the Eucharist such as the *Gloria,* the *Sursum Corda* and the *Sanctus.* The language is inclusive where possible, though there is no thorough rewriting. The hymns begin with the Trinity and end with the Beatific Vision. The eucharistic section is richer and the Churches of Christ tradition is acknowledged. There are different ways of saying and singing canticles and psalms. Timothy Dudley-Smith's hymn 'Tell out my soul the greatness of the Lord' is included as a version of the *Magnificat.*

The Churches or Disciples of Christ broke away from Presbyterianism in the U. S. A. in 1827. The Lord's Supper is central to their life and they practise blievers' baptism. Many congregations in Britain are now one with the United Reformed Church, though some remain independent. These are members of the Joint Litugical Goup.

The Methodist Church

The movement towards liturgical concern in the Methodist Church began when, after World War II, the design of churches placed the holy table as central, flanked by pulpit and lectern. It is not clear that there was a theology behind this. It might have been simply out of a desire to make the buildings look more like what churches were supposed to be. Dr Vincent Taylor's *Jesus and his Sacrifice* (1937) had shown the significance of the Supper in the ministry of Jesus and the book was widely welcomed in all the Churches by those anxious to revive eucharistic worship, not least the Anglo-Catholics, though Taylor himself was no sacramentalist. Methodists became much exercised about worship after an attack on its Methodist 'slovenliness' had been made at the Conference of 1957. The result was a Conference committee and a report which examined the history and character of Christian worship, emphasising its corporate nature, 'belonging to one another' and to the whole company of heaven. Orders were suggested which embodied the essential elements of adoration, confession, proclamation and hearing of the Gospel, affirmation of faith, thanksgiving and dedication. There was a judicious section on children's worship, limited by the custom of parallel Sunday School and the children remaining for part of the service except when it was deliberately family worship. The relation of children to Holy Communion was not then on the agenda. As we have seen, the Roman Catholics have had Children's Masses and the Church of Scotland has now an order for when children communicate. The question of baptised children receiving the Sacrament was not to the fore as it has become since, witness the World Council of Churches, 1982 Lima Report, *Baptism, Eucharist and Ministry*. The keeping of the Christian Year is recommended and the choice of appropriate hymns which are suited to the various points of the liturgy (a word which the Report does not use). Weekly Communion is not practicable in Methodism, but people must be helped to see that there is 'some correspondence between what is done on Communion Sundays and what is done on other Sundays'. Some of the prayers from the service of Holy Communion might be introduced into the Order for non-Communion Sundays the Report outlines. There is the implication that Communion is not an after-meeting as had been the custom in many Churches, but the principal service of the Sundays when it was appointed. The Report ends with practical suggestions.

A few years later, the Faith and Order Committee set about the task of revising the 1936 *Book of Offices* which resulted in the *Methodist Service Book* of 1975. The guiding spirit in this was the Revd A. Raymond George, the doyen of Methodist liturgists. The book is based on the principle that the Eucharist, Word and Sacrament, is the norm of Christian worship, and the order of service prescribed when there is no

Sacrament resembles a 'dry Mass', though that is not a term many Methodists would find it natural to use! The outline is preparation, Word, response, the last including thanksgiving (a Eucharistic Prayer without reference to the Supper), dedication and intercession. The Eucharist follows Dix's four-action shape. The Lord's Prayer follows the inter-cessions in the ministry of the Word (a suggestion of J. M. Todd in the Joint Liturgical Group), and the Nicene Creed follows the Peace before the Offertory in the Lord's Supper, on the grounds that most Methodists were no longer used to reciting the creeds in their services of the Word. It has seemed an unnecessary rehearsal of the Preface of the Eucharistic Prayer. The service has the confession and absolution after the Collect for Purity, the collect for the day before the *Gloria* and provides for three lessons to be followed by the sermon and intercessions. A modern version of the Prayer of Humble Access follows the breaking of the bread before communion. There is but one anaphora of the classic pattern. The prayer is independent of Anglican revisions, though Dr Jasper attended the finalising sessions of the Faith and Order Committee. There is not the emphasis on the sacrifice of Christ that we have observed in the Congregationalist and United Reformed Eucharists, this in spite of the Wesley *Hymns on the Lord's Supper.* The Father is asked to 'accept our sacrifice of praise and thanksgiving'. The epiclesis asks that 'by the power of the Holy Spirit we who receive your gifts of bread and wine may share in the body and blood of Christ'.

The service has been widely accepted. There has been an increase in the number of Communion services in Methodism and the whole service is used without a break in many villages as well as in town and suburban churches. It does mean that 'Communion is no longer seen as the privilege of members'. The belief that Methodism practises the 'open table' is quite unhistorical; in the early days of Methodism some ticket of admission was required, usually a class ticket, as an indication of a genuine desire to 'flee from the wrath to come'. True, Wesley maintained that the Sacrament was a 'converting' as well as a 'confirming' ordinance. 'He meant that it was a means of grace to those who were seeking salvation but had not yet felt that they had received an assurance of it, as well as to those who had.' (They were rather in his state before, as a conscientious Church of England clergyman, his heart was 'strangely warmed' in Aldersgate Street in May 1738 (George in Westerfield-Tucker, ed., pp. 31–52).

In 1968, there was a supplement to the 1933 Methodist Hymnbook, *Hymns and Songs*. In 1983 there was published *Hymns and Psalms: A Methodist and Ecumenical Hymn Book*. It was hoped that this would serve more than the Methodist Church, particularly the United Reformed Church, whose representatives shared in its compilation, which accounts for some of its features – more metrical psalms and the relegation of 'O for a thousand tongues to sing' from No. 1 to No. 744. For the first time in Methodist history there is no hint of the order and spirituality of the 1780 collection. Its main sections are: God's Nature; God's World; God's People. The table of contents owes something to suggestions of Dr Erik Routley in the 1970s. It did not succeed in its ecumenical purpose and, as we have mentioned, the URCs produced their own book. *Hymns and Psalms* is much richer in hymns for the Eucharist and hymns of social justice than its predecessors. It is also stronger in Wesley scholarship, though it has fewer Wesley hymns. It does not include many popular modern songs or choruses, which means that in many churches it is supplemented by other, non-Methodist collections such as *Mission Praise* which may be more likely to be taken on church weekends or student retreats.

No more than the ASB was the 1975 *Service Book* expected to last for many decades in a period of change and development. There will be a new book before long. Its experimental rites offer Eucharists for the different seasons of the Christian Year: Advent, Christmas and Epiphany, Lent and Passiontide, Easter, including Ascensiontide, and Pentecost, with three services for ordinary seasons. This is all very different from the austere economy of 1975 with its one anaphora.

Initiation

This has occupied much serious thought and not a little argument since the 1950s. There was a strong movement in the Church of England against indiscriminate baptism and a refusal by some clergy to baptise children whose parents would not comply with demands to attend church regularly and fulfil the responsibilities the service implied. The role of parents was stressed and that of godparents somewhat diminished. The latter had often become a nominal recognition of best friends rather than the prescribed religious responsibility.

There was also, in a less Christian society with fewer infant baptisms, a questioning of this custom outside the Baptist Church. This increased with the growth of evangelicalism and the insistence on personal faith and testimony. Congregationalists and Methodists had from the 1940s advocated infant baptism in the powerful words of Bernard Lord Manning:

> Baptism is not dedication. In baptism the main thing is not what men do, but what God has done. It is a sign that Christ claims all men as his own and that he has redeemed them to a new way of life. That is why we baptise children. We do not baptise them because we or they have faith . . . We do not baptise them in order to make them children of God . . . We baptise children because they are already God's. They are not outside his Kingdom until it occurs to them to enter it, or until it occurs to us to push them into it. The water of baptism declares that they are already entitled to all God's mercies to men in the passion of Christ . . . Christ redeemed us on the first Good Friday without any thought or action on our part. It is right therefore, that, as he acted in the first instance, without waiting for any sign of faith from us, so baptism, the sign of the benefits of his kingdom should come to us without waiting for any faith or desire on our part. Every time we baptise a child, we declare to the whole world in the most solemn manner that God does for us what he does without our merits and even without our knowledge. In baptism, perhaps more plainly than anywhere else, God commends his love towards us in that *while we were yet sinners* Christ died for us. (Manning, pp. 47–8; cf. Flemington, p. 137)

Alexander Schmemann, the Russian Orthodox liturgist, has said very much the same thing, in pointing out that the Western debate on infant versus adult baptism is alien to the Orthodox Church because faith in baptism is not personal faith but Christ's. Personal faith, itself a gift of God, may bring us or make us bring our children to the font but baptism 'depends totally and exclusively on Christ's faith; is the very gift of his faith, his true *grace*: "As many of you as have been baptised into Christ have put on Christ" says St Paul (Galatians 3:27); but what does it mean to "put on Christ" if not that in baptism we receive his life as our life and thus his faith, his love, his desire as the very "content" of our life?' (Schmemann, 1976, pp. 67f.). Nothing was more prominent in the reports of the Methodist Faith and Order Committee in the decades after World War II than the reiteration of the validity of infant baptism and its gospel authenticity. But by 1985 Methodists were recognising that they needed to provide for infant dedication and to recognise that there were those among them who could not conscientiously accept infant baptism. Some indeed expressed bitter resentment that their parents had foisted this upon them when they themselves could not consent to it or know what was going on. Such objectors seem to forget that a great deal has to be done for a child before full consciousness and understanding and that it is in those months and early years that what is done and the love shown or withheld may form a person's whole life and character.

There has been further confusion. Baptism has come to be regarded as a rite of passage. Confirmation marks another stage, entry upon adolescence. Natural theology has taken over. The thought of baptism as death, burial with Christ as in Romans 6, has been ignored by those rejoicing in the gift of a child and anxious to celebrate human life and to praise God in creation. Gordon Rupp never tired of pointing out the 'upside down' language of the Prayer Book rite: 'You began as a Christian not with baby-talk, but with the thought of death and dying – you were baptised into the death of Christ and you rose again to new life. You began old – that quaint stuff about the "old Adam" beginning to die in you' (Rupp, 1978, p. 15). The 'old Adam' may no longer be in the liturgies but in some of them, as the Joint Liturgical Group's *Initiation and Eucharist* emphasises and as the new series of the 1994 Scottish *Book of Common Order* says, 'the image of burial with Christ in the water of baptism is given a heightened place'.

There is also the insistence that baptism must be no longer a 'hole and corner affair', a private family ceremony on

Sunday afternoons or at home, but during Sunday worship with the recipient, child or adult, received 'into the congregation of Christ's flock'. The baptised baby will often be carried down the aisle and shown to the people.

The Roman Catholic rite of 1969 for the baptism of infants shows some reordering. The child is named and the parents are briefly admonished as to their duties, as are the godparents. There is then a welcome and signing with the cross by priest, parents and godparents. The child or children may then be removed to a separate place during the liturgy of the Word, which consists of suitable New Testament passages, a homily and intercessions with invocation of the saints during which if the children have been taken out they are brought back. The exorcism is in the form of a prayer followed by the pre-baptismal anointing. The baptismal party then goes to the font for, first, the blessing of the water, which, like all such prayers, includes those biblical references to water most relevant to Christian baptism – the flood, the crossing of the Red Sea, Jesus's baptism in Jordan and the emission of water and blood from his side. The Father and the Son are asked to send the Holy Spirit upon the water of the font, that 'all who are buried with Christ in the death of baptism' may 'rise also with him to newness of life'. There are two other forms of blessing, with more emphasis on new birth in Christ. There follows renunciation of sin and profession of faith, again with options. The actual baptism is by immersion or pouring three times in the name of the Father, the Son and the Holy Spirit. There is anointing with chrism, the clothing in a white garment which should be provided by the parents, the giving of the candle, the opening of the ears (effeta, *ephphathe*) and the conclusion with the saying of the Lord's Prayer and one of many blessings. The service may include songs at various points. A distinctive feature is the number of alternatives.

The new rites nearly all include some blessing of the water. The Methodist rite of 1975 and the Church of England of 1980 also provide for the sign of the cross and the giving of a candle. Exorcisms and anointing have gone. *The Book of Common Order* of 1994 has this declaration immediately before baptism:

N . . .
for you Jesus Christ came into the world:
for you he lived and showed God's love;
for you he suffered the darkness of Calvary
and cried at the last 'It is accomplished'
for you he triumphed over death
and rose in newness of life;
for you he ascended to reign at God's right hand.
All this he did for you, N.,
though you do not know it yet.
And so the word of Scripture is fulfilled
'We love because God loved us first'.

It has also a promise to the parents that there will always be a place and a home for the child in the Church:

Tell *her* of *her* baptism
and unfold to *her* the treasure
she has been given today.

The parents themselves must promise to bring up the child in the faith and duties and the life and worship of the Church. There is a fine prayer for the child in her home and a prayer for the congregation that they may all be touched again with the grace of baptism. There is also a prayer of joy in the communion of saints remembering those who have passed through the waters of death into life eternal and asking that 'we may follow them expectantly and faithfully in the strength of our baptism'.

There is an insistence in the Churches today that in baptism liturgy and spirituality be united and that the whole of our Christian life be seen as an 'improvement' of our baptism, in the Puritan phrase. Alexander Schmemann from the Russian Orthodox Church disliked the term 'spirituality', which smacks of techniques, and preferred 'the Christian life'. 'This stems from Baptism, in the death in Christ of the old man, in the rising again in Christ of the new life, in the gift of the Holy Spirit which makes us "kings, priests, and prophets", in the participation in the hidden, yet real, life of "the eighth day", the day without evening of the kingdom' (Schmemann, 1976, pp. 108, 129).

Confirmation is still practised and the Methodist Church adopted it in its 1975 *Service Book* as an addition to the 'Public Reception into Full Membership'. There is a general understanding that baptism makes church members, or more exactly, incorporates those who receive it into Christ. There was a long battle in the Church of England culminating in the early 1950s with the publication of G. W. H. Lampe's *The Seal of the Spirit* which contested the view of Mason, Dix and Ratcliff, that Confirmation, a rite to complete water baptism, was the greater sacrament. For whereas the Holy Spirit in baptism conveyed exorcism, pardon and new life in Christ, the Spirit in Confirmation, a rite reserved for the bishop, empowered for holiness. Lampe's arguments prevailed on the whole and, as a result, there has been – and not only in the Church of England – a belief that baptism admits to communion and there is no need to wait on another rite for this; but many are uneasy about children communicating without understanding, even though for the most mature Christians, the mystery remains. Is not another rite necessary to renew the gifts of the Spirit, that those who have been baptised may be joined in the solemn union of the other sacrament and empowered to live their lives as members of Christ? Whatever view is held, or policy adopted, Confirmation is for those baptised as infants, making their own the faith professed on their behalf at baptism and, for adults, a public renewal of vows and a prayer for the continuous working of the Spirit in sanctification. Roman and Anglican and Methodist services all pray for the sevenfold gifts of the Spirit of Isaiah 11. The Church of Scotland rite does not. It welcomes candidates to the Lord's table and to the full privileges of church membership, praying for an increase of the Holy Spirit.

CHAPTER 10

CRITIQUE AND NEW DIRECTIONS

The revisions of the revisions are partly in response to criticisms, partly to meet ever new development and understanding. The extensive work of revision was done, for instance, before the feminist clamour for inclusive language, which, among other documents, resulted in the Anglican *Making Women Visible* and the Methodist 'Inclusive Language and Imagery about God' (1992). Such reports are too cautious for more extreme feminists, as they are reluctant to use the feminine pronouns for God or add 'Mother' to 'Father' in liturgical address – although one of the experimental Methodist anaphoras does so – but the reports realise that it is no longer possible to use 'man' for both male and female, for humanity, as of old. The classics are no longer widely known. Greek, for instance, had two words, one for the male, the other for the human race. In English, 'man' can no longer be used with one or other meaning at the back of one's mind. The status of women as more than wives and mothers, and of equal professional standing with men, and sometimes of greater ability, is, of course, the decisive factor although adverse discrimination is not banished from society.

We have already noted criticisms of Dix's four-action shape as artificial. Some think that 'He took' cannot bear the weight of offertory, although Kilpatrick maintains that it is 'a term doubly justified, first because it establishes the beginning of the sacrificial action, and secondly because it locates this beginning at the end of the transition from the profane to the sacred' (Kilpatrick, p. 85).

There may be confusion here between presenting gifts, taking them and offering. What is offered, and when? Bread and wine, Christ himself, his body and blood, our praise and thanksgiving, ourselves? And what of other gifts besides bread and wine, money and produce of the earth? From Justin Martyr there has been a collection of money for the poor, but this is not the matter of the Sacrament. Only bread and wine are that, and some would say only unleavened bread and fermented wine, while there is the question as to whether bread and wine should be used in cultures where they are not staple. More of that below. And all this fails to reckon with the Orthodox 'Great Entrance' and the awesomeness of the Offertory in relation to the incarnation and Passion.

'He broke' was simply necessary to share bread, and the Joint Liturgical Group endorsed the view of the late Dr Angus Higgins that fraction was not an important symbolic action at the Last Supper, although, removed from the Eucharistic Prayer, it has become very prominent in modern celebrations where it is done in the sight of the people with the crack of the wafer, if such be used, and the words:

We break this bread
To share in the body of Christ

And the response:

Though we are many, we are one body,
because we all share in one bread.

This is not likely to be changed.

G. D. Kilpatrick, like Stuart Gibbons, the Congregationalist in the 1960s, thought that the epiclesis 'was an unfortunate development in the association of the Spirit with the Eucharist'. The Bible knows nothing of it; it conflicts with the biblical idea of sacrifice, where the consecration is not in the course of the sacrificial action but at its beginning; it tends to secularise the preceding parts of the Eucharistic Prayer and diminish their importance; it is not the best ground for interpreting eucharistic consecration which is the covenant. The Eastern Church is right in finding Western rites defective in omitting the Spirit, but this is best repaired by associating the Spirit with the work of creation and redemption and with the sacrifice of Christ, who 'through the eternal Spirit offered himself without spot to God' (Hebrews 9:14). Also Pentecost should be added to the saving acts. Kilpatrick introduces the text from Hebrews into his own Prayer of Thanksgiving, which also in recalling the institution makes it clear that its words are not consecratory. He also opposes the acclamation, 'Christ has died, Christ is risen, Christ will come again', an attempt to be ecumenical, which suggests, he maintains, that Christ is not with his Church during the Liturgy. It is an ill-judged imitation of the Orthodox and the Roman Catholics (Kilpatrick, pp. 92f., 111f.).

A further criticism is of 'liturgical fundamentalism', the tendency to regard the fourth century as a golden age of liturgy and to go back even earlier and take Hippolytus, supposedly as early as 215, as a model text. The former was the time of the post-Constantinian increase in congregations and the introduction of court ceremonial and pagan ideas, and the latter has to be reconstructed from translations into five languages, the Latin one dating from about 500CE. In any case, the service may represent the desires and convictions of its author rather than the practice of his Church. There is great uncertainty about the earliest Christian worship, as we have seen. This is not to deny the necessity of the historical quest, because Christianity is a historical religion, grounded upon past events from which it must not be separated and of which the true interpretation must ever be sought, though the result may be a plurality of traditions and understanding. Josef Jungmann rightly said, 'It is by studying the past that we can best learn how to shape the future' (Jungmann, 1960, p. 8). At the same time, liturgy, like theology, must be aware of contemporary situations, developments and needs. We do not live in the fourth century, nor the first, nor at the time of the Reformation, nor in the years immediately after World War II, nor in the 1960s. Liturgical work must be carried on in a perpetual tension between the past and the present, our inheritance and the need of its cash – or credit card – value in the world in which we live (see Bradshaw in Stevenson, ed., pp. 134–45; cf. Kilpatrick, p. 81). This tension is seen in two fields: the anthropological and the cultural.

The new liturgies have recovered the Word, but may have become too reliant on the verbal, even though the verbosity of Reformation exhortations has gone. The abandonment of the Latin Mass for the vernacular was a great victory for intelligibility and communication 'understanded of the people'. But a whole dimension of non-verbal communication and of symbolic power was lost. Music in worship may have something of the effect of the non-verbal. Some find that the settings of John Tavener, so much influenced by Orthodoxy, heighten worship because the words are not always clear; the sound has priority. And there is credibility in the complaints of the literary, many of them agnostics, that modern English is inelegant and 'candy-floss', unworthy of the transcendent. Some uneducated, almost illiterate people have a gut feeling which is similar. It is middle-class semi-intellectuals who lust for intelligibility. Others crave for the numinous, even if the term would be strange to them, and it has been maintained by J. G. Davies in *Everyday God* that this is not compatible with an incarnational religion. Liturgy may be over-symbolised and it was in the post-Tridentine rite, to say nothing of the Middle Ages. Again it is a question of balance.

We must not ignore those large congregations whose worship is still primarily of the Word. The worship may consist of modern music and hymnody. It is not eucharistic but its centre is an exposition of Scripture, not controlled by the clock, delivered by a master, such as John Stott. If some Christians reduce the Word to short readings and brief homilies and thereby believe that they exalt the Sacrament, others are able to listen enthralled for a long time to preaching from the Bible. This makes Christ real to them and they are not concerned with liturgy.

Victor Turner, the social anthropologist, has been considered to be ignorant of sacramental theology and liturgical history, and he writes in the jargon of his subject. Yet he has unearthed serious weaknesses in Vatican II's *Constitution on the Liturgy.* He has claimed that it was influenced by two obsolescent theories – structural-formalism and behaviourism. The first holds that the shape of the liturgy reflects that of society and must always seek to be 'relevant' to the current social trends and fashions. This robs it of its power to change them, though it may be forever changing itself. The second rests on belief in 'conditioning'! Authority may impose its own beliefs, and control the faithful to respond to what it deems good for them. This ignores folk-religion (it may need to correct, if not oppose, it in the interests of Christian truth but must understand where people are) and does not realise the need for the archaic and the liminal. It needs to pass over the threshold of consciousness, to enter the depths of being which entertain the primordial, the mysterious, inexpressible source, which the language of tradition, not always intelligible, though not simply nostalgic or archaic, enables us somehow to reach (Stevenson, ed., *passim*).

There is, however, the whole matter covered by the ugly word 'inculturation'. We have already noted the criticisms of the Church of South India liturgy that it is too much a colonialist imposition despite its good intentions and that even when it seeks to be Indian it may be Brahmanist and far from the needs of the low caste and poor. What it is easy to forget is that inculturation has taken place from the beginnings of Christianity. 'The notion of absolute and general fixity in the whole range of liturgical phenomena during even the period of the Counter-Reformation is valid only in terms of official curial policy. For the living Church, whether in Europe or elsewhere, it is more fable than fact.' In one sense 'inculturation is nothing other than the continuation of God's own humble incarnation in our midst by Word, faith and sacrament' (Kavanagh in *Studia Liturgica*, 1990, pp. 96, 104).

As we have said, 'relevance' is not the sole criterion of liturgy, and although Christianity must seek integration within very different cultures, 'it needs too', in the words of Adrian Hastings, 'to retain in each a dimension of strangeness.' Yet this may not be secured by authoritatively imposing a liturgy which in many respects is the product of Western culture on the Southern hemisphere, which, like the Far East, will increasingly dominate Christianity in the future. This raises again the simple matter of the eucharistic elements. 'To insist upon a wheat 'eucharist' in a rice society is a great deformation of the 'eucharist's' essential meaning, while a rice eucharist which may seem odd to the European onlooker and invalid to the Roman canonist, is in point of fact the true and requisite translation of the old tradition in a culturally new context – as requisite a translation in a climate where wheat does not grow as was that of the words from Aramaic to Greek' (Hastings in *Studia Liturgica*, 1990, pp. 19–27).

There may be a two-way process here. Many Western Christians are taking to the forms of other cultures, witness 'liturgical dance', though not all of this is in the style of Africans dancing from a funeral, or lepers dancing to bring their financial offerings to God. The liveliness of Black worship has also infected many in the West, uninspired with the respectable sobriety of formal liturgy. There is a longing for life and freedom which is making the liturgical movement, in spite of the vast learning it has engendered, possibly a passing phase. One may be unhappy with many manifestations of the charismatic and of the Toronto blessing, which are not of themselves distinctively Christian and carry irrationalism to a dangerous extent, but awareness of other cultures in what, in some ways, is now one world, does have its effect on Western patterns, witness ethnic dress, and worship cannot be exempt, though the injunction of St Paul, disturbed by the charismatic movement in Corinth, may still be needed: 'Let all things be done decently and in order' (1 Corinthians 14:40).

We must take seriously the fact that we live in a 'post-modern' society, much as we may deplore some of its menacing concepts and excesses. But many of the values of 'modernism' and the Enlightenment are now at a discount – metaphysics, truth established by painstaking historical research, the attempt to establish the meaning of a text by study of its author and the situation in which it was written. Every argument and hypothesis is 'deconstructed' and we are to live in a welter of fragmentation and a babel of cacophonous voices. But this has led to a 'rebirth of religion' over against the secularism which, from Bonhoeffer until the 1970s, many Christian theologians were regarding as the condition in which the gospel must operate, if not as the authentic development of Christianity in the world of science and technology, a world come of age. We must learn to live *before* God in a world *without* God, said Bonhoeffer. The secular theologians revelled in the dictum of the early Barth, 'Religion is not salvation', and thought true Christianity might have its opportunity through its death. Religion, in fact, is very much alive, but is strongest in the fundamentalisms of the major faiths and has 'undergone displacement, migration and transformation' outside the Churches, in the New Age, for instance, which in Britain is widely dispersed to include wealthy management consultants and the much maligned 'travellers'. Professor Richard H. Roberts has cited the 'ritual event' of the now fallen Michael Jackson's Bucharest concert, globally broadcast, as 'a very important example of an eclectic post-modern functioning of quasi-religion . . . It was a carefully crafted ritual involving ecstasies and mass hysteria' (Roberts in Ford and Stamps, ed., *passim*). Ian Ramsey long ago saw the very much more restrained, less eclectic performances of the Beatles and other pop groups as for many people, particularly the young of those days, 'disclosure situations' of the beyond of our lives.

For the Church to try to baptise this into Christ may result in the dangers of the nine o'clock service at Sheffield. We must not be bemused by numbers but take to heart the lessons of Scripture that God's truth may often be the possession of the few, who nevertheless hold it in trust and use it on behalf of the many. Professor Roberts thinks that what is involved is a 'principled eclecticism', the mobilisation of all the resources which the Churches possess, the total inheritance. 'The Tradition as a whole in its variety offers enormous resources, symbolic, mythic, narrative, ethical, theological' (Ford and Stamps, ed., p. 195). This would suggest that liturgical scholarship is more necessary than ever, even though it may appear 'modern' rather than 'post-modern'. There will have to be pluralism, without any one strain being dominant to the suppression of others. The authority will not be an ultramontane institution, but the full, ecumenical, catholic gospel itself, the wholeness of Christ.

There are many who are concerned with 'Christian Worship and the Quest for Just Society', to quote the title of a paper by Susan J. White. This may mean the opposite of inculturation, for social justice is very much a concept of

Western Christianity. Liberation theology, which has won so much support from Latin American theologians, emanates from Germany and a somewhat selective reading of Scripture. To some extent it is imposed on countries whose populations number millions of Catholics whose faith is burgeoning and is 'anti-political, anti-intellectual, spontaneous, devotional, fervent, characterized by the cult of (often unofficial) saints, relics and shrines' (Paul Johnson cited by Kavanagh, p. 100). History shows that it is often this type of religion which survives when theologies which preach political involvement are long forgotten. But social justice is a corollary of the gospel and there is much to be learned from the 'base communities' of Latin American Christianity and the hope which the Eucharist brings of global transformation and cultural revolution. The Eucharist survives and becomes more full of meaning when so much else is questioned, as in the 1960s, or when many supporters are removed amid Latin American poverty and oppression, or as with the Orthodox liturgy in times of Islamic and Communist persecution. In Latin America the Mass has been an adjunct of dictatorship, but there is a belief and a longing that it may be freed from this and that 'if only we get the liturgy right . . . a just and humane society will follow almost inevitably' (Susan J. White).

Susan White, however, goes on to raise the questions of those Western theologians, both Christian and Jewish, who wonder if worship is possible after the Holocaust. She does not refer to a feeling among some men of letters, like Theodor Adorno, that to write poetry after Auschwitz is barbaric, or quote George Steiner. 'The world of Auschwitz lies outside speech as it lies outside reason.' She cites the Roman Catholic liturgist, David Power, who asks:

> Can we in truth celebrate the Eucharist after the Nazi holocaust and in the face of imminent nuclear holocaust, and in a world half-populated by refugees in the same way as we did before the occurrence of such horrors?

To this we may add Nicholas Lash's confession that he is 'almost tempted to say that in the shadow cast by the Holocaust, a shadow eclipsing God in the eclipse of relationship, the Christian *requires permission* from the Jew to sing the Easter "Alleluia" . . . The victors, the rich, the powerful, those who call the tune (whether individuals, classes, nations or alliances of nations) always require "permission" to sing the songs of Easter from the vanquished, the poor and the weak' (Lash, p. 211). In the end White would probably agree with Ulrich Simon in *The Theology of Auschwitz* that the only way we can come to terms with Auschwitz is liturgically. Only when we see it and all injustice and the crimes against humanity in the context of the crucifixion-resurrection of Christ do we find not only the hope which saves us from decline into total despair and bitterness which may add to destructiveness, but the courage to withstand the abuse of power which becomes increasingly more likely as technology advances. But such liturgy cannot be 'clap-happy', nor deny the tragic element in the gospel, as some liberationists, though not all, would seem to do, as well as some charismatics.

Modern liturgy is much concerned with its environment. There are those who think that church buildings are unnecessary and, worse, inimical to the understanding of Christ, who, as Chrysostom said, in words already quoted, 'purified the whole earth, and made every place suitable for prayer'. The whole earth finally became a temple. Buildings root the gospel very much in this world. They are expensive and prodigal of resources, the cause of quarrels and imprison the gospel, often confining liturgy to certain forms and, as sermons in stones, fixing particular ideas of God, who does not dwell in temples made with hands. They may lead to a splendour and display not easily reconcilable with Christ's humility and a service which may be manifest in a rather pompous liturgical presidency rather than in one who took the form of a slave. Alexander Schmemann has told how for many people forced to worship in cellars and garages with the bare necessities of liturgy in the first years of Russian emigration there was a fulness of liturgical experience they never found in churches of magnificence and grandiose design (Schmemann, 1975, pp. 92f.). Buildings are, moreover, temporary. Even though they may last for centuries there will come a day when not one stone will be left upon another, as Keble dared to assert when he chose that passage from the

Gospels as his text for the opening of his new church at Hursley. Yet buildings are witnesses to God-in-Christ, sacramentals and a home for God's people, as well as objects of devotion and love and, often, of creative beauty in a world in which many edifices are ugly in the interests of what is most ugly in human life. They are, above all, places of worship, giving space for the proclamation of the gospel, its expression in worship and for the communion, both corporately and privately, of souls with God.

'Space' is one of the key-words of modern liturgical architecture, giving opportunity for openness and movement even within the confining walls. The sense of space does not necessarily demand a large building. It probably means that pews should go. They originated as partitioned places in which attendants at Mass might find quiet for meditation without the distractions of these who might be engaged in secular activities until the elevation. They then became essential for listening to sermons, or going to sleep in the course of them. They were socially divisive, rented accommodation, and, as in theatres, people paid more for the best seats. They excluded those who had not paid for them, who were often ejected if they wandered into regular members' pews. They kept out the poor and the strangers, whom Scripture would always accommodate. And today when such restrictions have largely vanished they are immovable furniture, preventing drama or dance or, in some cases, processions. Altar rails are now out of fashion, originally intended to keep dogs from the altar; now they seem to resemble barriers to the unrestricted freedom of divine grace. They do, however, help the infirm to kneel. Altars, or holy tables, might well be square rather than oblong. They should be bare of all but what is needed for the Sacrament. The primitive westward position is almost universal, as it was in Reformed rites, though some, like the poet R. S. Thomas, have felt that the eucharistic mystery is best conveyed with the priest's back to the congregation as he leads them to the throne of God's grace.

If the congregation is not all the time regimented in rows, the fashion of the circle may symbolise exclusiveness. It may resemble a separated group which it is not easy to enter, though it must not be forgotten that the early Church was just that, tests of membership were severe, there must be no conformity to the world and worship soon became a mystery which only the initiated could share. But there is now a feeling, not universal, that, although a deep dedication is the ultimate requirement, all sorts and conditions of people should be welcomed and led into it and the church itself will be a mixed community of people at various stages of discipleship and the intensely devout perhaps leavened and humanised by those whose reasons for belonging are different and range from the need for friendship to the aesthetic.

W. H. Vanstone once wrote a short piece in which he said that modern worship with its warmth and friendliness, its 'transatlantic manners', Christian names and the rest, gives people a place and makes them feel at home as though they belonged, part of a society of friends. Older liturgies gave space. This people also need. They should find room for that which they cannot share, 'for the thought too private to be spoken or the feeling too obscure to be articuated; that they should feel free from the hidden pressure or manipulation of too marked attention, or too immediate involvement; that they should find their privacy left intact save only for what they themselves wish to disclose or choose to share' (Vanstone in Martin and Mullen, eds., pp. 143–8). It is surprising that Vanstone does not mention the need for contemplation, which many found in the old Latin Mass. But place and space are both necessary in worship, and liturgy should provide for them.

Posture will vary at different points in the service. Keble's church at Hursley in Hampshire has pews like prie-dieux suggesting that the main purpose of worship was to kneel in prayer. Standing is now the vogue in many places and this has ancient antecedents, though it may tire the older worshippers and be impossible for some of the handicapped, causing a rather painful distinction.

The completed cathedral at Portsmouth, due to the genius of David Stancliffe, is a symbol of Christian pilgrimage both in life and worship, with the large assembly place for penitence and preparation, proceeding to initiation around the font, which someone complained looks like a coffin, not realising that that is part of its meaning (Romans 6).

Christians must always be 'improving their baptism. This is Christian 'spirituality', the living out of 'the sacrament of the Spirit', which is baptism. There is then advance to the ministry of the Word which may be proclamatory and prophetic, or meditative, in both leading to prayer. And so to Eucharist, the table fellowship of thanksgiving, which re-presents Christ's once-for-all sacrifice and unites our sufferings and needs, and joys also, with the death from which comes life and victory.

Portsmouth Cathedral has at the extreme east end the pyx with the reserved Sacrament, housed in an arch which symbolises the ascent into heaven, the goal and consummation of the Christian life and of God's purpose in the universe. At the west end in the rafters is a place for private retreat.

Such an arrangement is only possible in large churches, although much could be done on a smaller scale. It is good to keep it in mind as a symbol of what should happen in worship. It teaches us that the Christian life has liturgical shape. This is the basis of the course in Christian ethics devised by Stanley Hauerwas at Duke University, North Carolina. Ethics is taught as worship. Christians are not only called to do 'the right thing' but expected to be holy, and holiness is living life to the praise of God through loving him and our neighbour. Hence the link between ethics and worship should be very strong.

The course is organised around the basic movements of the liturgy, the gathered Church, transcending all divisions of age, gender, nation, class or race, brought together by worship which takes them out of the world in the sense that they are called by Christ and see it from a different perspective and profess different values from those who are not of him, greeting one another in the name of the Trinity. The awareness of God leads, as it did with Isaiah in the Temple, to the confession of sin, and the course examines the nature of sin and shows that sin is a more determinative notion than injustice; it challenges the liberal preoccupation with injustice, as possibly evidenced in Susan White's lecture above, while it tolerates adultery and abortion. In some ways the course may be deemed reactionary: instead of liturgy being influenced by the concerns of humanity in our time, it is the other way on – behaviour is governed by worship, which is not something to be contrived in response to what one generation conceives as human needs and notions but is given and is the controlling factor of Christian life.

The centrality of Scripture and preaching raises the whole question of authority. Congregations are trained to stand under the Word of God. 'Moreover, that the Church is directed to preach on the same texts year after year challenges the modernist assumption characteristic of fundamentalism and historical criticism that the text of the Bible has *a* meaning.'

This leads to a discussion on the character necessary for ministers of the Word; this in turn involves a general consideration of Christian, in distinction to other, virtues and of the place of humility in the Christian life.

Christians respond to the Word in baptism, which introduces a discussion of the sacraments as those 'summary' acts which bind Christians to the life of Christ. Baptism raises the question of death in all its aspects – shades of the Portsmouth Cathedral font – not only suicide and abortion, but the death of the 'bachelor' in both sexes in marriage. Again the difference from 'the world' is obvious. Christian sex ethics cannot be abstracted from the age-old Christian practice of singleness and lifelong monogamous marriage, while abortion is prohibited because there can be no 'unwanted' child born among Christians.

The Eucharist is the summing up of all that God has done in Christ which brings worshippers to the 'great thanksgiving'. This gives an opportunity to discuss christological issues: the person of Christ and atonement. Theology must not be separated from worship. 'Sacrificial doctrines of the atonement too often result in the Eucharist being understood as a sacrifice God demands rather than God's sacrifice for the sake of the world in which we are graciously included.'

Capital punishment must be discussed eucharistically, not simply from a desire for retribution or humane sentiment. Human sacrifice has been ended for all times through Christ's cross. This is a crucial example of the Church's stake in limiting the power of the State to punish. The Eucharist also demands questions of economics – what does our sharing in Christ's body say about 'ownership'? – and the ethics of war. Dare we rise from Christ's table and go out to kill our fellow human beings? The burden of proof is on Christians who feel it right to participate in war as the lesser of evils, the cruel necessity for the defeat of oppression.

The 'sending out' raises the questions of Christian service of God in the world through a survey of Christian political history. The Church can never be a 'sect'. But service is through worship. There are lectures on the Church in the Third Reich and a challenge to the assumption that democracy is the most Christian form of government.

The course is limitless. Music and prayer and aesthetics should have a larger part in it. Both in the creation of beauty and in the growth of holiness, the Spirit anticipates the transfiguration of the cosmos (Hauerwas in Ford and Stamps, ed., pp. 35–47).

We ought to note developments in Orthodoxy particularly the work of Alexander Schmemann (1921–83). He was born in Estonia, but his parents emigrated to Paris where he was brought up and educated, not entirely in Russian émigré circles. He was formed by such authorities as Georges Florovsky from the Orthodox but also by Roman Catholics, especially Jean Daniélou and Louis Bouyer. In 1946, having taught in St Serge, he accepted a post at St Vladimir's seminary, New York where he remained until the end of his life.

Schmemann was much exercised by what he saw as the crisis of contemporary Orthodoxy. Liturgy and theology were estranged from one another and from real life. Theology had become a jargon-ridden preoccupation of professionals; liturgy was an act of worship for which people could escape to the sanctuary, 'a departure out of the world for a little while, as a "vent" or break in earthly existence' instead of being the whole life of the people of God, the joyous encounter with the Kingdom of God, the reign of Christ everywhere, even though, we may add, this does not evade the tragic element in his humiliation (Schmemann, 1966, p. 25). There is some parallel with Hauerwas here and his connection of ethics with worship, although Hauerwas is very Western in his categories of thought. Liturgy is not cult, nor is it a department of theology, a subject on the syllabus. It is the source of theology, something done to make possible and express the living relationship with the life, death, resurrection and glorification of Jesus Christ, his ascension to heaven and the descent of the Spirit. The foundation is in the *lex orandi*, the law of praying, 'the epiphany and experience of the Church of herself and her faith' (Grisbrooke in *Studia Liturgica*, 1993, p. 156). A possible danger here is that the critical vocation of the theologian may be disallowed and also the unity one sees in Pascal, which, according to T. S. Eliot, may be the highest stage of civilised human beings, of the profoundest scepticism with the deepest faith.

Schmemann's understanding of liturgical reform was in these terms, not of modernising the Church's worship. As well as welcoming the revival of Communion, long neglected, he saw three defects in its practice: the profusion of symbolism, as illustration not as manifestation of reality, the practice of secret prayers instead of listening to and sharing in the prayers of the liturgy, and the distinction between clergy and laity during communion. This distinction is necessary in the life of the Church for the clergy have a particular role in the ministry of the sacraments, while the laity are ordained into the ministry of Christ to the world, but 'the entire assembly, in the mutual submission of all ministries one to another, constitutes a single body for the realization of the priesthood of Jesus Christ' (Schmemann, 1988, pp. 243, 94f.).

But Schmemann, like Louis Bouyer, was saddened that in the Roman Church and elsewhere 'some fifty years of constructive work within the Liturgical Movement was swept away by a hasty acceptance of such principles as the famous "relevance", or "urgent needs of modern society" "the celebration of life" or "social justice" (*pace* Susan White). The result is a disintegration of liturgy and this in spite of some excellent ideas and a great deal of liturgical competence' (Grisbrooke, 1993, p. 147).

One of Schmemann's major contributions was his emphasis on eschatology as integral to liturgical theology. There is an inter-relationship between eschatology, the Eucharist and the Church. Schmemann deplored the Western emphasis on consecratory formulae which had invaded the

East, the heart of the Eucharist being seen as the recitation of the words of Christ and the invocation of the Holy Spirit on the elements. The Eucharist is 'the Sacrament of the Kingdom', a movement of ascent to the heavenly sanctuary and 'the table of Christ', and thereby a foretaste of the Kingdom which always is and is always coming to be. It is our weekly journey into heaven from which we return to live life in Christ in the world, destined for God's rule. Eschatology, 'the doctrine of the final destiny of the world and man', has been reduced to the doctrine of God 'as the Judge and Avenger' and to the question of one's personal fate after death. The whole newness, the uniqueness of the Christian *leitourgia* was in its eschatological nature as the presence here and now of the future *parousia*, as the epiphany of that which is to come, of 'the life of the world to come'. 'The sincere believer goes to Church "to touch other worlds"' (Dostoevsky).

> All he knows is that he has left his everyday life and has come where everything is *different* and yet so essential, so vital, so desirable, so vital that it illumines and gives meaning to his entire life. Likewise he knows, even if he cannot express it in words, that this *other* reality makes life worth living, for everything proceeds to it, everything is referred to it, everything is to be judged by it – by the kingdom of God it manifests. (Schmemann, 1987, pp. 42f., 47ff.)

CHAPTER 11

THE LITURGY OF TIME

The Daily Office

The origins of non-eucharistic worship in the Christian Church are difficult to recover. Gregory Dix thought that 'the sanctification of time' replaced the early dominance of eschatology after the Constantinian establishment when it was obvious that the Church would have to be part of continuing human history, and when in protest against worldliness Christians would retreat into the eremetic and, soon, the coenobitic (monastic community) life. C. W. Dugmore believed that from the first some Christians had worshipped in Jewish synagogues, as Jesus did, and when they were excluded maintained Jewish traditions of daily, weekly and yearly cycles with Jewish forms of prayer, christianised by the name of Jesus and the mighty acts of God continued in the gospel. The New Testament supports this, not only in the style of its prayers, but in its sense and details of time, though because of their belief in Jesus Christ, Christians may very soon have become a worshipping entity distinct from the Jews.

It is natural to suppose that the first Christians would want to worship God morning and evening, but also would be encouraged to pray at night, in obedience to the command to watch, and at cockcrow and at the times of the Lord's Passion. This would often be in private, but where possible Christians would come together. Fewer numbers than the Jews' ten males would constitute a quorum: 'Where two or three are gathered together in my name, there am I in the midst.' The accounts of the disciples persevering in prayer could imply fixed and regular times, while the eschatological emphasis of Christian prayer, supremely the Lord's Prayer, could well mean an awareness of time as they looked for the Lord's return praying towards the east, as did Qumran. The *Didache* 8:3 orders the Lord's Prayer to be said three times a day, which perhaps has foundation in the Gethsemane stories of Matthew and Mark in which Jesus comes to his disciples three times and finds them sleeping in spite of his command to 'watch and pray'. 'The observance of fixed times of prayer, far from being opposed to the expectation of an imminent *parousia,* was, on the contrary, the very expression of it' (Bradshaw, 1981, pp. 37ff.).

Paul Bradshaw has meticulously traced, with fine detail and judicious balance, the keeping of hours of prayer in the centres of the early Church. And although the evidence does not conclusively suggest that the times of prayer were kept corporately in the early Church, the individual's prayer was seen as part of the prayer of the whole Church. As Cyprian said, 'when one prays, he does not pray for himself alone . . . Our prayer is public and common; and when we pray, we pray not for one but for the whole people, because we the whole people are one' (Bradshaw, 1981, pp. 65f.). We may believe that Christians came together when they could apart from the eucharistic assembly, and once Constantine had established the peace of the Church, there was opportunity for regular meetings for daily prayers. This led to what modern scholars have called 'the Cathedral Office', a form which included psalmody, canticles such as the *Benedicite* and those in the New Testament, hymns and possibly, though these may have disappeared with the early charismatic movement, 'spiritual songs' (Colossians 3:16), readings from the Hebrew Scriptures and Christian writings and prayers, which, at first extempore, became written and collected. There may also have been preaching. These services would certainly have been said, or sung, morning and evening. These were obvious and convenient times; their observance came to be linked with the Jewish morning and evening sacrifices, seen as a Christian fulfilment. They were full of praise and thanksgiving, 'truly divine pleasures' said Eusebius, but also penitence, on the evidence of Chrysostom. Some Christians, the especially devout, would keep other hours. They may have engaged in devotions at the normal division of the Roman working day, the third, sixth and ninth hours (9.00, 12.00 and 15.00), which are mentioned in the Gospels.

A full account is given by Egeria travelling in Jerusalem at the end of the fourth century. Psalms were an essential part. A psalm might be sung by a cantor while the congregation meditated on it and responded with 'Alleluia', or, as a development, with a refrain consisting of a verse or part of a verse from the psalm itself. The other, less ancient method, was for the Psalter to be used as a hymnbook, the psalms sung in unison (Bradshaw, 1981, pp. 83f.).

The Cathedral Office was gradually supplanted by the worship of the monasteries. The monks had all the time there was to pray, although the Rule of St Benedict skilfully combined this with manual and, where there were the gifts, scholarly work. The principal differences from the Cathedral Office were in the keeping of 'hours' and in the use of the Psalter. Psalm 119:164 – 'Seven times a day do I praise thee' – seemed to enjoin seven daily offices, while in the same psalm, 'I remember thy name in the night O Lord' (v. 55) and other references to night prayer in the psalms demanded night prayer. Thus there arose the monastic offices of lauds, prime, terce, sext, none, vespers and compline with the night office variously known as vigils, nocturns, or mattins.

The Cathedral Office, like the synagogue services, had used the Psalter rather as a modern hymbook, selecting psalms appropriate for the occasion or time of day. Certain psalms were especially suitable for the morning, such as Psalm 63, while Psalms 148, 149 and 150 are in several sources known as 'morning hymns' and were retained as such in the Monastic Offices. Similarly Psalm 141 is an evening psalm and Psalms 15, 142, 132 and 130 are known as 'candlelight psalms'. Augustine once remarked that 'A love of Psalmody gave birth to monasticism'. The monasteries adopted a new policy, previously unknown, of reciting the whole Psalter in its biblical order over a number of offices and a course of time which might vary from a day to a week, or even one office. In a few places this reading or chanting was made really continuous by the use of a shift system, which meant that the saying of the psalms never ceased. By taking over the offices, the psalms prevented them having a single structure or theme.

It also meant that discipline mattered more than edification, the number of psalms said rather than their meaning for the Christian life. Worship became 'a prolonged ascetical effort' and an element of competition entered in. Who could say the most psalms, or pray the most prayers? Paul, a hermit of the Sketic desert, 'improvised the first known rosary by carrying with him 300 pebbles with which to reckon the 300 prayers which were his daily toil; but he lost heart when news reached him of a neighbouring virgin who accomplished seven hundred a day in spite of fasting five days a week', (Kirk, p. 191). In the Byzantine offices, there might be a mechanical repetition of prayers, 'Lord have mercy' repeated forty times (cf. Schmemann, 1975, p. 148).

Monasticism was originally a lay movement of protest in opposition to the institutional Church, although it has been maintained that it was pre-Christian and that two forms of Christian life are demanded by some of the ascetic teaching of Jesus (O 'Neill in Williams, ed., pp. 270–87). Be that as it may, the monasticism of Antony, Pachomius and Cassian did not remain in the wilderness as its essential milieu, and became an ecclesiastical institution itself, with monasteries in great cities. Monks were an elite, a sort of honours school of the Christian life. Monasticism represented the ideal both in East and West to which Christians in the world must somehow seek to approximate. Alexander Schmemann has said that monasticism meant the replacement of life by prayer. 'If in the first early Christian view every undertaking could become a prayer, a ministry creating of and bearing witness to the kingdom, in monasticism prayer itself now became the sole undertaking replacing all other tasks' (Schmemann, 1975, p. 107). Worship became a devotional rule and Communion 'an individual act related to the individual needs of the believer' (Schmemann, 1975, pp. 150f.). Hence in the West there arose and still prevails the unfortunate Pelagian expression 'making my communion', with a diminished conception of sharing with the Church in the celebration of the act which is greater than the making of the worlds. The Eucharist became inserted into the liturgy of time, the chief of the offices, not the anticipation of the Kingdom, which takes the Church out of time altogether into the *eschaton*, where time is no more, death is swallowed up in victory and we are all one in the divine love.

The history of the office in the West in the Middle Ages is complex and in places obscure. As with the Eucharist, Rome took over, although the Rule of St Benedict (530), with its offices capable of being compassed within a reasonable time and aware of the need not to impose burdens of devotion too great to be borne, is immensely important. If we summarise ten centuries in a few statements, the developments are these:

1. The 'Cathedral Office' was displaced by the monastic even in secular churches and the office increasingly confined to the clergy.

2. 'Collectories' became enlarged and came to include more than collects, indeed model offices. This was the origin of the breviary, the full Latin title of which has been translated by J. D. Crichton as 'A short conspectus or order for the offices of the whole year' (Jones, Wainwright, Yarnold, p. 379). They consisted of 200 to 300 folios and could not include lectionaries which would have made them impossible to handle. There was a time in the thirteenth century when the provision of Scripture was generous but by the time of the Reformation, Scripture was much reduced until the readings became short 'chapters' or sentences. The thirteenth-century office, which owed a good deal to the chapel of Innocent III (d. 1217) and his successors came to be known as 'Franciscan'. It had to be modified because of the Franciscan itinerancy. Offices could not always be said in choir and were often recited privately. This eventually resulted in shorter readings from Scripture, but the number of festivals not least those of the Blessed Virgin Mary (also the Office of the Dead) increased and these tended to replace the office of the day instead of being additions to it. Lessons from mythical and spurious lives of the saints were introduced and the simplicity of services based on psalmody and Scripture was lost.

3. There was much variety. The orders had their own offices and centres such as Milan or Lyons. In England, as with the Mass, there were the variations of Sarum, Hereford

and York, Lincoln and, in Wales, Bangor. The basic differences were not great, but the commemoration of local saints overlaid and sometimes ousted the ferial office.

4. The books required were numerous and confusing. As Cranmer wrote in the preface to the 1549 Prayer Book:

> Moreover the number and hardness of the rules called the Pie and the manifold changings of the service, was the cause, that to turn the Book only was so hard and intricate a matter, that many times there was more business to find out what should be read, than to read it when it was found out. [A criticism that could be made of some modern office books.]

There was not dissimilar dissatisfaction in the Roman Church itself and the Spanish Cardinal Quinones provided a reformed and simplified breviary, though he had in mind private use by individual clerics rather than corporate worship. He kept the hours, though combined mattins and lauds, and the weekly recitation of the psalter, though with three psalms only for each office. It meant that the office consisted mostly of psalms and Scripture. The whole of the New Testament was to be read in the course of the year.

Quinones' reforms had papal support and were welcomed for a time but did not survive the Council of Trent. The lack of provision for congregational and choral use was an undoubted deficiency. They did influence the *Book of Common Prayer.* The offices of the two books of 1549 and 1552 were the result of long gestation due to Cranmer's native caution and Henry VIII's unpredictable oscillations and fondness for services still in Latin.

E. C. Ratcliff said of the Cranmerian reform, 'The intention and spirit of the new Offices are summed up, not by the verse, "Seven times a day do I praise thee", but by "Thy word is a lantern unto my feet"'. Cranmer reduced the seven plus one offices to two, mattins and evensong in 1549, Morning and Evening Prayer, as they were called in 1552. He did this by skilful combination of mattins, lauds and prime and vespers and compline. They are both services of the Word with two longish lessons at each. The Old Testament is to be read through once a year except for certain 'least edifying books and chapters', in fact from Leviticus. Parts of the Apocrypha are included. The New Testament is to be read three times a year, apart from Revelation which is confined to two chapters. The Psalter is to be read through once a month, with special psalms for Sundays and holy days, which take precedence. This last pertains to lessons also.

The Apostles' Creed follows the second canticle in both offices. The Athanasian Creed seems to have been added as an afterthought, in place of the Apostles' Creed after the *Benedictus* at mattins on the great festivals and, in 1552, on the principal saints' days as well. The *Benedicite,* from lauds, replaces the *Te Deum* in the morning office in Lent in 1549. It is an alternative to it in 1552.

Cranmer's full liturgy is, above all, a Book of *Common* Prayer. The offices are to be read in public and the people are summoned by the church bell. The offices became for a long time the principal services by which Church of England worship was judged and this is due to several factors: the English were not good communicants (the Venerable Bede complained of this); the morning service became shortened to Morning Prayer, with the litany and ante-communion being dropped; sermons and hymns, both missing from Cranmer, were introduced; and the services inspired fine choral settings.

In 1552, Cranmer added a sonorous penitential introduction to mattins, and evensong which is movingly beautiful but has helped him to gain the reputation of being obsessed with sin. In 1662 an anthem and State prayers were added. In 1552, at Evening Prayer, the *Cantate Domino* (Psalm 98) could replace the *Magnificat* for Protestant reasons, bearing in mind the Marian devotion which had surrounded the latter in the Middle Ages; and the *Deus Misereatur* (Psalm 67) became an alternative to the *Nunc Dimittis.*

There has always been in Anglicanism a hankering for the full scheme of hours. In 1627 John Cosin published *A Collection of Private Devotions for the Houres of Prayer.* It was intended for the Anglican ladies-in-waiting at the court of Queen Henrietta Maria, who were being shamed by the much more intense disciplines of the Catholics who had accompanied Charles I's consort from France. The foundation, says Cosin, is the Lord's own prayer, which may begin, continue and perfect 'our most holy devotions', 'thereby supplying, with the fulness of that one, whatsoever may be defective in all our other prayers'. The collection has offices for the first, third, sixth and ninth hours, vespers and compline. The offices include hymns. There is much other material for private devotion, for instance, a first-person adaptation of Cranmer's General Confession. There are short prayers to accompany particular times of day, rising, dressing and going to sleep. There is guidance as to how to prepare for the Sacrament and receive absolution. There are prayers for the high moments of the Eucharist and for all circumstances of life and death (Stanwood, ed.).

The book was greeted with howls of Puritan rage as a subversive instrument of Counter-Reformation, as politically disloyal as it was religiously retrograde. The tradition, however, was retained in the Church of England, particularly among non-jurors, those who having taken oaths to the Stuarts, did not feel they could conform under William and Mary after 1689. John Wesley, though he did not use Cosin's *Devotions,* or the offices for all the canonical hours had as part of his Oxford rule, which he later republished for Methodists, the repetition of a collect at nine, twelve and three, besides the use of Morning and Evening Prayer supplemented by long periods of meditation. His very first publication in 1733, with many subsequent editions, was *A Collection of Forms of Prayer for Every Day of the Week* mostly filched from the non-juror, Nathaniel Spinckes. We have seen that he objected to the imprecatory psalms in the Prayer Book.

The English Reformation, in its more Protestant forms, changed the character of the sanctification of time. Sunday became the Christian's market day, the supreme occasion of public worship and teaching. The other six days were for labour, though they were not thereby to be entirely secular. The book to be compared and contrasted with Cosin's *Devotions* is the work of another Anglican, Lewis Bayly's *The Practice of Piety.* Written about 1610, it reached its twenty-fifth edition by 1630, its fifty-ninth in 1735 and was last reissued in 1842. It was translated into three continental languages and in 1665 at Cambridge Massachusetts into the tongue of the local Indians. Thoroughly Calvinist, this manual prescribes a devotional discipline for the then new merchant class, the heads of large households and men of trade. The *Book of Common Prayer* is presupposed, but whereas for Cosin its complement is a reformed breviary, for Bayly the extra devotions are not set offices but compositions which could serve as a model for extemporaneous prayers. They are long and theological, verbose in comparison with Cosin. The whole household is to be gathered for prayer daily, which will not be to share in an office. Bayly expects the Bible to be read through in the course of the year and shows how this may be done – three chapters a day and the Prayer Book psalms.

But we must not be misled into thinking that Bayly's style of devotion came into existence with the Reformers, whereas Cosin is Catholic. Though *The Practice of Piety* is much more a handbook of theology for laymen than any medieval primer – and it may be argued that it thereby does not enable its users to know God quite as do the offices of worship and praise where so much is received unconsciously and without rational thought – Bayly, like other English Puritans and the later German Pietists whom they influenced, borrows a scheme of recollection from the Spanish humanist Ludovicus Vives (1492–1540), who came to England in 1523 as tutor to Princess, later Queen Mary. The bed is always to remind the sleeper of his grave, his rising of his resurrection from the dead. Should he hear the cock crow, he must remember Peter's denial and penitence with many tears. The putting on of clothes is to carry the mind back to man's primeval innocence and fallen shame. The sun streaming through the windows is to be a sign of the sun of righteousness, risen with healing in his wings (cf. Wakefield, 1969, pp. 61–3).

There is a distinction, adumbrated above, which needs to be spelled out and which has modern expression, in the Protestant and Catholic attitude to the liturgy of time. Protestants were always conscious of the Pauline injunction 'Let all things be done unto edifying'. Cosin would not have demurred. But there seems to be a feeling that this overshadows worship, which is more than an intellectual activity for moral improvement. In 1957, Martin Thornton wrote *Pastoral Theology: A Reorientation* in which he seeks a recovery of the office, to which at the appropriate time a group may turn aside from either work or pleasure, a study group or drinking in the pub. Feelings are not important, nor understanding. It is the barrack square drill of the Christian. Enjoyment is secondary and the benefits are in obedience and an uncalculated growth in grace.

It is remarkable that there has been a turn to offices among the successors of the Puritans. In 1941, Nathaniel Micklem published *Prayers and Praises* which he had first written in Latin, which, intended for private prayer, consists of offices for morning and evening for every day of the week. They are enriched by hymns from the Free Church tradition, especially Watts, Wesley and Olney, together with Gerhardt. Psalms are mostly represented by extracted verses; Scripture by short passages, chiefly from the New Testament. The prayers are from Scripture, the *Book of Common Prayer,* the breviary, Lancelot Andrewes, Jeremy Taylor, Archbishop Laud. It is to accompany, not replace, the reading and study of the Bible and personal prayers, as well as those prompted by the news bulletin or newspaper. It is compiled with 'dry seasons' in mind when extempore inspiration fails, but, above all, as an offering of praise to God 'to whom everything in his house shall cry "Glory"'.

One of the first tasks of the Joint Liturgical Group was a revision of the Daily Office. The resulting structure was as follows:

MORNING

Sentence or Versicle and Response
Venite
Psalm
Lessons (a) Old Testament
(b) Epistle
Silence
Canticle or hymn
Here may be said The Creed
Lord's Prayer
Collects (a) of the day
(b) morning
Here may follow the Intercessions or other prayers

EVENING

Sentence or Versicle and Responses
Psalm
Lesson – Gospel
Silence
Act of penitence
Collect – evening

Here may follow the thanksgiving or other prayers.

The *Venite* omits the four admonitory verses of Psalm 95 and replaces them with the last verse of Psalm 96, which some would feel is a mishandling of Scripture, imported from the United States. The Psalter replaces the monthly reading of the psalms with one four times a year, with a maximum of twenty-five verses on each occasion. Nine or so psalms are omitted as unsuitable. The two-year lectionary plans to read the whole of the New Testament once a year and nearly the whole of the Old Testament once every two years. Apocryphal books are given as alternatives to Old Testament passages in a few weeks. Each day has its own canticles, the *Benedictus* is used on Tuesday evening, Keble's 'Hail Gladdening Light', his translation of *Phos hilaron,* on Thursday evening, *Salvator mundi,* attributed to Henry Allon, a Congregational minister, on Friday morning, Revelation 4:11, 5:12 and 15:3, 4 on Friday evening and Saturday morning, and the Easter Anthems on Saturday evening. There is a fine selection of classical hymns which may be alternatives. The second edition of the Office in 1978 had a large number of extra canticles from Scripture. The second morning collect was especially composed by the Revd A. Raymond George to replace the one from the Prayer Book asking God who has brought us safely to the beginning of this day to defend us in the same by his almighty power. It runs:

> Eternal God and Father by whose power we are created and by whose love we are redeemed. Guide and strengthen us by thy Spirit, that we may give ourselves to thy service and live this day in love to one another and to thee; through Jesus Christ our Lord. Amen.

By 1978 this was in the 'you' form.

The 1968 edition attracted some attention because a Baptist minister, Stephen Winward, wrote the introductory essay. It is to be compared with what we have said about Nathaniel Micklem's introduction to his *Prayers and Praises*, although it is even more emphatic about the centrality of the office in Christian devotion.

The Methodist Sacramental Fellowship had devised offices and committed its members to saying them from its inception. There have been several revisions. Many Christians have come to use the offices of the ecumenical community at Taizé with their mantra-like repetitions and silences as well as sung responses.

The deposited Church of England Prayer Book of 1927/8 offered many variations, which, it was said, violated the integrity of offices and abandoned the principle of uniformity (Ratcliff, in Clarke, ed., p. 270). To some this destroys the very nature of the office which is basically a rule, 'a disciplined response to the love of God, crystallized into a system out of the living experience of the organic Church', as Martin Thornton idealistically wrote (Thornton, 1965, p. 27).

The Anglican offices in the *Alternative Service Book* of 1980, very closely follow the revisions of the Joint Liturgical Group, with the *Venite* revised, a variety of canticles, as alternatives to those traditional, and the JLG collect as an alternative to that for the morning in the Prayer Book. The *Te Deum* and *Benedictus* are transposed in the morning. The versicles and responses after the creed and Lord's Prayer are altered somewhat to make them less like what Dean Inge rather naughtily described as a conversation between two deaf men, neither of whom exactly hears what the other is saying. There is provision for a sermon in both offices.

These offices have not achieved great popularity and they have been overtaken in some places by *Celebrating Common Prayer* (1992), a version of the Anglican Franciscan Daily Office. (As has been implied, the Franciscans have had a great influence on the development of the office.)

The book provides a fourfold office – morning, midday, evening and night. Each day of the week is devoted to a season of the Christian Year – Sunday, Easter; Monday, Pentecost; Tuesday, Advent; Wednesday, Christmas; Thursday, Epiphany; Friday, Lent and Passiontide; Saturday, the

Kingdom season (the eve of All Saints Day to the eve of Advent Sunday), a new Anglican season, abandoning the Joint Liturgical Group lectionary and calendar for November. During the seasons themselves, the appropriate office is said daily except at midday. Each office is divided into preparation, the word of God, prayers and conclusion. There is a choice of alternatives in each section (*pace* Ratcliff). There is a selection of appropriate psalms in the offices as in the Cathedral Office, using the Psalter like a hymnbook, although all the psalms are printed in the version of the Standard Book of Common Prayer of the Episcopal Church of the United States, with collects following each psalm, translated from the Roman *Liturgy of the Hours*. There are over seventy canticles and a wealth of collects and intercessions. A simple celebration is provided with families and children in mind.

Celebrating Common Prayer is but one instance of the desire that worship should not be only on Sundays, which indeed may give less opportunity than of old, but should be a joyful partnership of Christians every day. The *Book of Common Order* has daily services and the Episcopal Church of Scotland published *Daily Prayer* in 1990 with morning and evening offices and compline. The offices have four themes: incarnation; returning to God; the suffering Christ; new life (the Lord: the Spirit), with 'other times' material, such as antiphons, for festivals. There is also, as in *Celebrating Common Prayer,* a commendation. The Psalter is from the *Book of Alternative Services* of the Anglican Church of Canada, though it is identical with that of the United States, apart from variations in the translation of the collects after each psalm.

The Roman Church began the revision of its offices in the 1960s as a result of the Constitution on the Sacred Liturgy of Vatican II. The revisers preferred 'The Liturgy of the Hours' to 'The Divine Office' since 'it is distributed throughout the day, thus creating privileged moments which help direct all activities towards the ideal of ceaseless prayer'. The English translators have, however, gone back to 'The Divine Office'. The term 'breviary' has been abandoned (Martimort, p. 156).

Vatican II decreed that lauds and vespers are the two most important offices. Mattins can be said at any time of the day with fewer psalms and longer lessons. Prime – originally to prevent lazy monks returning to bed between lauds and work

– is suppressed and only one of terce, sext and none need be said. Compline is to be revised as the prayer for the end of the day (cf. Cosin). The Psalter is to be distributed over a greater period than a week. It has been spread over four weeks, though on the great seasons and greater feasts there are appropriate psalms. No office has more than three psalms, though the third in lauds is an Old Testament canticle, and in vespers one from the New Testament. The tradition found in Cassian and Egeria of meditation and prayer after each psalm has been restored by the provision of collects which gather up the sentiments and round off the psalmody. They are optional. Antiphons to be sung before or after each psalm, or as refrains in the course of the chant are retained. They go back to the Ambrosian and Benedictine offices. They may be an adapted, key verse of a psalm or poetic compositions, from the Old Testament or the Gospel, or hagiographical for saints' days, or sung alone, not as the accompaniment to a psalm.

The readings are to be longer with better selections from the Fathers and the Acts of the Martyrs and historical truth in the lives of the saints. These last have been widely selected but, apart from Vatican II and some papal texts, they do not include twentieth-century authors, which is a deprivation in more ways than one. Hymns are to be used more extensively, as the beginning of each office. This is happening and hymns from cultures other than the traditional Eastern and Western are being composed. They must be, in Augustine's definition, 'songs with praise to God' and end with a doxology.

There is an 'Office of Readings' to replace mattins. A two-year cycle of Scripture is proposed, each year to present the history of salvation, with responses and patristic readings to correspond. In the other offices, the psalms are followed by readings of a few verses. The aim is of 'setting forth some passage of Sacred Scripture in a striking way, or highlighting some shorter sentence that may receive less attention in the continuous cycle of Scripture readings'.

There is the hope that the offices will no longer be thought of as a clerical possession and Sunday vespers in particular is to be celebrated with the people. This may lead to a displacement of the Benediction of the Blessed Sacrament.

In spite of all the reforms, there are those like Grisbrooke and Bradshaw, who feel that the monastic office is still in control, the norm from which all revision proceeds. 'We need to discover and create a truly "cathedral office", a pattern of daily prayer appropriate to our own age' (Bradshaw, 1992, pp. 153f.).

Kalendar

The liturgy of time begins with Sunday, the day of resurrection, the weekly celebration of the paschal mystery, known as 'the Lord's day' by the Seer of Patmos. By the end of the first century, it had replaced the Jewish sabbath as the Christian day of assembly, a sign of the new order in Christ and the new resurrection life which Christians lived in him. It was a day of celebration and of joy even in the midst of trials and persecutions. There was to be no penitence, no kneeling for prayer, no fasting. It is the first day of the week, the day of creation, but also the eighth day, coming after the seventh, the day which is a sign of eternal life, in which the Church celebrates the great sabbath of the Kingdom. The Letter of Barnabas (*c.* 80CE), commenting on Jesus's words critical of the Jewish sabbath says that he means:

> It is not the sabbaths now celebrated that please me, but the sabbath which I made, and on which, after bringing all things to their rest, I will begin an eighth day, that is a new world. That is why we celebrate as a joyous feast the eighth day on which Jesus rose from the dead and, after appearing to his disciples, ascended into heaven.

Wednesday, Friday and Saturday soon attained a special place in Christian worship. Wednesday, the day of Judas's pact with the chief priests, to betray Jesus, and Friday, the day of his death, were fast days, though also days of assembly (they became eucharistic in Africa, a custom which spread across the West) and teaching. Origen wrote his commentaries for these days. Saturday, in reaction to the Jewish sabbath, was an aliturgical day in many places, but a fast day in Rome and Alexandria from the third century to recall the Lent and paschal fasts. In the East, Saturday became a feast day, with the only eucharistic celebration apart from Sunday, and a day of honouring saints. In the tenth century, following Alcuin, the West began to hold Masses in honour of Our Lady on Saturdays.

Ember days, possibly a corruption of *quatuor tempora*, four seasons, originated in the fourth and fifth centuries in Rome to mark the beginning of each natural, agricultural season with days of fasting and prayer. These included assemblies at the three stational churches and they became occasions for ordination. The custom gradually spread throughout the West, where ordinations are preceded by days of fasting and special prayer. The East knows nothing of such days.

It is obvious that Christians would become especially conscious of the crucifixion and resurrection of the Lord at the time of the annual celebration of the Jewish Passover, although this does not seem to have been a special festival until early in the second century, and in Rome not until the second half of it. It was the only feast which depended on a lunar calendar. Even then there were two ways of calculating the date of Easter. The Churches of Asia Minor kept the actual day of the Jewish Passover, the fourteenth of Nisan. The other Churches, including Rome held the festival on the following Sunday, 'the first day of the week'. Pope Victor (189–98) intervened and the second way became normative. In the West after the Council of Nicaea in 325, Easter was celebrated on the Sunday following the first full moon after the spring equinox.

There was at first a unitive celebration, a fast for one or two days commemorating the bridegroom's being taken away from the Church, culminating in a nocturnal assembly, during which there was a transition from death to life, sorrow to joy, marked by the Eucharist. This became the Easter vigil with readings from Old and New Testaments preceding the Eucharist. It was an obvious time for baptism, bearing in mind Romans 6, especially when baptisms were mostly of adults. The baptismal water was blessed at Easter in the West even when adult baptism became the exception, but it disappeared in the East from the eleventh century.

It became a festival of light with the paschal candle, the candle of candles, for these were vital in the ancient world to banish darkness, though also sometimes to herald orgies. For Christians this reminded them of Christ, the Light of the World and they sang the hymn 'Hail gladdening light'. This was the origin of the *Exultet,* the proclamation of paschal joy in the form of a lengthy thanksgiving.

This came to be preceded by a period of preparation especially for those to be baptised, also for penitents to be reconciled. This involved fasting and was the origin of Lent. But the commemoration gradually became more historical as the Church continued in time. The Gospels become more detailed as they recount the days before the resurrection and it was inevitable that worship would re-live the Gospels, although the tradition, which is still maintained, is not to harmonise but to concentrate each day on one of the Passion narratives as a whole. Egeria's three-year travels in the Holy Land in the fourth century show that by this time Holy Week, known as 'The Great Week', was observed in Jerusalem beginning with a commemoration of the raising of Lazarus on the Saturday before what we know as Palm Sunday, though Egeria does not. On the Sunday there was a procession of palms late in the afternoon. All ages joined in, babies 'on their parents' shoulders'. It led to the Church of the Anastasis (or Resurrection) and concluded with the evening ('Cathedral') office. The Eucharist had been celebrated in the morning. There were services of the Word every day, some at great length. Judas's betrayal on the Wednesday was accompanied by groans at the infamy of the deed.

Maundy Thursday's worship began at two in the afternoon with a Eucharist concentrating on Judas's betrayal and death, followed by a second on the theme of the Last Supper, the anaphora being said for the only time 'behind the cross', which seems to have been a vestibule to the rear of the stump of rent rock which was the supposed site of Calvary. There was then a hurried, straggling procession to the Mount of Olives to keep vigil at four stations, one being Gethsemane. There was a return to Calvary for the story of the trial before Pilate and, just before sunrise, some of the more vigorous worshippers went to pray on Mount Sion at the column where Christ was scourged. On Good Friday from eight in the morning until twelve there was veneration of the relic of the cross, then a three-hour service based on the Passion throughout Scripture, ending with John 19:30 when Jesus gives up his spirit. The usual Holy Week three o'clock service followed, after which, at the Holy Sepulchre, there was read St John's account of Christ's burial.

Good Friday was not known everywhere. At Antioch in 388 Chrysostom spoke of 'the way of the cross'. Augustine in 400 referred to 'the most holy triduum of the crucified, buried and risen Lord', but in 450 at Rome, according to Leo the Great's sermons, Good Friday was unknown. The Mass of the Pre-Sanctified, communion from the reserved Sacrament on days when the Eucharist was not celebrated, probably began as early as the second century. The Orthodox have it every Wednesday and Friday in Lent, but not on Good Friday, when it has been a distinctive part of the Roman Liturgy.

If the days before Easter came to have a solemn and mournful commemoration, the days after, fifty until Pentecost, even earlier became a time of rejoicing, 'the great Sunday'. It was an octave of Sundays and a week of weeks. The English designation of the Sunday after Easter as 'Low Sunday' ought not to suggest that it is an anti-climax after the great festival. 'Low' may be a corruption of 'laudes', the opening word of the sequence sung between the gradual and the Gospel (Lowther Clarke, p. 208).

The celebratory note was interrupted as the chronology of Acts began to influence the liturgy of time, and the Ascension was kept not as part of the Easter ceremonies as Luke 24 and the Fourth Gospel would suggest, but forty days after. This happened in the fourth century, a time when the Cappadocian Fathers in particular, now that christological questions were settled, turned their attention to the doctrine of the Holy Spirit. Pentecost became more than the climax and conclusion of the Easter season – John, after all, makes the giving of the Spirit an event of Easter evening – a great feast in its own right, preceded by a fast.

Easter and Pentecost coincide with two Jewish feasts, Passover and the harvest Feast of Weeks, which had come to commemorate the giving of the Law. Why is there no Christian parallel to the Feast of Tabernacles, which is important in St John's account of the ministry of Jesus (John 7:10, 37–8), and which had come to reflect messianic and eschatological expectations? It included the reading of Zechariah 14, which not only prophesies the Messiah's coming and reign, but continuous day ('at evening time there shall be light') and living water flowing out from Jerusalem.

There was at this feast the ritual drawing of water by day and the illumination of one of the Temple courts on the first night. Hence Jesus's declarations at the feast that he can provide living water for the thirsty, a reference, says John, to the Spirit which flows from him (cf. Revelation 7:17, 21:7, 22:1f.) and his glorification through the cross; and he is the Light of the World (cf. Revelation 21; 23ff., 22:5). References to the Feast of Tabernacles have also been found in the synoptic account of Jesus's entry into Jerusalem. Was its commemoration split for Christians between the Easter celebrations, the entry into Jerusalem and the new feast of Epiphany connected with the Lord's baptism? The latter in the Gentile Churches which kept the Roman calendar was held in January, the beginning of its year. In those Churches the story of the entry was also read in December at the end of the year as a preface to the eschatological passages, which accounts for its occurring as the Gospel for the first Sunday in Advent as well as for Palm Sunday (cf. Schmemann, 1975, pp. 123f.).

It is significant that the kalendar commemorates only three births – Jesus, John the Baptist, and the new birth of Paul, his conversion. The true birthday of the Christian was the day of his or her death. Christmas is not mentioned until 354 and was undoubtedly instituted at Rome to direct the pagan celebrations at the winter solstice into a Christian feast. Epiphany is of Eastern origin. It may have first, as we have seen, been concerned chiefly with the Lord's baptism, which some Eastern Christians regarded as the incarnation of the Word in the humanity of Jesus. But there was much pagan celebration to be christianised. January 6th was connected with the virgin birth of Dionysus, who changed springs of water into wine. It could then also celebrate the birth of Jesus, especially in an age which had fought christological battles and wanted to accord supernatural, divine honours to the only-begotten Son and also, with the birth stories of Matthew and Luke in its possession, venerate his Mother, the Theotokos. Epiphany cannot be much older than Christmas, if at all. Both feasts came to be celebrated in both parts of the Church. In the West Epiphany became associated with the visit of the Wise Men, a manifestation of Christ to the Gentiles (pagans), as well as with the baptism. In the East the celebrations of December 25th did not separate the Magi from the other nativity stories. At vespers on December 24th, the Byzantine Church sings:

> Lord, every creature you have made brings you its testimony of gratitude: the angels bring their song, the heavens its star, the magi their gifts, the shepherds their wonder, the earth its cave, the wilderness its manger, and we bring a Virgin Mother.

Around 386CE, Egeria attests the celebrations of the presentation of Christ in the Temple on the fortieth day after Christmas, the end of the Christmas season. It was the sixth century before the feast was accepted in Syria and Constantinople and the second half of the seventh century before it was kept in Rome. At Constantinople it was called 'the Meeting of our great God and Saviour Jesus Christ with Simeon the Just when the latter took him in his arms'. In the middle of the eighth century a new name appeared among the Franks, 'The Purification of the Blessed Virgin Mary'. After a while, this title prevailed and was dominant for many centuries, even in the *Book of Common Prayer,* where it is now the second name but in bolder print. In the Roman Church, Mary and, as we have seen, candles took over.

Advent fulfilled the need in the West for 'a pre-Christmas Lent', gradually instituted from the end of the fourth century. But, as the name suggests, it became a time of expectation, not only of the Nativity, but of the glorious return of the Lord at the end of time. *Adventus* had been an old pagan term, which now came to represent the biblical '*parousia*'. Isaiah and John the Baptist were the prophetic voices most heard in the lections. There was, much later, an unfortunate concentration on the 'four last things', death, judgement, heaven and hell. But, traditionally, Advent is in two stages; the first recalls Christ's two comings, the second celebrates him, beginning with the ninth-century antiphons, 'the great Os'.

The East does not keep Advent as in the West, though in the Syrian rite there are the 'weeks of the annunciations, five, to Zechariah, to Mary, followed by the Visitation, the Birth of John the Baptist, and to Joseph. In the Byzantine rite, there is commemoration of the saints of the old Covenant, who 'lead the dance for the birth of the Saviour' (see Martimort, ed., pp. 11–95).

The commemoration of saints began with the martyrs. Churches were often built at their tombs. Jesus himself is called a martyr ('witness') in Revelation 1:5 and 3:14. Their deaths, such as those of Stephen, Ignatius of Antioch, Polycarp, and in the next century Cyprian, were occasions of great awe, the crown of noble lives. Local traditions were decisive in days when there was no easy world church communication. After the peace of the Church there were no more martyrs. Christian 'athletes' were commemorated and Mary, the Theotokos, had four feasts to begin with. The apostles and New Testament characters did not appear at first since there were no local traditions. There were more and more imaginative discoveries and a proliferation of relics. There was an interval of 600 years with no new saints until the new martyr, Thomas à Becket, in 1170. Then the cult increased to overlay liturgy. It was drastically reduced by the Reformers but has persisted in Rome, not least under John Paul II, while Anglicans who have no process of canonisation, which in Rome, is an industry, have now a list of commemorations which includes some non-Anglicans, such as Thomas Aquinas and John Bunyan.

CONCLUSION

Ritual is a necessity of human life in both joy and sorrow. We need to express our feelings corporately, but also to reach to the mystery which transcends questioning. This may not always be verbal but accompanied by actions, such as dancing. When Anna Pavlova was asked what she was saying in a particular dance, she replied, 'If I could tell you I would not dance.' Even more has singing been inescapable, sometimes spontaneous. After the Hillsborough football disaster in 1989, the crowds could not refrain from singing the 'Kop National Anthem' (so named after a stand at Liverpool's football ground), 'You'll never walk alone', from the musical *Carousel*. It was included in the service at Liverpool's Anglican Cathedral. We have already quoted Ulrich Simon as saying that the only way to bear the unspeakable horrors of Auschwitz, to contemplate them and still maintain hope in a world where such atrocities are possible, is somehow to come to terms with them liturgically. And this does not mean re-enactment, which would be both blasphemous and injurious. We have to find a form which expresses the inexpressible horror and grief, which does not seek to explain it or try to fit it into a beneficent, overruling purpose, which is impossible and almost sinfully shallow, but which will not deny the hope by which alone we and our neighbours can go on living.

The Hillsborough ritual was a memorial of the victims, an act of remembrance and thanksgiving for their lives and loves and comradeship. In some way it brought them back through remembrance and it united those who joined in. For a short time, differences, contentions and rancours were forgotten. And hope was affirmed amid the distress. Such rituals will have different cultural expressions.

In Christianity all this points to the centrality of the Eucharist, which while confronting the tragedy of life seen in Christ's passion, is also a feast of joy, a way of showing our delight in one another, in the blessings of this life and, above all, in the God who gives us Christ. This is now recognised in almost all Churches, that the great Sacrament which has caused so much enmity and pain, could be the means of unity. This requires open hospitality at the Lord's table for those who believe, who love God much and want to love him more. The one and only qualification for admission should be, as Adrian Hastings has said, the willingness to say 'amen' to the Eucharistic Prayer. Or, as J. N. Figgis wrote much earlier, 'I think we can say as far as Creed goes that a man is a Christian or a non-Christian in so far as he can enter into the spirit of Watts' hymn, "When I survey the wondrous Cross".'

Eucharistic consecration is now seen in the thanksgiving, or even the rite as a whole and not in the words of institution or these and the epiclesis. This is one reason why the ancient custom of standing for the prayer has been revived in some places among some people. But the poetic power of the consecrated bread and wine, evidenced in our time by John Betjeman and Elizabeth Jennings, to name only two, does not diminish. Transubstantiation, or some equivalent belief, will not die. There is a craving for the act and moment of change, for 'tiny words/Full of more than this world can ever contain' (Elizabeth Jennings).

Worship is not entertainment, though God is to be enjoyed. It should have no other motive than to glorify him and bring us into his presence. It is our journey into heaven, our pass to the royal enclosure, as E. C. Ratcliff once put it. It cannot be seen simply as a tool for conversion, though God may use it for this. Nor is worship essentially a health card for the benefit of self and friends, though intercession is all-important. Its theological rationale must be explored and understood. We must always go to church in love for our friends and enemies, in remembrance of their needs and longing that they and the world may be healed.

We have noted that in a time of liturgical renewal, so wonderfully ecumenical, there is a reaction against set forms, a desire for 'liveliness' above all and awareness that where Christianity seems strongest and least in decline, the worship may be of a different culture from the great liturgical traditions of East and West. This may make us uneasy, defensive and sad. We must have faith in the old maxim *semper reformanda* ('always to be reformed'). None of our liturgical achievements and glories escape a judgement which we may feel when the orders which bring us to Christ and heaven, have little meaning for many. Yet we must not surrender or degrade Christian truth, or trivialise the gospel in order to make it attractive. It is almost incredible that there should be included in Christian worship, as has happened, a vulgar ditty such as:

> God is good to me, God is good to me,
> He gives me jelly to fill my belly.

That profanes both the awe-some act of God in Christ 'greater than the making of the worlds', and the hunger of the large part of humanity. We must not think that we are following the guidance of the Holy Spirit when we are pandering to a consumerist culture. There should always be a strangeness in worship, a difference from the contemporary and a challenge to it.

We are left with a conundrum of divine providence. Was there ever a time when the Church had such treasure for its worship, the whole tradition of the past and a new creativity of beauty, prayers and liturgies, and offices which bring many of us to the throne of grace and equip us for the liturgy of life? And yet in Europe, the Churches continue to decline and worldwide, in spite of African enthusiasm and Latin American liberation, the finality of Christ is challenged. We fear a dark age in which Christianity is torn apart by fundamentalism and a strange alliance of faiths and fashions with what some would feel is a dangerous leaning to 'the world' in the pejorative sense. This is not to deny the need to revere other faiths at their best and highest, to learn from them and to be rebuked by them while ever seeking and trying to practise the truth as it is in Jesus. In this quest and task, worship is essential, because, although governed by theology it takes us to realms beyond reason and the values of a passing age. It is the sacrament of love. It may lead to sacristy-mindedness and a putting of second things first. It has not been free from un-Christlike acrimonies or the stain of sin. But it preserves the faith and unites God's people in contemplation of those things which eye has not seen, nor ear heard, nor have they entered into the human heart, but which God has prepared for those who love him. As Nathaniel Micklem wrote:

> The whole drama of redemption is, as it were, present together before our eyes as visibly occurrent, and the promise of our inheritance is sealed by the Lord himself upon our wondering hearts. (Micklem, ed., p. 256)

REFERENCES

Books

Arnold, J. H. and Wyatt, E. G. P., eds, *Walter Howard Frere: Papers* (Oxford: Oxford University Press, 1940).

Austin, G. OP, ed., *Fountain of Life* (Washington DC: Pastoral Press, 1991).

Balthasar H. Urs von, *The Glory of the Lord I. Seeing the Form* (Edinburgh: T. & T. Clark, 1982).

Bossy J., *Christianity in the West 1400–1700* (Oxford: Oxford University Press, 1983).

Bouyer, L., *Life and Liturgy* (London: Sheed and Ward, 1956).

Bradshaw, P. F., *Daily Prayer in the Early Church* (London: Alcuin/SPCK, 1981).

Bradshaw, P. F., *The Search for the Origins of Christian Worship* (London: Alcuin/SPCK, 1992).

Bradshaw, P. F., ed., *The Canons of Hippolytus* (London: Alcuin/Grow, 1987).

Cabasilas, N. A., *Commentary on the Divine Liturgy* (London: SPCK, 1977).

Chadwick, O., *The Mind of the Oxford Movement* (London: A. & C. Black, 1960).

Clarke, W. K. L., ed., *Liturgy and Worship* (London: SPCK, 1932).

Cross, F. L., *St Cyril of Jerusalem's Lectures on the Christian Sacraments* (London: SPCK, 1951).

Cullmann, O., *Early Christian Worship* (London: SCM Press, 1953).

Cuming, G. J., *The Durham Book* (Oxford: Oxford University Press, 1961).

Cuming, G. J., *A History of Anglican Worship* (London and Basingstoke: Macmillan, 1982).
Cuming, G. J., *The Godly Order* (London: Alcuin/SPCK, 1983).
Cuming, G. J., ed., *The Liturgy of St. Mark* (Rome: Pontificium Institutum Studiorum Orientalium, 1990).
Davies, H., *The Worship of the English Puritans* (London: Dacre Press, 1948).
Davies, H., *Worship and Theology in England 1900–1965* (Oxford: Oxford University Press, 1965).
Dearmer, P., *The Art of Public Worship* (Oxford: Mowbrays, 1919).
Dix, G., *The Shape of the Liturgy* (London: Dacre Press, 1945).
Dix, G., *The Treatise of the Apostolic Tradition of St Hippolytus of Rome* (1937; revised edn London: SPCK, 1968).
Dodd, C. H., *History and the Gospel* (Cambridge: Cambridge University Press, 1938).
Dowden, J., *The Workmanship of the Prayer Book* (London: Methuen, 1899).
Dowden, J., *Further Studies in the Prayer Book* (London: Methuen, 1908).
Dudley, M., ed., *Like a two-edged Sword* (Norwich: The Canterbury Press, 1995).
Duffy, E., *The Stripping of the Altars* (New Haven and London: Yale University Press, 1992).
Eusebius, *The History of the Church from Christ to Constantine* trs Williamson (Harmondsworth: Penguin, 1965).
Fisher, J. D. C., *Christian Initiation: The Reformation Period* (London: Alcuin/SPCK, 1970).
Flemington, W. F., *The New Testament Doctrine of Baptism* (London: SPCK, 1948).
Ford, D. F. and Stamps, D. L., eds, *The Essentials of Christian Community* (Edinburgh: T. & T. Clark, 1996).
Frere, W. H., *Some Principles of Liturgical Reform* (London: John Murray, 1911).
Grisbrooke, W. J., *The Liturgical Portions of the Apostolic Constitutions* (London: Alcuin/Grow, 1990).
Hall, B., *Humanists and Protestants* (Edinburgh: T. & T. Clark, 1990).
Hart, T., ed., *Justice the True and Only Mercy: Essays on the Life and Theology of Peter Taylor Forsyth* (Edinburgh: T. & T. Clark, 1995).

Hindmarsh, D. B., *John Newton and the English Evangelical Tradition* (Oxford: Clarendon Press, 1996).

Hort, A. F., ed., *Life and Letters of F. J. A. Hort* (London: Macmillan, 1896).

Hunter, J., *The Coming Church* (London: Williams and Norgate, 1905).

Jasper, R. C. D., ed., *Walter Howard Frere: Correspondence* (London: SPCK, 1954).

Jasper, R. C. D., ed., *The Daily Office* (London: SPCK, 1968 and 1978).

Jasper, R. C. D., ed., *Initiation and Eucharist* (London: SPCK, 1972).

Jasper, R. C. D., and Bradshaw, P. F., eds, *A Companion to the Alternative Service Book* (London: SPCK, 1986).

Jasper, R. C. D., and Cuming, G. J., eds, *Prayers of the Eucharist* (New York: Pueblo Publishing Company, 1987).

Jeremias, J., *The Eucharistic Words of Jesus* (London: SCM Press 1966).

Jungmann, J. A., *The Place of Christ in Liturgical Prayer* (London: Geoffrey Chapman, 1965).

Jungmann, J. A., *The Mass* (Minnesota: Liturgical Press, 1976).

Jungmann, J. A.,*The Eucharistic Prayer* (Wheathampstead: Anthony Clarke, 1978).

Jungmann, J. A., *The Early Liturgy to the Time of Gregory the Great* (London: Darton, Longman and Todd, 1960).

Kilpatrick, G. D., *The Eucharist in Bible and Liturgy* (Cambridge: Cambridge University Press, 1983).

Kirk, K. E., *The Vision of God* (London: Longmans, 1932).

Lampe, G. W. H., *The Seal of the Spirit* (London: Longmans, 1951 and SPCK, 1967).

Lash, N., *Easter in Ordinary* (London: SCM Press, 1988).

MacCulloch, D., *Thomas Cranmer* (New Haven and London: Yale University Press, 1996).

MacKinnon, D., *Themes in Theology* (Edinburgh: T. & T. Clark, 1986).

McLachlan, H. J., *Socinianism in Seventeenth Century England* (Oxford: Oxford University Press, 1951).

Manning, B. L., *Essays in Orthodox Dissent* (London: Independent Press, 1939).

Martimort, A. G., ed., *The Church at Prayer Vol. IV, The Liturgy and Time* (London: Geoffrey Chapman, 1986).

Mascall, E. L., *Corpus Christi* (2nd edn. London: Longmans, 1965).
Maxwell, W. D. *John Knox's Genevan Service Book (1556)* (Edinburgh: Oliver and Boyd, 1931).
Maxwell, W. D., *An Outline of Christian Worship* (Oxford; Oxford University Press, 1936; 3rd impression 1945).
Micklem, N., ed., *Christian Worship* (Oxford: Oxford University Press, 1936).
Nuttall, G. F., *The Holy Spirit in Puritan Faith and Experience* (Oxford: Blackwell, 1946).
Nuttall, G. F., *The Puritan Spirit* (London: Epworth Press, 1967).
Petuchowski, J. J. and Brooke, M., eds, *The Lord's Prayer and Jewish Liturgy* (London: Burns & Oates, 1978).
Power, D. N. OMI, *Culture and Theology* (Washington DC: The Pastoral Press, 1990).
Ratcliff, E. C., *Liturgical Studies* (London: SPCK, 1978).
Rupp, E. G., *The Sixty Plus and Other Sermons* (London: Collins Fount, 1978).
Schmemann, A., *The World as Sacrament* (London: Darton, Longman and Todd, 1966).
Schmemann, A., *An Introduction to Liturgical Theology* , 2nd edn. (London: The Faith Press, 1975)
Schmemann, A., *Of Water and the Spirit* (London: SPCK, 1976).
Schmemann, A., *The Eucharist* (New York: St. Vladimir's Seminary Press, 1987).
Schillebeeckx, E., *The Eucharist* (London: Sheed and Ward, 1968, 1977).
Spinks, B. D., ed., *Addai and Mari: A Test for Students* (Nottingham: Grove Books, 1980).
Spinks, B. D., *Freedom or Order?* (Pennsylvania: Pickwick Publications 1984).
Spinks, B. D., *Worship: Prayers from the East* (Washington DC: The Pastoral Press, 1993).
Srawley, J. H., *The Early History of the Liturgy,* 2nd edn. (Cambridge: Cambridge University Press, 1947).
Stanwood, P. G., ed., *John Cosin: A Collection of Private Devotions* (Oxford: Oxford University Press, 1967).
Stephens, W. P., *The Theology of Huldrych Zwingli* (Cambridge: Cambridge University Press, 1986).

Stevenson, K. W., *Eucharist and Offering* (New York: Pueblo Publishing Company, 1986).

Stevenson, K. W., ed., *Liturgy Reshaped* (London: SPCK, 1982).

Sykes, S. W., ed., *Sacrifice and Redemption* (Cambridge: Cambridge University Press, 1991).

Taft, R. F., *The Great Entrance* (Rome: Pontificium Institutum Studiorum Orietalium, 1978).

Thornton, M., *The Rock and the River* (London: SPCK, 1965).

Wakefield, G. S., *Puritan Devotion* (London: Epworth Press, 1957).

Wakefield, G. S., *The Life of the Spirit in the World of Today* (New York: Macmillan Company, and London: Epworth Press, 1969).

Westerfield-Tucker, K. B., ed., *The Sunday Service of the Methodists* (Nashville, TN: Kingswood Books, 1996).

Wigan, B. J., *The Liturgy in English*, 2nd edn. (Oxford: Oxford University Press, 1964).

Williams, R., ed., *The Making of Orthodoxy* (Cambridge: Cambridge University Press, 1989).

Wilkinson, J., *Egeria's Travels* (London: SPCK, 1971)

Whyte, A., *Bunyan Characters: Second Series* (Edinburgh: Oliphant, Anderson and Ferrier, 1894).

Yarnold, E., *The Awe-Inspiring Rites of Initiation*, 2nd edn. (Edinburgh: T. & T. Clark, 1994).

Articles

Collinson, P., 'Thomas Cranmer', in Geoffrey Rowell, ed., *The English Religious Tradition and the Genius of Anglicanism* (Wantage: Ikon, 1992).

Dunn, J. D. G., 'Whatever happened to the Lord's Supper?', *Epworth Review* 19 (January 1982), pp. 35ff.

Franklin, R. W., 'The People's Work: Anti-Jansenist Prejudice in the Benedictine Movement for Popular Participation in the nineteenth century', *Studia Liturgica* 19 (1989), pp. 60–7.

Grisbrooke, W. J., 'An Orthodox Approach to Liturgical Theology: The Work of Alexander Schmemann', *Studia Liturgica* 23 (1993), pp. 140–57.

Hastings, A., 'Western Christianity confronts other Cultures', *Studia Liturgica* 20 (1990), pp. 19–27.

Hauerwas, S., 'The Liturgical Shape of the Christian Life: Teaching Ethics as Worship', in D. F. Ford and D. L. Stamps, eds, *Essentials of Christian Community* (Edinburgh: T. & T. Clark, 1996), pp. 35–48.

Kavanagh, A., OSB, 'Liturgical Inculturation: Looking to the Future', *Studia Liturgica* 20, (1990), pp. 101–6.

MacKinnon, D. M., 'Sacrament and Common Meal', in D. E. Nineham, ed., *Studies in the Gospels* (Oxford: Blackwell, 1955), pp. 201 ff.

Stephens, W. P., 'Zwingli's Sacramental Views', Pittsburgh Theological Monographs 1984, pp. 155–69.

Trowell, S., 'Unitarian and/or Anglican; The Relationship of Unitarianism to the Church from 1667 to 1698', *Bulletin of the John Rylands Library* 78.1 (Spring 1996), pp. 77–101.

Vanstone, W. H., 'Parish Church and Prayer Book', in D. Martin and P. Mullen, eds, *No Alternative* (Oxford: Blackwell, 1981), pp. 143–8.

Waller, R., 'James Martineau', in *Truth, Liberty, Religion* (Oxford: Manchester College, 1986), pp. 227–64.

Webb, R. K., 'The Unitarian Background', in *Truth, Liberty, Religion* (Oxford: Manchester College, 1986), pp. 3–33.

White, S. J., 'Christian Worship and the Quest for a Just Society', *Methodist Sacramental Fellowship Bulletin* 125 (1996), pp. 23–37.

FOR FURTHER READING

Baumstark, A., *Comparative Liturgy* (Oxford: Mowbray, 1958).

Brightman, F. E., *Liturgies Eastern and Western* (Oxford: Clarendon Press, 1896).

Brightman, F. E., *The English Rite* (London: Rivingtons, 1916).

Brooks, P. N., *Thomas Cranmer's Doctrine of the Eucharist* (London and Basingstoke: Macmillan, 1975).

Buchanan C. O., *Modern Anglican Liturgies 1958–68* (Oxford: Oxford University Press, 1968).

Buchanan, C. O., *Further Anglican Liturgies (1968–75)* (Nottingham: Grove Books, 1979).

Buchanan C. O., *Latest Anglican Liturgies (1976–84)* (London: SPCK/Nottingham: Grove Books, 1984).

Crichton, J. D., *Christian Celebration: the Mass* (London: Geoffrey Chapman, 1971).

Crichton, J. D., *Christian Celebration: the Prayer of the Church* (London: Geoffrey Chapman, 1976).

Davies, J. G., ed., *A New Dictionary of Liturgy and Worship* (London: SCM Press, 1989).

Davies, J. G., *Liturgical Dance* (London: SCM Press, 1984).

Davies, H., *Worship and Theology in England* 1534 to the present in three books, 2nd edn. (Grand Rapids: Eerdmans, 1996).

Fenwick, J. and Spinks, B. D., *Worship in Transition: The Twentieth Century Liturgical Movement* (Edinburgh: T. & T. Clark, 1995).

Fisher, J. D. C., *Baptism in the Medieval West* (London: SPCK, 1965).

Frere, W. H., *The Anaphora* (London: SPCK, 1938).

Hardy, D. W. and Ford, D. F., *Jubilate: Theology in Praise*

(London: Darton, Longman and Todd, 1984).
Forrester, D. and Murray, D., eds, *Studies in the History of Worship in Scotland*, 2nd edn. (Edinburgh: T. & T. Clark, 1996).
Forrester, D., McDonald, J. I. H. and Tellini, G., *Encounter with God*, 2nd edn. (Edinburgh: T. & T. Clark, 1996).
Heron, A., *Table and Tradition* (Edinburgh: The Handsel Press, 1983).
Jagger, P. J., *Christian Initiation 1552–1969* (London: Alcuin/SPCK, 1970).
Jones, C., Wainwright, G. and Yarnold E., eds, *The Study of Liturgy* (London: SPCK, 1978 and 1992).
Jungmann, J. A., *The Mass of the Roman Rite* (New York: 1951–6).
Klauser T., *A Short History of Western Liturgy* (Oxford: Oxford University Press, 1969).
Lietzmann, H., *Mass and Lord's Supper* (Leiden: Brill, 1953).
Marshall, I. H., *Last Supper and Lord's Supper* (Exeter: Paternoster, 1980).
Moule, C. F. D., *Worship in the New Testament* (London: Lutterworth, 1961).
Rattenbury, J. E., *The Eucharistic Hymns of John and Charles Wesley* (London: Epworth Press, 1948).
Rupp, E. G., *Patterns of Reformation* (London: Epworth Press, 1969).
Wainwright, G., *Eucharist and Eschatology* (London: Epworth Press, 1971 and New York: Oxford University Press, 1981).
Wainwright, G., *Doxology* (London: Epworth Press, 1979).
Wainwright, G., *Worship with One Accord* (New York: Oxford University Press, 1997).
Wainwright, G. and Thurian, M., *Baptism and Eucharist: Ecumenical Convergence in Celebration* (Geneva: World Council of Churches, 1983).
Watson, J. R., *The English Hymn, A Critical and Historical Study* (Oxford: Clarendon Press, 1997).
Whitaker, E. C., *Documents of Baptismal Liturgy* (London: SPCK, 1977)
Whitaker, E. C., *The Baptismal Liturgy* (London: SPCK, 1981).
White, J. F., *Documents of Christian Worship* (Edinburgh: T. & T. Clark, 1992).
White S. J., *Groundwork of Christian Worship* (London: Epworth Press, 1997).

INDEX